# The Rhetoric and Poetics of Aristotle

*The Rhetoric - translated by John Henry Freese*

*The Poetics - translated by Ingram Bywater*

 PANTIANOS CLASSICS

Published by Pantianos Classics

ISBN-13: 978-1540454980

The translation of the Rhetoric was first published in 1924

The translation of the Poetics was first published in 1920

# Contents

**The Rhetoric** ............................................................................ 6
**Book I** ...................................................................................... 6
   Chapter 1.................................................................................. 6
   Chapter 2.................................................................................. 9
   Chapter 3................................................................................ 14
   Chapter 4................................................................................ 16
   Chapter 5................................................................................ 18
   Chapter 6................................................................................ 21
   Chapter 7................................................................................ 24
   Chapter 8................................................................................ 29
   Chapter 9................................................................................ 30
   Chapter 10.............................................................................. 34
   Chapter 11.............................................................................. 37
   Chapter 12.............................................................................. 40
   Chapter 13.............................................................................. 43
   Chapter 14.............................................................................. 46
   Chapter 15.............................................................................. 47
**Book II** ................................................................................... 52
   Chapter 1................................................................................ 52
   Chapter 2................................................................................ 53
   Chapter 3................................................................................ 56

Chapter 4 .................................................................................. 58
Chapter 5 .................................................................................. 61
Chapter 6 .................................................................................. 63
Chapter 7 .................................................................................. 66
Chapter 8 .................................................................................. 67
Chapter 9 .................................................................................. 69
Chapter 10 ................................................................................ 71
Chapter 11 ................................................................................ 72
Chapter 12 ................................................................................ 73
Chapter 13 ................................................................................ 75
Chapter 14 ................................................................................ 76
Chapter 15 ................................................................................ 76
Chapter 16 ................................................................................ 77
Chapter 17 ................................................................................ 77
Chapter 18 ................................................................................ 78
Chapter 19 ................................................................................ 79
Chapter 20 ................................................................................ 81
Chapter 21 ................................................................................ 83
Chapter 22 ................................................................................ 85
Chapter 23 ................................................................................ 87
Chapter 24 ................................................................................ 95
Chapter 25 ................................................................................ 97
Chapter 26 ................................................................................ 99

# Book III ............................................................................... 101

Chapter 1 ................................................................................ 101
Chapter 2 ................................................................................ 102
Chapter 3 ................................................................................ 105
Chapter 4 ................................................................................ 107

Chapter 5 ............................................................................ 107
Chapter 6 ............................................................................ 109
Chapter 7 ............................................................................ 109
Chapter 8 ............................................................................ 111
Chapter 9 ............................................................................ 112
Chapter 10 .......................................................................... 114
Chapter 11 .......................................................................... 116
Chapter 12 .......................................................................... 120
Chapter 13 .......................................................................... 121
Chapter 14 .......................................................................... 122
Chapter 15 .......................................................................... 125
Chapter 16 .......................................................................... 126
Chapter 17 .......................................................................... 128
Chapter 18 .......................................................................... 131
Chapter 19 .......................................................................... 132

# **The Poetics of Aristotle ........................................... 134**

Preface ............................................................................... 134
Aristotle on the Art of Poetry ............................................ 141

# The Rhetoric

## Book I

### Chapter 1

Rhetoric is a counterpart of Dialectic; for both have to do with matters that are in a manner within the cognizance of all men and not confined to any special science. Hence all men in a manner have a share of both; for all, up to a certain point, endeavor to criticize or uphold an argument, to defend themselves or to accuse. Now, the majority of people do this either at random or with a familiarity arising from habit. But since both these ways are possible, it is clear that matters can be reduced to a system, for it is possible to examine the reason why some attain their end by familiarity and others by chance; and such an examination all would at once admit to be the function of an art.
Now, previous compilers of "Arts" of Rhetoric have provided us with only a small portion of this art, for proofs are the only things in it that come within the province of art; everything else is merely an accessory. And yet they say nothing about enthymemes which are the body of proof, but chiefly devote their attention to matters outside the subject; for the arousing of prejudice, compassion, anger, and similar emotions has no connection with the matter in hand, but is directed only to the dicast. The result would be that, if all trials were now carried on as they are in some States, especially those that are well administered, there would be nothing left for the rhetorician to say. For all men either think that all the laws ought so to prescribe, or in fact carry out the principle and forbid speaking outside the subject, as in the court of Areopagus, and in this they are right. For it is wrong to warp the dicast's feelings, to arouse him to anger, jealousy or compassion, which would be like making the rule crooked which one intended to use. Further, it is evident that the only business of the litigant is to prove that the fact in question is or is not so, that it has happened or not; whether it is important or unimportant, just or unjust, in all cases in which the legislator has not laid down a ruling, is a matter for

the dicast himself to decide; it is not the business of the litigants to instruct him.

First of all, therefore, it is proper that laws, properly enacted, should themselves define the issue of all cases as far as possible, and leave as little as possible to the discretion of the judges; in the first place, because it is easier to find one or a few men of good sense, capable of framing laws and pronouncing judgements, than a large number; secondly, legislation is the result of long consideration, whereas judgements are delivered on the spur of the moment, so that it is difficult for the judges properly to decide questions of justice or expediency. But what is most important of all is that the judgement of the legislator does not apply to a particular case, but is universal and applies to the future, whereas the member of the public assembly and the dicast have to decide present and definite issues, and in their case love, hate, or personal interest is often involved, so that they are no longer capable of discerning the truth adequately, their judgement being obscured by their own pleasure or pain.

All other cases, as we have just said, should be left to the authority of the judge as seldom as possible, except where it is a question of a thing having happened or not, of its going to happen or not, of being or not being so; this must be left to the discretion of the judges, for it is impossible for the legislator to foresee such questions. If this is so, it is obvious that all those who definitely lay down, for instance, what should be the contents of the exordium or the narrative, or of the other parts of the discourse, are bringing under the rules of art what is outside the subject; for the only thing to which their attention is devoted is how to put the judge into a certain frame of mind. They give no account of the artificial proofs, which make a man a master of rhetorical argument.

Hence, although the method of deliberative and forensic Rhetoric is the same, and although the pursuit of the former is nobler and more worthy of a statesman than that of the latter, which is limited to transactions between private citizens, they say nothing about the former, but without exception endeavor to bring forensic speaking under the rules of art. The reason of this is that in public speaking it is less worth while to talk of what is outside the subject, and that deliberative oratory lends itself to trickery less than forensic, because it is of more general interest. For in the assembly the judges decide upon their own affairs, so that the only thing necessary is to prove the truth of the statement of one who recommends a measure, but in the law courts this is not sufficient; there it is useful to win over the hearers, for the decision concerns other interests than those of the judges, who, having only themselves to consider and listening merely for their own pleasure, surrender to the pleaders but do not give a real decision.

That is why, as I have said before, in many places the law prohibits speaking outside the subject in the law courts, whereas in the assembly the judges themselves take adequate precautions against this.

It is obvious, therefore, that a system arranged according to the rules of art is only concerned with proofs; that proof is a sort of demonstration, since we are most strongly convinced when we suppose anything to have been demonstrated; that rhetorical demonstration is an enthymeme, which, generally speaking, is the strongest of rhetorical proofs and lastly, that the enthymeme is a kind of syllogism. Now, as it is the function of Dialectic as a whole, or of one of its parts, to consider every kind of syllogism in a similar manner, it is clear that he who is most capable of examining the matter and forms of a syllogism will be in the highest degree a master of rhetorical argument, if to this he adds a knowledge of the subjects with which enthymemes deal and the differences between them and logical syllogisms. For, in fact, the true and that which resembles it come under the purview of the same faculty, and at the same time men have a sufficient natural capacity for the truth and indeed in most cases attain to it; wherefore one who divines well in regard to the truth will also be able to divine well in regard to probabilities.

It is clear, then, that all other rhetoricians bring under the rules of art what is outside the subject, and have rather inclined to the forensic branch of oratory. Nevertheless, Rhetoric is useful, because the true and the just are naturally superior to their opposites, so that, if decisions are improperly made, they must owe their defeat to their own advocates; which is reprehensible. Further, in dealing with certain persons, even if we possessed the most accurate scientific knowledge, we should not find it easy to persuade them by the employment of such knowledge. For scientific discourse is concerned with instruction, but in the case of such persons instruction is impossible; our proofs and arguments must rest on generally accepted principles, as we said in the Topics, when speaking of converse with the multitude. Further, the orator should be able to prove opposites, as in logical arguments; not that we should do both (for one ought not to persuade people to do what is wrong), but that the real state of the case may not escape us, and that we ourselves may be able to counteract false arguments, if another makes an unfair use of them. Rhetoric and Dialectic alone of all the arts prove opposites; for both are equally concerned with them. However, it is not the same with the subject matter, but, generally speaking, that which is true and better is naturally always easier to prove and more likely to persuade. Besides, it would be absurd if it were considered disgraceful not to be able to defend oneself with the help of the body, but not disgraceful as far as speech is concerned, whose use is more characteristic of man than that of the body. If it is argued that one who makes an unfair use of such faculty of speech may do a great deal of harm, this objection applies equally to all good things except virtue, and above all to those things which are most useful, such as strength, health, wealth, generalship; for as these, rightly used, may be of the greatest benefit, so, wrongly used, they may do an equal amount of harm.

It is thus evident that Rhetoric does not deal with any one definite class of subjects, but, like Dialectic, [is of general application]; also, that it is useful; and further, that its function is not so much to persuade, as to find out in each case the existing means of persuasion. The same holds good in respect to all the other arts. For instance, it is not the function of medicine to restore a patient to health, but only to promote this end as far as possible; for even those whose recovery is impossible may be properly treated. It is further evident that it belongs to Rhetoric to discover the real and apparent means of persuasion, just as it belongs to Dialectic to discover the real and apparent syllogism. For what makes the sophist is not the faculty but the moral purpose. But there is a difference: in Rhetoric, one who acts in accordance with sound argument, and one who acts in accordance with moral purpose, are both called rhetoricians; but in Dialectic it is the moral purpose that makes the sophist, the dialectician being one whose arguments rest, not on moral purpose but on the faculty.

Let us now endeavor to treat of the method itself, to see how and by what means we shall be able to attain our objects. And so let us as it were start again, and having defined Rhetoric anew, pass on to the remainder of the subject.

## Chapter 2

Rhetoric then may be defined as the faculty of discovering the possible means of persuasion in reference to any subject whatever. This is the function of no other of the arts, each of which is able to instruct and persuade in its own special subject; thus, medicine deals with health and sickness, geometry with the properties of magnitudes, arithmetic with number, and similarly with all the other arts and sciences. But Rhetoric, so to say, appears to be able to discover the means of persuasion in reference to any given subject. That is why we say that as an art its rules are not applied to any particular definite class of things.

As for proofs, some are artificial, others inartificial. By the latter I understand all those which have not been furnished by ourselves but were already in existence, such as witnesses, tortures, contracts, and the like; by the former, all that can be constructed by system and by our own efforts. Thus we have only to make use of the latter, whereas we must invent the former.

Now the proofs furnished by the speech are of three kinds. The first depends upon the moral character of the speaker, the second upon putting the hearer into a certain frame of mind, the third upon the speech itself, in so far as it proves or seems to prove.

The orator persuades by moral character when his speech is delivered in such a manner as to render him worthy of confidence; for we feel confidence in a greater degree and more readily in persons of worth in regard to everything in general, but where there is no certainty and there is room for doubt, our confidence is absolute. But this confidence must be due to the speech itself, not to any preconceived idea of the speaker's character; for it is not the case, as some writers of rhetorical treatises lay down in their "Art," that the worth of the orator in no way contributes to his powers of persuasion; on the contrary, moral character, so to say, constitutes the most effective means of proof. The orator persuades by means of his hearers, when they are roused to emotion by his speech; for the judgements we deliver are not the same when we are influenced by joy or sorrow, love or hate; and it is to this alone that, as we have said, the present-day writers of treatises endeavor to devote their attention. (We will discuss these matters in detail when we come to speak of the emotions.) Lastly, persuasion is produced by the speech itself, when we establish the true or apparently true from the means of persuasion applicable to each individual subject.

Now, since proofs are effected by these means, it is evident that, to be able to grasp them, a man must be capable of logical reasoning, of studying characters and the virtues, and thirdly the emotions—the nature and character of each, its origin, and the manner in which it is produced. Thus it appears that Rhetoric is as it were an offshoot of Dialectic and of the science of Ethics, which may be reasonably called Politics. That is why Rhetoric assumes the character of Politics, and those who claim to possess it, partly from ignorance, partly from boastfulness, and partly from other human weaknesses, do the same. For, as we said at the outset, Rhetoric is a sort of division or likeness of Dialectic, since neither of them is a science that deals with the nature of any definite subject, but they are merely faculties of furnishing arguments. We have now said nearly enough about the faculties of these arts and their mutual relations.

But for purposes of demonstration, real or apparent, just as Dialectic possesses two modes of argument, induction and the syllogism, real or apparent, the same is the case in Rhetoric; for the example is induction, and the enthymeme a syllogism, and the apparent enthymeme an apparent syllogism. Accordingly I call an enthymeme a rhetorical syllogism, and an example rhetorical induction. Now all orators produce belief by employing as proofs either examples or enthymemes and nothing else; so that if, generally speaking, it is necessary to prove any fact whatever either by syllogism or by induction—and that this is so is clear from the Analytics—each of the two former must be identical with each of the two latter. The difference between example and enthymeme is evident from the Topics, where, in discussing syllogism and induction, it has previously been said that the proof from a number of particular cases that such is the rule, is called in Dialectic induction, in Rhetoric example; but when, certain things being posited, something different results by reason of them, alongside of them, from their being true, either universally or in most cases, such a conclusion in Dialectic is called a syllogism, in Rhetoric an enthymeme. It is evident that Rhetoric enjoys both these advantages—for what has been said in the Methodica holds good also in this case—for rhetorical speeches are sometimes characterized by examples and sometimes by enthymemes, and orators themselves may be similarly distinguished by their fondness for one or the other. Now arguments that depend on examples are not less calculated to persuade, but those which depend upon enthymemes meet with greater approval. Their origin and the way in which each should be used will be discussed later; for the moment let us define more clearly these proofs themselves.

Now, that which is persuasive is persuasive in reference to some one, and is persuasive and convincing either at once and in and by itself, or because it appears to be proved by propositions that are convincing; further, no art has the particular in view, medicine for instance what is good for Socrates or Callias, but what is good for this or that class of persons (for this is a matter that comes within the province of an art, whereas the particular is infinite and cannot be the subject of a true science); similarly, therefore, Rhetoric will not consider what seems probable in each individual case, for instance to Socrates or Hippias, but that which seems probable to this or that class of persons. It is the same with Dialectic, which does not draw conclusions from any random premises—for even madmen have some fancies—but it takes its material from subjects which demand reasoned discussion, as Rhetoric does from those which are common subjects of deliberation.

The function of Rhetoric, then, is to deal with things about which we deliberate, but for which we have no systematic rules; and in the presence of such hearers as are unable to take a general view of many stages, or to follow a lengthy chain of argument. But we only deliberate about things which seem to admit of issuing in two ways; as for those things which cannot in the past, present, or future be otherwise, no one deliberates about them, if he supposes that they are such; for nothing would be gained by it. Now, it is possible to draw conclusions and inferences partly from what has been previously demonstrated syllogistically, partly from what has not, which however needs demonstration, because it is not probable. The first of these methods is necessarily difficult to follow owing to its length, for the judge is supposed to be a simple person; the second will obtain little credence, because it does not depend upon what is either admitted or probable. The necessary result then is that the enthymeme and the example are concerned with things which may, generally speaking, be other than they are, the example being a kind of induction and the enthymeme a kind of syllogism, and deduced from few premises, often from fewer than the regular syllogism; for if any one of these is well known, there is no need to mention it, for the hearer can add it himself. For instance, to prove that Dorieus was the victor in a contest at which the prize was a crown, it is enough to say that he won a victory at the Olympic games; there is no need to add that the prize at the Olympic games is a crown, for everybody knows it.

But since few of the propositions of the rhetorical syllogism are necessary, for most of the things which we judge and examine can be other than they are, human actions, which are the subject of our deliberation and examination, being all of such a character and, generally speaking, none of them necessary; since, further, facts which only generally happen or are merely possible can only be demonstrated by other facts of the same kind, and necessary facts by necessary propositions (and that this is so is clear from the Analytics), it is evident that the materials from which enthymemes are derived will be sometimes necessary, but for the most part only generally true; and these materials being probabilities and signs, it follows that these two elements must correspond to these two kinds of propositions, each to each. For that which is probable is that which generally happens, not however unreservedly, as some define it, but that which is concerned with things that may be other than they are, being so related to that in regard to which it is probable as the universal to the particular. As to signs, some are related as the particular to the universal, others as the universal to the particular. Necessary signs are called tekmēria; those which are not necessary have no distinguishing name. I call those necessary signs from which a logical syllogism can be constructed, wherefore such a sign is called tekmērion; for when people think that their arguments are irrefutable, they think that they are bringing forward a tekmērion, something as it were proved and concluded; for in the old language tekmar and peras have the same meaning (limit, conclusion).

Among signs, some are related as the particular to the universal; for instance, if one were to say that all wise men are just, because Socrates was both wise and just. Now this is a sign, but even though the particular statement is true, it can be refuted, because it cannot be reduced to syllogistic form. But if one were to say that it is a sign that a man is ill, because he has a fever, or that a woman has had a child because she has milk, this is a necessary sign. This alone among signs is a tekmērion; for only in this case, if the fact is true, is the argument irrefutable. Other signs are related as the universal to the particular, for instance, if one were to say that it is a sign that this man has a fever, because he breathes hard; but even if the fact be true, this argument also can be refuted, for it is possible for a man to breathe hard without having a fever. We have now explained the meaning of probable, sign, and necessary sign, and the difference between them; in the Analytics we have defined them more clearly and stated why some of them can be converted into logical syllogisms, while others cannot.

We have said that example is a kind of induction and with what kind of material it deals by way of induction. It is neither the relation of part to whole, nor of whole to part, nor of one whole to another whole, but of part to part, of like to like, when both come under the same genus, but one of them is better known than the other. For example, to prove that Dionysius is aiming at a tyranny, because he asks for a bodyguard, one might say that Pisistratus before him and Theagenes of Megara did the same, and when they obtained what they asked for made themselves tyrants. All the other tyrants known may serve as an example of Dionysius, whose reason, however, for asking for a bodyguard we do not yet know. All these examples are contained under the same universal proposition, that one who is aiming at a tyranny asks for a bodyguard.

We have now stated the materials of proofs which are thought to be demonstrative. But a very great difference between enthymemes has escaped the notice of nearly every one, although it also exists in the dialectical method of syllogisms. For some of them belong to Rhetoric, some syllogisms only to Dialectic, and others to other arts and faculties, some already existing and others not yet established. Hence it is that this escapes the notice of the speakers, and the more they specialize in a subject, the more they transgress the limits of Rhetoric and Dialectic. But this will be clearer if stated at greater length.

I mean by dialectical and rhetorical syllogisms those which are concerned with what we call "topics," which may be applied alike to Law, Physics, Politics, and many other sciences that differ in kind, such as the topic of the more or less, which will furnish syllogisms and enthymemes equally well for Law, Physics, or any other science whatever, although these subjects differ in kind. Specific topics on the other hand are derived from propositions which are peculiar to each species or genus of things; there are, for example, propositions about Physics which can furnish neither enthymemes nor syllogisms about Ethics, and there are propositions concerned with Ethics which will be useless for furnishing conclusions about Physics; and the same holds good in all cases. The first kind of topics will not make a man practically wise about any particular class of things, because they do not deal with any particular subject matter; but as to the specific topics, the happier a man is in his choice of propositions, the more he will unconsciously produce a science quite different from Dialectic and Rhetoric. For if once he hits upon first principles, it will no longer be Dialectic or Rhetoric, but that science whose principles he has arrived at. Most enthymemes are constructed from these specific topics, which are called particular and special, fewer from those that are common or universal. As then we have done in the Topics, so here we must distinguish the specific and universal topics, from which enthymemes may be constructed. By specific topics I mean the propositions peculiar to each class of things, by universal those common to all alike. Let us then first speak of the specific topics, but before doing so let us ascertain the different kinds of Rhetoric, so that, having determined their number, we may separately ascertain their elements and propositions.

## Chapter 3

The kinds of Rhetoric are three in number, corresponding to the three kinds of hearers. For every speech is composed of three parts: the speaker, the subject of which he treats, and the person to whom it is addressed, I mean the hearer, to whom the end or object of the speech refers. Now the hearer must necessarily be either a mere spectator or a judge, and a judge either of things past or of things to come. For instance, a member of the general assembly is a judge of things to come; the dicast, of things past; the mere spectator, of the ability of the speaker. Therefore there are necessarily three kinds of rhetorical speeches, deliberative, forensic, and epideictic.

The deliberative kind is either hortatory or dissuasive; for both those who give advice in private and those who speak in the assembly invariably either exhort or dissuade. The forensic kind is either accusatory or defensive; for litigants must necessarily either accuse or defend. The epideictic kind has for its subject praise or blame.

Further, to each of these a special time is appropriate: to the deliberative the future, for the speaker, whether he exhorts or dissuades, always advises about things to come; to the forensic the past, for it is always in reference to things done that one party accuses and the other defends; to the epideictic most appropriately the present, for it is the existing condition of things that all those who praise or blame have in view. It is not uncommon, however, for epideictic speakers to avail themselves of other times, of the past by way of recalling it, or of the future by way of anticipating it.

Each of the three kinds has a different special end, and as there are three kinds of Rhetoric, so there are three special ends. The end of the deliberative speaker is the expedient or harmful; for he who exhorts recommends a course of action as better, and he who dissuades advises against it as worse; all other considerations, such as justice and injustice, honor and disgrace, are included as accessory in reference to this. The end of the forensic speaker is the just or the unjust; in this case also all other considerations are included as accessory. The end of those who praise or blame is the honorable and disgraceful; and they also refer all other considerations to these. A sign that what I have stated is the end which each has in view is the fact that sometimes the speakers will not dispute about the other points. For example, a man on trial does not always deny that an act has been committed or damage inflicted by him, but he will never admit that the act is unjust; for otherwise a trial would be unnecessary. Similarly, the deliberative orator, although he often sacrifices everything else, will never admit that he is recommending what is inexpedient or is dissuading from what is useful; but often he is quite indifferent about showing that the enslavement of neighboring peoples, even if they have done no harm, is not an act of injustice. Similarly, those who praise or blame do not consider whether a man has done what is expedient or harmful, but frequently make it a matter for praise that, disregarding his own interest, he performed some deed of honor. For example, they praise Achilles because he went to the aid of his comrade Patroclus, knowing that he was fated to die, although he might have lived. To him such a death was more honorable, although life was more expedient.

From what has been said it is evident that the orator must first have in readiness the propositions on these three subjects. Now, necessary signs, probabilities, and signs are the propositions of the rhetorician; for the syllogism universally consists of propositions, and the enthymeme is a syllogism composed of the propositions above mentioned. Again, since what is impossible can neither have been done nor will be done, but only what is possible, and since what has not taken place nor will take place can neither have been done nor will be done, it is necessary for each of the three kinds of orators to have in readiness propositions dealing with the possible and the impossible, and as to whether anything has taken place or will take place, or not. Further, since all, whether they praise or blame, exhort or dissuade, accuse or defend, not only endeavor to prove what we have stated, but also that the same things, whether good or bad, honorable or disgraceful, just or unjust, are great or small, either in themselves or when compared with each other, it is clear that it will be necessary for the orator to be ready with propositions dealing with greatness and smallness and the greater and the less, both universally and in particular; for instance, which is the greater or less good, or act of injustice or justice; and similarly with regard to all other subjects. We have now stated the topics concerning which the orator must provide himself with propositions; after this, we must distinguish between each of them individually, that is, what the three kinds of Rhetoric, deliberative, epideictic, and forensic, are concerned with.

## Chapter 4

We must first ascertain about what kind of good or bad things the deliberative orator advises, since he cannot do so about everything, but only about things which may possibly happen or not. Everything which of necessity either is or will be, or which cannot possibly be or come to pass, is outside the scope of deliberation. Indeed, even in the case of things that are possible advice is not universally appropriate; for they include certain advantages, natural and accidental, about which it is not worth while to offer advice. But it is clear that advice is limited to those subjects about which we take counsel; and such are all those which can naturally be referred to ourselves and the first cause of whose origination is in our own power; for our examination is limited to finding out whether such things are possible or impossible for us to perform.

However, there is no need at present to endeavor to enumerate with scrupulous exactness or to classify those subjects which men are wont to discuss, or to define them as far as possible with strict accuracy, since this is not the function of the rhetorical art but of one that is more intelligent and exact, and further, more than its legitimate subjects of inquiry have already been assigned to it. For what we have said before is true: that Rhetoric is composed of analytical science and of that branch of political science which is concerned with Ethics, and that it resembles partly Dialectic and partly sophistical arguments. But in proportion as anyone endeavors to make of Dialectic or Rhetoric, not what they are, faculties, but sciences, to that extent he will, without knowing it, destroy their real nature, in thus altering their character, by crossing over into the domain of sciences, whose subjects are certain definite things, not merely words. Nevertheless, even at present we may mention such matters as it is worth while to analyze, while still leaving much for political science to investigate.

Now, we may say that the most important subjects about which all men deliberate and deliberative orators harangue, are five in number, to wit: ways and means, war and peace, the defence of the country, imports and exports, legislation.

Accordingly, the orator who is going to give advice on ways and means should be acquainted with the nature and extent of the State resources, so that if any is omitted it may be added, and if any is insufficient, it may be increased. Further, he should know all the expenses of the State, that if any is superfluous, it may be removed, or, if too great, may be curtailed. For men become wealthier, not only by adding to what they already possess, but also by cutting down expenses. Of these things it is not only possible to acquire a general view from individual experience, but in view of advising concerning them it is further necessary to be well informed about what has been discovered among others.

In regard to war and peace, the orator should be acquainted with the power of the State, how great it is already and how great it may possibly become; of what kind it is already and what additions may possibly be made to it; further, what wars it has waged and its conduct of them. These things he should be acquainted with, not only as far as his own State is concerned, but also in reference to neighboring States, and particularly those with whom there is a likelihood of war, so that towards the stronger a pacific attitude may be maintained, and in regard to the weaker, the decision as to making war on them may be left to his own State. Again, he should know whether their forces are like or unlike his own, for herein also advantage or disadvantage may lie. With reference to these matters he must also have examined the results, not only of the wars carried on by his own State, but also of those carried on by others; for similar results naturally arise from similar causes.

Again, in regard to the defense of the country, he should not be ignorant how it is carried on; he should know both the strength of the guard, its character, and the positions of the guard-houses (which is impossible for one who is unacquainted with the country), so that if any guard is insufficient it may be increased, or if any is superfluous it may be disbanded, and greater attention devoted to suitable positions.

Again, in regard to food, he should know what amount of expenditure is sufficient to support the State; what kind of food is produced at home or can be imported; and what exports and imports are necessary, in order that contracts and agreements may be made with those who can furnish them; for it is necessary to keep the citizens free from reproach in their relations with two classes of people—those who are stronger and those who are useful for commercial purposes.

With a view to the safety of the State, it is necessary that the orator should be able to judge of all these questions, but an understanding of legislation is of special importance, for it is on the laws that the safety of the State is based. Wherefore he must know how many forms of government there are; what is expedient for each; and the natural causes of its downfall, whether they are peculiar to the particular form of government or opposed to it. By being ruined by causes peculiar to itself, I mean that, with the exception of the perfect form of government, all the rest are ruined by being relaxed or strained to excess. Thus democracy, not only when relaxed, but also when strained to excess, becomes weaker and will end in an oligarchy; similarly, not only does an aquiline or snub nose reach the mean, when one of these defects is relaxed, but when it becomes aquiline or snub to excess, it is altered to such an extent that even the likeness of a nose is lost. Moreover, with reference to acts of legislation, it is useful not only to understand what form of government is expedient by judging in the light of the past, but also to become acquainted with those in existence in other nations, and to learn what kinds of government are suitable to what kinds of people. It is clear, therefore, that for legislation books of travel are useful, since they help us to understand the laws of other nations, and for political debates historical works. All these things, however, belong to Politics and not to Rhetoric.

Such, then, are the most important questions upon which the would-be deliberative orator must be well informed. Now let us again state the sources whence we must derive our arguments for exhortation or discussion on these and other questions.

## Chapter 5

Men, individually and in common, nearly all have some aim, in the attainment of which they choose or avoid certain things. This aim, briefly stated, is happiness and its component parts. Therefore, for the sake of illustration, let us ascertain what happiness, generally speaking, is, and what its parts consist in; for all who exhort or dissuade discuss happiness and the things which conduce or are detrimental to it. For one should do the things which procure happiness or one of its parts, or increase instead of diminishing it, and avoid doing those things which destroy or hinder it or bring about what is contrary to it.

Let us then define happiness as well-being combined with virtue, or independence of life, or the life that is most agreeable combined with security, or abundance of possessions and slaves, combined with power to protect and make use of them; for nearly all men admit that one or more of these things constitutes happiness. If, then, such is the nature of happiness, its component parts must necessarily be: noble birth, numerous friends, good friends, wealth, good children, numerous children, a good old age; further, bodily excellences, such as health, beauty, strength, stature, fitness for athletic contests, a good reputation, honor, good luck, virtue. For a man would be entirely independent, provided he possessed all internal and external goods; for there are no others. Internal goods are those of mind and body; external goods are noble birth, friends, wealth, honor. To these we think should be added certain capacities and good luck; for on these conditions life will be perfectly secure. Let us now in the same way define each of these in detail.

Noble birth, in the case of a nation or State, means that its members or inhabitants are sprung from the soil, or of long standing; that its first members were famous as leaders, and that many of their descendants have been famous for qualities that are highly esteemed. In the case of private individuals, noble birth is derived from either the father's or the mother's side, and on both sides there must be legitimacy; and, as in the case of a State, it means that its founders were distinguished for virtue, or wealth, or any other of the things that men honor, and that a number of famous persons, both men and women, young and old, belong to the family.

The blessing of good children and numerous children needs little explanation. For the commonwealth it consists in a large number of good young men, good in bodily excellences, such as stature, beauty, strength, fitness for athletic contests; the moral excellences of a young man are self-control and courage. For the individual it consists in a number of good children of his own, both male and female, and such as we have described. Female bodily excellences are beauty and stature, their moral excellences self-control and industrious habits, free from servility. The object of both the individual and of the community should be to secure the existence of each of these qualities in both men and women; for all those States in which the character of women is unsatisfactory, as in Lacedaemon, may be considered only half-happy.

Wealth consists in abundance of money, ownership of land and properties, and further of movables, cattle, and slaves, remarkable for number, size, and beauty, if they are all secure, liberal, and useful. Property that is productive is more useful, but that which has enjoyment for its object is more liberal. By productive I mean that which is a source of income, by enjoyable that which offers no advantage beyond the use of it—at least, none worth mentioning. Security may be defined as possession of property in such places and on such conditions that the use of it is in our own hands; and ownership as the right of alienation or not, by which I mean giving the property away or selling it. In a word, being wealthy consists rather in use than in possession; for the actualization and use of such things is wealth.

A good reputation consists in being considered a man of worth by all, or in possessing something of such a nature that all or most men, or the good, or the men of practical wisdom desire it.

Honor is a token of a reputation for doing good; and those who have already done good are justly and above all honored, not but that he who is capable of doing good is also honored. Doing good relates either to personal security and all the causes of existence; or to wealth; or to any other good things which are not easy to acquire, either in any conditions, or at such a place, or at such a time; for many obtain honor for things that

appear trifling, but this depends upon place and time. The components of honor are sacrifices, memorials in verse and prose, privileges, grants of land, front seats, public burial, State maintenance, and among the barbarians, prostration and giving place, and all gifts which are highly prized in each country. For a gift is at once a giving of a possession and a token of honor; wherefore gifts are desired by the ambitious and by those who are fond of money, since they are an acquisition for the latter and an honor for the former; so that they furnish both with what they want.
Bodily excellence is health, and of such a kind that when exercising the body we are free from sickness; for many are healthy in the way Herodicus is said to have been, whom no one would consider happy in the matter of health, because they are obliged to abstain from all or nearly all human enjoyments.
Beauty varies with each age. In a young man, it consists in possessing a body capable of enduring all efforts, either of the racecourse or of bodily strength, while he himself is pleasant to look upon and a sheer delight. This is why the athletes in the pentathlon are most beautiful, because they are naturally adapted for bodily exertion and for swiftness of foot. In a man who has reached his prime, beauty consists in being naturally adapted for the toils of war, in being pleasant to look upon and at the same time awe-inspiring. In an old man, beauty consists in being naturally adapted to contend with unavoidable labors and in not causing annoyance to others, thanks to the absence of the disagreeable accompaniments of old age.
Strength consists in the power of moving another as one wills, for which purpose it is necessary to pull or push, to lift, to squeeze or crush, so that the strong man is strong by virtue of being able to do all or some of these things.
Excellence of stature consists in being superior to most men in height, depth, and breadth, but in such proportion as not to render the movements of the body slower as the result of excess.
Bodily excellence in athletics consists in size, strength, and swiftness of foot; for to be swift is to be strong. For one who is able to throw his legs about in a certain way, to move them rapidly and with long strides, makes a good runner; one who can hug and grapple, a good wrestler; one who can thrust away by a blow of the fist, a good boxer; one who excels in boxing and wrestling is fit for the pancratium, he who excels in all for the pentathlon.
A happy old age is one that comes slowly with freedom from pain; for neither one who rapidly grows old nor one who grows old insensibly but with pain enjoys a happy old age. This also depends upon bodily excellences and good fortune; for unless a man is free from illness and is strong, he will never be free from suffering, nor will he live long and painlessly without good fortune. Apart from health and strength, however,

there is a power of vitality in certain cases; for many live long who are not endowed with bodily excellences. But a minute examination of such questions is needless for the present purpose.

The meaning of numerous and worthy friends is easy to understand from the definition of a friend. A friend is one who exerts himself to do for the sake of another what he thinks is advantageous to him. A man to whom many persons are so disposed, has many friends; if they are virtuous, he has worthy friends.

Good fortune consists in the acquisition or possession of either all, or the most, or the most important of those goods of which fortune is the cause. Now fortune is the cause of some things with which the arts also are concerned, and also of many which have nothing to do with art, for instance, such as are due to nature (though it is possible that the results of fortune may be contrary to nature); for art is a cause of health, but nature of beauty and stature. Speaking generally, the goods which come from fortune are such as excite envy. Fortune is also a cause of those goods which are beyond calculation; for instance, a man's brothers are all ugly, while he is handsome; they did not see the treasure, while he found it; the arrow hit one who stood by and not the man aimed at; or, one who frequented a certain place was the only one who did not go there on a certain occasion, while those who went there then for the first time met their death. All such instances appear to be examples of good fortune. The definition of virtue, with which the topic of praise is most closely connected, must be left until we come to treat of the latter.

## Chapter 6

It is evident, then, what things, likely to happen or already existing, the orator should aim at, when exhorting, and what when dissuading; for they are opposites. But since the aim before the deliberative orator is that which is expedient, and men deliberate, not about the end, but about the means to the end, which are the things which are expedient in regard to our actions; and since, further, the expedient is good, we must first grasp the elementary notions of good and expedient in general.

Let us assume good to be whatever is desirable for its own sake, or for the sake of which we choose something else; that which is the aim of all things, or of all things that possess sensation or reason; or would be, if they could acquire the latter. Whatever reason might assign to each and whatever reason does assign to each in individual cases, that is good for each; and that whose presence makes a man fit and also independent; and independence in general; and that which produces or preserves such things, or on which such things follow, or all that is likely to prevent or destroy their opposites.

Now things follow in two ways—simultaneously or subsequently; for instance, knowledge is subsequent to learning, but life is simultaneous with health. Things which produce act in three ways; thus, healthiness produces health; and so does food; and exercise as a rule. This being laid down, it necessarily follows that the acquisition of good things and the loss of evil things are both good; for it follows simultaneously on the latter that we are rid of that which is bad, and subsequently on the former that we obtain possession of that which is good. The same applies to the acquisition of a greater in place of a less good, and a less in place of a greater evil; for in proportion as the greater exceeds the less, there is an acquisition of the one and a loss of the other. The virtues also must be a good thing; for those who possess them are in a sound condition, and they are also productive of good things and practical. However, we must speak separately concerning each—what it is, and of what kind. Pleasure also must be a good; for all living creatures naturally desire it. Hence it follows that both agreeable and beautiful things must be good; for the former produce pleasure, while among beautiful things some are pleasant and others are desirable in themselves.

To enumerate them one by one, the following things must necessarily be good. Happiness, since it is desirable in itself and self-sufficient, and to obtain it we choose a number of things. Justice, courage, self-control, magnanimity, magnificence, and all other similar states of mind, for they are virtues of the soul. Health, beauty, and the like, for they are virtues of the body and produce many advantages; for instance, health is productive of pleasure and of life, wherefore it is thought to be best of all, because it is the cause of two things which the majority of men prize most highly. Wealth, since it is the excellence of acquisition and productive of many things. A friend and friendship, since a friend is desirable in himself and produces many advantages. Honor and good repute, since they are agreeable and produce many advantages, and are generally accompanied by the possession of those things for which men are honored. Eloquence and capacity for action; for all such faculties are productive of many advantages. Further, natural cleverness, good memory, readiness to learn, quick-wittedness, and all similar qualities; for these faculties are productive of advantages. The same applies to all the sciences, arts, and even life, for even though no other good should result from it, it is desirable in itself. Lastly, justice, since it is expedient in general for the common weal.

These are nearly all the things generally recognized as good; in the case of doubtful goods, the arguments in their favor are drawn from the following. That is good the opposite of which is evil, or the opposite of which is advantageous to our enemies; for instance, if it is specially advantageous to our enemies that we should be cowards, it is clear that courage is specially advantageous to the citizens. And, speaking generally, the opposite of what our enemies desire or of that in which they rejoice, appears to be advantageous; wherefore it was well said:

"Of a truth Priam would exult."

This is not always the case, but only as a general rule, for there is nothing to prevent one and the same thing being sometimes advantageous to two opposite parties; hence it is said that misfortune brings men together, when a common danger threatens them.

That which is not in excess is good, whereas that which is greater than it should be, is bad. And that which has cost much labor and expense, for it at once is seen to be an apparent good, and such a thing is regarded as an end, and an end of many efforts; now, an end is a good. Wherefore it was said:

"And they would [leave Argive Helen for Priam and the Trojans] to boast of,"

and,

"It is disgraceful to tarry long,"

and the proverb,

"[to break] the pitcher at the door."

And that which many aim at and which is seen to be competed for by many; for that which all aim at was recognized as a good, and the majority may almost stand for "all." And that which is the object of praise, for no one praises that which is not good. And that which is praised by enemies; for if even those who are injured by it acknowledge its goodness, this amounts to a universal recognition of it; for it is because of its goodness being evident that they acknowledge it, just as those whom their enemies praise are worthless. Wherefore the Corinthians imagined themselves insulted by Simonides, when he wrote,

"Ilium does not blame the Corinthians."

And that which one of the practically wise or good, man or woman, has chosen before others, as Athene chose Odysseus, Theseus Helen, the goddesses Alexander (Paris), and Homer Achilles.

And, generally speaking, all that is deliberately chosen is good. Now, men deliberately choose to do the things just mentioned, and those which are harmful to their enemies, and advantageous to their friends, and things which are possible. The last are of two kinds: things which might happen, and things which easily happen; by the latter are meant things that happen without labor or in a short time, for difficulty is defined by labor or length of time. And anything that happens as men wish is good; and what they wish is either what is not evil at all or is less an evil than a good, which will be the case for instance, whenever the penalty attached to it is unnoticed or light. And things that are peculiar to them, or which no one else possesses, or which are out of the common; for thus the honor is greater. And things which are appropriate to them; such are all things befitting them in respect of birth and power. And things which they think they lack, however unimportant; for none the less they deliberately choose to acquire them. And things which are easy of accomplishment, for being easy they are possible; such things are those in which all, or most men, or those who are equals or inferiors have been successful. And things whereby they will gratify friends or incur the hatred of enemies. And all things that those whom they admire deliberately choose to do. And those things in regard to which they are clever naturally or by experience; for they hope to be more easily successful in them. And things which no worthless man would approve, for that makes them the more commendable. And things which they happen to desire, for such things seem not only agreeable, but also better. Lastly, and above all, each man thinks those things good which are the object of his special desire, as victory of the man who desires victory, honor of the ambitious man, money of the avaricious, and so in other instances. These then are the materials from which we must draw our arguments in reference to good and the expedient.

## Chapter 7

But since men often agree that both of two things are useful, but dispute which is the more so, we must next speak of the greater good and the more expedient. Let one thing, then, be said to exceed another, when it is as great and something more—and to be exceeded when it is contained in the other. "Greater" and "more" always imply a relation with less; "great" and "small," "much" and "little" with the general size of things; the "great" is that which exceeds, and that which falls short of it is "small"; and similarly "much" and "little." Since, besides, we call good that which is desirable for its own sake and not for anything else, and that which all things aim at and which they would choose if they possessed reason and practical wisdom; and that which is productive or protective of good, or on which such things follow; and since that for the sake of which anything is done is the end, and the end is that for the sake of which everything else is done, and that is good for each man which relatively to him presents all these conditions, it necessarily follows that a larger number of good things is a greater good than one or a smaller number, if the one or the smaller number is reckoned as one of them; for it exceeds them and that which is contained is exceeded.
And if that which is greatest in one class surpass that which is greatest in another class, the first class will surpass the second; and whenever one class surpasses another, the greatest of that class will surpass the greatest

of the other. For instance, if the biggest man is greater than the biggest woman, men in general will be bigger than women; and if men in general are bigger than women, the biggest man will be bigger than the biggest woman; for the superiority of classes and of the greatest things contained in them are proportionate. And when this follows on that, but not that on this [then "that" is the greater good]; for the enjoyment of that which follows is contained in that of the other. Now, things follow simultaneously, or successively, or potentially; thus, life follows simultaneously on health, but not health on life; knowledge follows subsequently on learning [but not learning on knowledge]; and simple theft potentially on sacrilege, for one who commits sacrilege will also steal. And things which exceed the same thing by a greater amount [than something else] are greater, for they must also exceed the greater. And things which produce a greater good are greater; for this we agreed was the meaning of productive of greater. And similarly, that which is produced by a greater cause; for if that which produces health is more desirable than that which produces pleasure and a greater good, then health is a greater good than pleasure. And that which is more desirable in itself is superior to that which is not; for example, strength is a greater good than the wholesome, which is not desirable for its own sake, while strength is; and, this we agreed was the meaning of a good. And the end is a greater good than the means; for the latter is desirable for the sake of something else, the former for its own sake; for instance, exercise is only a means for the acquirement of a good constitution. And that which has less need of one or several other things in addition is a greater good, for it is more independent (and "having less need" means needing fewer or easier additions). And when one thing does not exist or cannot be brought into existence without the aid of another, but that other can, then that which needs no aid is more independent, and accordingly is seen to be a greater good.

And if one thing is a first principle, and another not; if one thing is a cause and another not, for the same reason; for without cause or first principle nothing can exist or come into existence. And if there are two first principles or two causes, that which results from the greater is greater; and conversely, when there are two first principles or two causes, that which is the first cause or principle of the greater is greater. It is clear then, from what has been said, that a thing may be greater in two ways; for if it is a first principle but another is not, it will appear to be greater, and if it is not a first principle [but an end], while another is; for the end is greater and not a first principle. Thus, Leodamas, when accusing Callistratus, declared that the man who had given the advice was more guilty than the one who carried it out; for if he had not suggested it, it could not have been carried out. And conversely, when accusing Chabrias, he declared that the man who had carried out the advice was more guilty than the one who had given it; for it could not have been carried out, had there not been some one to do so, and the reason why people devised plots was that others might carry them out.

And that which is scarcer is a greater good than that which is abundant, as gold than iron, although it is less useful, but the possession of it is more valuable, since it is more difficult of acquisition. From another point of view, that which is abundant is to be preferred to that which is scarce, because the use of it is greater, for "often" exceeds "seldom,"; whence the saying:

"Water is best."

And, speaking generally, that which is more difficult is preferable to that which is easier of attainment, for it is scarcer; but from another point of view that which is easier is preferable to that which is more difficult; for its nature is as we wish. And that, the contrary or the deprivation of which is greater, is the greater good. And virtue is greater than non-virtue, and vice than non-vice; for virtues and vices are ends, the others not. And those things whose works are nobler or more disgraceful are themselves greater; and the works of those things, the vices and virtues of which are greater, will also be greater, since between causes and first principles compared with results there is the same relation as between results compared with causes and first principles. Things, superiority in which is more desirable or nobler, are to be preferred; for instance, sharpness of sight is preferable to keenness of smell for sight is better than smell. And loving one's friends more than money is nobler, whence it follows that love of friends is nobler than love of money. And, on the other hand, the better and nobler things are, the better and nobler will be their superiority; and similarly, those things, the desire for which is nobler and better, are themselves nobler and better, for greater longings are directed towards greater objects. For the same reason, the better and nobler the object, the better and nobler are the desires.

And when the sciences are nobler and more dignified, the nobler and more dignified are their subjects; for as is the science, so is the truth which is its object, and each science prescribes that which properly belongs to it; and, by analogy, the nobler and more dignified the objects of a science, the nobler and more dignified is the science itself, for the same reasons. And that which men of practical wisdom, either all, or more, or the best of them, would judge, or have judged, to be a greater good, must necessarily be such, either absolutely or in so far as they have judged as men of practical wisdom. The same may be said in regard to everything else; for the nature, quantity, and quality of things are such as would be defined by science and practical wisdom. But our statement only applies to goods; for we defined that as good which everything, if possessed of practical wisdom, would choose; hence it is evident that that is a greater good to which practical wisdom assigns the superiority. So also are those things which better men possess, either absolutely, or in so far as they are better; for instance courage is better than strength. And what the better man would choose, either absolutely or in so far as he is better; thus, it is better to suffer wrong than to commit it, for that is what the juster man would choose. And that which is more agreeable rather than that which is less so; for all things pursue pleasure and desire it for its own sake; and it is by these conditions that the good and the end have been defined. And that is more agreeable which is less subject to pain and is agreeable for a longer time. And that which is nobler than that which is less noble; for the noble is that which is either agreeable or desirable in itself. And all things which we have a greater desire to be instrumental in procuring for ourselves or for our friends are greater goods, and those as to which our desire is least are greater evils. And things that last longer are preferable to those that are of shorter duration, and those that are safer to those that are less so; for time increases the use of the first and the wish that of the second; for whenever we wish, we can make greater use of things that are safe.

And things in all cases follow the relations between coordinates and similar inflections; for instance, if "courageously" is nobler than and preferable to "temperately," then "courage" is preferable to "temperance," and it is better to be "courageous" than "temperate." And that which is chosen by all is better than that which is not; and that which the majority choose than that which the minority choose; for, as we have said, the good is that which all desire, and consequently a good is greater, the more it is desired. The same applies to goods which are recognized as greater by opponents or enemies, by judges, or by those whom they select; for in the one case it would be, so to say, the verdict of all mankind, in the other that of those who are acknowledged authorities and experts. And sometimes a good is greater in which all participate, for it is a disgrace not to participate in it; sometimes when none or only a few participate in it, for it is scarcer. And things which are more praiseworthy, since they are nobler. And in the same way things which are more highly honored, for honor is a sort of measure of worth; and conversely those things are greater evils, the punishment for which is greater. And those things which are greater than what is acknowledged, or appears, to be great, are greater. And the same whole when divided into parts appears greater, for there appears to be superiority in a greater number of things. Whence the poet says that Meleager was persuaded to rise up and fight by the recital of
"All the ills that befall those whose city is taken; the people perish, and fire utterly destroys the city, and strangers carry off the children."
Combination and building up, as employed by Epicharmus, produce the same effect as division, and for the same reason; for combination is an exhibition of great superiority and appears to be the origin and cause of

great things. And since that which is harder to obtain and scarcer is greater, it follows that special occasions, ages, places, times, and powers, produce great effects; for if a man does things beyond his powers, beyond his age, and beyond what his equals could do, if they are done in such a manner, in such a place, and at such a time, they will possess importance in actions that are noble, good, or just, or the opposite. Hence the epigram on the Olympian victor:

"Formerly, with a rough basket on my shoulders, I used to carry fish from Argos to Tegea."

And Iphicrates lauded himself, saying, "Look what I started from!" And that which is natural is a greater good than that which is acquired, because it is harder. Whence the poet says:

"Self-taught am I."

And that which is the greatest part of that which is great is more to be desired; as Pericles said in his Funeral Oration, that the removal of the youth from the city was like the year being robbed of its spring. And those things which are available in greater need, as in old age and illness, are greater goods. And of two things that which is nearer the end proposed is preferable. And that which is useful for the individual is preferable to that which is useful absolutely; that which is possible to that which is impossible; for it is the possible that is useful to us, not the impossible. And those things which are at the end of life; for things near the end are more like ends.

And real things are preferable to those that have reference to public opinion, the latter being defined as those which a man would not choose if they were likely to remain unnoticed by others. It would seem then that it is better to receive than to confer a benefit; for one would choose the former even if it should pass unnoticed, whereas one would not choose to confer a benefit, if it were likely to remain unknown. Those things also are to be preferred, which men would rather possess in reality than in appearance, because they are nearer the truth; wherefore it is commonly said that justice is a thing of little importance, because people prefer to appear just than to be just; and this is not the case, for instance, in regard to health. The same may be said of things that serve several ends; for instance, those that assist us to live, to live well, to enjoy life, and to do noble actions; wherefore health and wealth seem to be the greatest goods, for they include all these advantages. And that which is more free from pain and accompanied by pleasure is a greater good; for there is more than one good, since pleasure and freedom from pain combined are both goods. And of two goods the greater is that which, added to one and the same, makes the whole greater. And those things, the presence of which does not escape notice, are preferable to those which pass unnoticed, because they appear more real; whence being wealthy would appear to be a greater good than the appearance of it. And that which is held most dear, sometimes alone, sometimes accompanied by other things, is a greater good. Wherefore he who puts out the eye of a one-eyed man and he who puts out one eye of another who has two, does not do equal injury; for in the former case, a man has been deprived of that which he held most dear.

# Chapter 8

These are nearly all the topics from which arguments may be drawn in persuading and dissuading; but the most important and effective of all the means of persuasion and good counsel is to know all the forms of government and to distinguish the manners and customs, institutions, and interests of each; for all men are guided by considerations of expediency, and that which preserves the State is expedient. Further, the declaration of the authority is authoritative, and the different kinds of authority are distinguished according to forms of government; in fact, there are as many authorities as there are forms of government.

Now, there are four kinds of government, democracy, oligarchy, aristocracy, monarchy, so that the supreme and deciding authority is always a part or the whole of these. Democracy is a form of government in which the offices are distributed by the people among themselves by lot; in an oligarchy, by those who possess a certain property-qualification; in an aristocracy, by those who possess an educational qualification, meaning an education that is laid down by the law. In fact, in an aristocracy, power and office are in the hands of those who have remained faithful to what the law prescribes, and who must of necessity appear best, whence this form of government has taken its name. In a monarchy, as its name indicates, one man alone is supreme over all; if it is subject to certain regulations, it is called a kingdom; if it is unlimited, a tyranny.

Nor should the end of each form of government be neglected, for men choose the things which have reference to the end. Now, the end of democracy is liberty, of oligarchy wealth, of aristocracy things relating to education and what the law prescribes, . . . , of tyranny self-protection. It is clear then that we must distinguish the manners and customs, institutions, and interests of each form of government, since it is in reference to this that men make their choice. But as proofs are established not only by demonstrative, but also by ethical argument—since we have confidence in an orator who exhibits certain qualities, such as goodness, goodwill, or both—it follows that we ought to be acquainted with the characters of each form of government; for, in reference to each, the character most likely to persuade must be that which is characteristic of it. These characters will be understood by the same means; for characters reveal themselves in accordance with moral purpose, and moral purpose has reference to the end.

We have now stated what things, whether future or present, should be the aim of those who recommend a certain course; from what topics they should derive their proofs of expediency; further, the ways and means of being well equipped for dealing with the characters and institutions of each form of government, so far as was within the scope of the present occasion; for the subject has been discussed in detail in the Politics.

## Chapter 9

We will next speak of virtue and vice, of the noble and the disgraceful, since they constitute the aim of one who praises and of one who blames; for, when speaking of these, we shall incidentally bring to light the means of making us appear of such and such a character, which, as we have said, is a second method of proof; for it is by the same means that we shall be able to inspire confidence in ourselves or others in regard to virtue. But since it happens that men, seriously or not, often praise not only a man or a god but even inanimate things or any ordinary animal, we ought in the same way to make ourselves familiar with the propositions relating to these subjects. Let us, then, discuss these matters also, so far as may serve for illustration.

The noble, then, is that which, being desirable in itself is at the same time worthy of praise, or which, being good, is pleasant because it is good. If this is the noble, then virtue must of necessity be noble, for, being good, it is worthy of praise. Virtue, it would seem, is a faculty of providing and preserving good things, a faculty productive of many and great benefits, in fact, of all things in all cases. The components of virtue are justice, courage, self-control, magnificence, magnanimity, liberality, gentleness, practical and speculative wisdom. The greatest virtues are necessarily those which are most useful to others, if virtue is the faculty of conferring benefits. For this reason justice and courage are the most esteemed, the latter being useful to others in war, the former in peace as well. Next is liberality, for the liberal spend freely and do not dispute the possession of wealth, which is the chief object of other men's desire. Justice is a virtue which assigns to each man his due in conformity with the law; injustice claims what belongs to others, in opposition to the law. Courage makes men perform noble acts in the midst of dangers according to the dictates of the law and in submission to it; the contrary is cowardice. Self-control is a virtue which disposes men in regard to the pleasures of the body as the law prescribes; the contrary is licentiousness. Liberality does good in many matters; the

contrary is avarice. Magnanimity is a virtue productive of great benefi
the contrary is little-mindedness. Magnificence is a virtue which produ
greatness in matters of expenditure; the contraries are little-mindedness
and meanness. Practical wisdom is a virtue of reason, which enables men
to come to a wise decision in regard to good and evil things, which have
been mentioned as connected with happiness.

Concerning virtue and vice in general and their separate parts, enough has been said for the moment. To discern the rest presents no difficulty; for it is evident that whatever produces virtue, as it tends to it, must be noble, and so also must be what comes from virtue; for such are its signs and works. But since the signs of virtue and such things as are the works and sufferings of a good man are noble, it necessarily follows that all the works and signs of courage and all courageous acts are also noble. The same may be said of just things and of just actions; (but not of what one suffers justly; for in this alone amongst the virtues that which is justly done is not always noble, and a just punishment is more disgraceful than an unjust punishment). The same applies equally to the other virtues. Those things of which the reward is honor are noble; also those which are done for honor rather than money. Also, those desirable things which a man does not do for his own sake; things which are absolutely good, which a man has done for the sake of his country, while neglecting his own interests; things which are naturally good; and not such as are good for the individual, since such things are inspired by selfish motives.

And those things are noble which it is possible for a man to possess after death rather than during his lifetime, for the latter involve more selfishness; all acts done for the sake of others, for they are more disinterested; the successes gained, not for oneself but for others; and for one's benefactors, for that is justice; in a word, all acts of kinds, for they are disinterested. And the contrary of those things of which we are ashamed; for we are ashamed of what is disgraceful, in words, acts, or intention; as, for instance, when Alcaeus said:

"I would fain say something, but shame holds me back,"

Sappho rejoined:

"Hadst thou desired what was good or noble, and had not thy tongue stirred up some evil to utter it, shame would not have filled thine eyes; but thou would'st have spoken of what is right."

Those things also are noble for which men anxiously strive, but without fear; for men are thus affected about goods which lead to good repute. Virtues and actions are nobler, when they proceed from those who are naturally worthier, for instance, from a man rather than from a woman. It is the same with those which are the cause of enjoyment to others rather than to ourselves; this is why justice and that which is just are noble. To take vengeance on one's enemies is nobler than to come to terms with them; for to retaliate is just, and that which is just is noble; and further, a courageous man ought not to allow himself to be beaten. Victory and honor also are noble; for both are desirable even when they are fruitless, and are manifestations of superior virtue. And things worthy of remembrance, which are the more honorable the longer their memory lasts; those which follow us after death; those which are accompanied by honor; and those which are out of the common. Those which are only possessed by a single individual, because they are more worthy of remembrance. And possessions which bring no profit; for they are more gentlemanly. Customs that are peculiar to individual peoples and all the tokens of what is esteemed among them are noble; for instance, in Lacedaemon it is noble to wear one's hair long, for it is the mark of a gentleman, the performance of any servile task being difficult for one whose hair is long. And not carrying on any vulgar profession is noble, for a gentleman does not live in dependence on others.

We must also assume, for the purpose of praise or blame, that qualities which closely resemble the real qualities are identical with them; for instance, that the cautious man is cold and designing, the simpleton good-natured, and the emotionless gentle. And in each case we must adopt a term from qualities closely connected, always in the more favorable sense; for instance, the choleric and passionate man may be spoken of as frank and open, the arrogant as magnificent and dignified; those in excess as possessing the corresponding virtue, the fool-hardy as courageous, the recklessly extravagant as liberal. For most people will think so, and at the same time a fallacious argument may be drawn from the motive; for if a man risks his life when there is no necessity, much more will he be thought likely to do so when it is honorable; and if he is lavish to all comers, the more so will he be to his friends; for the height of virtue is to do good to all. We ought also to consider in whose presence we praise, for, as Socrates said, it is not difficult to praise Athenians among Athenians. We ought also to speak of what is esteemed among the particular audience, Scythians, Lacedaemonians, or philosophers, as actually existing there. And, generally speaking, that which is esteemed should be classed as noble, since there seems to be a close resemblance between the two. Again, all such actions as are in accord with what is fitting are noble; if, for instance, they are worthy of a man's ancestors or of his own previous achievements; for to obtain additional honor is noble and conduces to happiness. Also, if the tendency of what is done is better and nobler, and goes beyond what is to be expected; for instance, if a man is moderate in good fortune and stout-hearted in adversity, or if, when he becomes greater, he is better and more forgiving. Such was the phrase of Iphicrates, "Look what I started from!" and of the Olympian victor:

"Formerly, with a rough basket on my shoulders, I used to carry fish from Argos to Tegea."
and of Simonides:
"Daughter, wife, and sister of tyrants."
Since praise is founded on actions, and acting according to moral purpose is characteristic of the worthy man, we must endeavor to show that a man is acting in that manner, and it is useful that it should appear that he has done so on several occasions. For this reason also one must assume that accidents and strokes of good fortune are due to moral purpose; for if a number of similar examples can be adduced, they will be thought to be signs of virtue and moral purpose.

Now praise is language that sets forth greatness of virtue; hence it is necessary to show that a man's actions are virtuous. But encomium deals with achievements—all attendant circumstances, such as noble birth and education, merely conduce to persuasion; for it is probable that virtuous parents will have virtuous offspring and that a man will turn out as he has been brought up. Hence we pronounce an encomium upon those who have achieved something. Achievements, in fact, are signs of moral habit; for we should praise even a man who had not achieved anything, if we felt confident that he was likely to do so. Blessing and felicitation are identical with each other, but are not the same as praise and encomium, which, as virtue is contained in happiness, are contained in felicitation.

Praise and counsels have a common aspect; for what you might suggest in counseling becomes encomium by a change in the phrase. Accordingly, when we know what we ought to do and the qualities we ought to possess, we ought to make a change in the phrase and turn it, employing this knowledge as a suggestion. For instance, the statement that "one ought not to pride oneself on goods which are due to fortune, but on those which are due to oneself alone," when expressed in this way, has the force of a suggestion; but expressed thus, "he was proud, not of goods which were due to fortune, but of those which were due to himself alone," it becomes praise. Accordingly, if you desire to praise, look what you would suggest; if you desire to suggest, look what you would praise. The form of the expression will necessarily be opposite, when the prohibitive has been changed into the non-prohibitive.

We must also employ many of the means of amplification; for instance, if a man has done anything alone, or first, or with a few, or has been chiefly responsible for it; all these circumstances render an action noble. Similarly, topics derived from times and seasons, that is to say, if our expectation is surpassed. Also, if a man has often been successful in the same thing; for this is of importance and would appear to be due to the man himself, and not to be the result of chance. And if it is for his sake that distinctions which are an encouragement or honor have been invented and established;

and if he was the first on whom an encomium was pronounced, as Hippolochus, or to whom a statue was set up in the market-place, as to Harmodius and Aristogiton. And similarly in opposite cases. If he does not furnish you with enough material in himself, you must compare him with others, as Isocrates used to do, because of his inexperience of forensic speaking. And you must compare him with illustrious personages, for it affords ground for amplification and is noble, if he can be proved better than men of worth. Amplification is with good reason ranked as one of the forms of praise, since it consists in superiority, and superiority is one of the things that are noble. That is why, if you cannot compare him with illustrious personages, you must compare him with ordinary persons, since superiority is thought to indicate virtue. Speaking generally, of the topics common to all rhetorical arguments, amplification is most suitable for epideictic speakers, whose subject is actions which are not disputed, so that all that remains to be done is to attribute beauty and importance to them. Examples are most suitable for deliberative speakers, for it is by examination of the past that we divine and judge the future. Enthymemes are most suitable for forensic speakers, because the past, by reason of its obscurity, above all lends itself to the investigation of causes and to demonstrative proof. Such are nearly all the materials of praise or blame, the things which those who praise or blame should keep in view, and the sources of encomia and invective; for when these are known their contraries are obvious, since blame is derived from the contrary things.

## Chapter 10

We have next to speak of the number and quality of the propositions of which those syllogisms are constructed which have for their object accusation and defence. Three things have to be considered; first, the nature and the number of the motives which lead men to act unjustly; secondly, what is the state of mind of those who so act; thirdly, the character and dispositions of those who are exposed to injustice. We will discuss these questions in order, after we have first defined acting unjustly. Let injustice, then, be defined as voluntarily causing injury contrary to the law. Now, the law is particular or general. By particular, I mean the written law in accordance with which a state is administered; by general, the unwritten regulations which appear to be universally recognized. Men act voluntarily when they know what they do, and do not act under compulsion. What is done voluntarily is not always done with premeditation; but what is done with premeditation is always known to the agent, for no one is ignorant of what he does with a purpose. The motives which lead men to do injury and commit wrong actions are depravity and incontinence. For if men have one or more vices, it is in that which makes him vicious that he shows himself unjust; for example, the illiberal in regard to money, the licentious in regard to bodily pleasures, the effeminate in regard to what makes for ease, the coward in regard to dangers, for fright makes him desert his comrades in peril; the ambitious in his desire for honor, the irascible owing to anger, one who is eager to conquer in his desire for victory, the rancorous in his desire for vengeance; the foolish man from having mistaken ideas of right and wrong, the shameless from his contempt for the opinion of others. Similarly, each of the rest of mankind is unjust in regard to his special weakness.

This will be perfectly clear, partly from what has already been said about the virtues, and partly from what will be said about the emotions. It remains to state the motives and character of those who do wrong and of those who suffer from it. First, then, let us decide what those who set about doing wrong long for or avoid; for it is evident that the accuser must examine the number and nature of the motives which are to be found in his opponent; the defendant, which of them are not to be found in him. Now, all human actions are either the result of man's efforts or not. Of the latter some are due to chance, others to necessity. Of those due to necessity, some are to be attributed to compulsion, others to nature, so that the things which men do not do of themselves are all the result of chance, nature, or compulsion. As for those which they do of themselves and of which they are the cause, some are the result of habit, others of longing, and of the latter some are due to rational, others to irrational longing. Now wish is a [rational] longing for good, for no one wishes for anything unless he thinks it is good; irrational longings are anger and desire. Thus all the actions of men must necessarily be referred to seven causes: chance, nature, compulsion, habit, reason, anger, and desire.

But it is superfluous to establish further distinctions of men's acts based upon age, moral habits, or anything else. For if the young happen to be irascible, or passionately desire anything, it is not because of their youth that they act accordingly, but because of anger and desire. Nor is it because of wealth or poverty; but the poor happen to desire wealth because of their lack of it, and the rich desire unnecessary pleasures because they are able to procure them. Yet in their case too it will not be wealth or poverty, but desire, that will be the mainspring of their action. Similarly, the just and the unjust, and all the others who are said to act in accordance with their moral habits, will act from the same causes, either from reason or emotion, but some from good characters and emotions, and others from the opposite. Not but that it does happen that such and such moral habits are followed by such and such consequences; for it may be that from the outset the fact of being temperate produces in the temperate man good opinions and desires in the matter of pleasant things, in the intemperate man the contrary. Therefore we must leave these distinctions on one side, but we must examine what are the usual consequences of certain conditions. For, if a man is fair or dark, tall or short, there is no rule that any such consequences should follow, but if he is young or old, just or unjust, it does make a difference. In a word, it will be necessary to take account of all the circumstances that make men's characters different; for instance, if a man fancies himself rich or poor, fortunate or unfortunate, it will make a difference. We will, however, discuss this later; let us now speak of what remains to be said here.

Things which are the result of chance are all those of which the cause is indefinite, those which happen without any end in view, and that neither always, nor generally, nor regularly. The definition of chance will make this clear. Things which are the result of nature are all those of which the cause is in themselves and regular; for they turn out always, or generally, in the same way. As for those which happen contrary to nature there is no need to investigate minutely whether their occurrence is due to a certain force of nature or some other cause (it would seem, however, that such cases also are due to chance). Those things are the result of compulsion which are done by the agents themselves in opposition to their desire or calculation. Things are the result of habit, when they are done because they have often been done. Things are the result of calculation which are done because, of the goods already mentioned, they appear to be expedient either as an end or means to an end, provided they are done by reason of their being expedient; for even the intemperate do certain things that are expedient, for the sake, not of expediency, but of pleasure. Passion and anger are the causes of acts of revenge. But there is a difference between revenge and punishment; the latter is inflicted in the interest of the sufferer, the former in the interest of him who inflicts it, that he may obtain satisfaction. We will define anger when we come to speak of the emotions. Desire is the cause of things being done that are apparently pleasant. The things which are familiar and to which we have become accustomed are among pleasant things; for men do with pleasure many things which are not naturally pleasant, when they have become accustomed to them.

In short, all things that men do of themselves either are, or seem, good or pleasant; and since men do voluntarily what they do of themselves, and involuntarily what they do not, it follows that all that men do voluntarily will be either that which is or seems good, or that which is or seems pleasant. For I reckon among good things the removal of that which is evil or seems evil, or the exchange of a greater evil for a less, because these two things are in a way desirable; in like manner, I reckon among pleasant things the removal of that which is or appears painful, and the exchange of a greater pain for a less. We must therefore make ourselves acquainted with the number and quality of expedient and pleasant things. We have already spoken of the expedient when discussing deliberative rhetoric; let us now speak of the pleasant. And we must regard our definitions as sufficient in each case, provided they are neither obscure nor too precise.

# Chapter 11

Let it be assumed by us that pleasure is a certain movement of the soul, a sudden and perceptible settling down into its natural state, and pain the opposite. If such is the nature of pleasure, it is evident that that which produces the disposition we have just mentioned is pleasant, and that that which destroys it or produces the contrary settling down is painful. Necessarily, therefore, it must be generally pleasant to enter into a normal state (especially when what is done in accordance with that state has come into its own again); and the same with habits. For that which has become habitual becomes as it were natural; in fact, habit is something like nature, for the distance between "often" and "always" is not great, and nature belongs to the idea of "always," habit to that of "often." That which is not compulsory is also pleasant, for compulsion is contrary to nature. That is why what is necessary is painful, and it was rightly said,
"For every act of necessity is disagreeable."
Application, study, and intense effort are also painful, for these involve necessity and compulsion, if they have not become habitual; for then habit makes them pleasant. Things contrary to these are pleasant; wherefore states of ease, idleness, carelessness, amusement, recreation, and sleep are among pleasant things, because none of these is in any way compulsory. Everything of which we have in us the desire is pleasant, for desire is a longing for the pleasant.
Now, of desires some are irrational, others rational. I call irrational all those that are not the result of any assumption. Such are all those which are called natural; for instance, those which come into existence through the body—such as the desire of food, thirst, hunger, the desire of such and such food in particular; the desires connected with taste, sexual pleasures, in a word, with touch, smell, hearing, and sight. I call those desires rational which are due to our being convinced; for there are many things which we desire to see or acquire when we have heard them spoken of and are convinced that they are pleasant.
And if pleasure consists in the sensation of a certain emotion, and imagination is a weakened sensation, then both the man who remembers and the man who hopes will be attended by an imagination of what he remembers or hopes. This being so, it is evident that there is pleasure both for those who remember and for those who hope, since there is sensation. Therefore all pleasant things must either be present in sensation, or past in

recollection, or future in hope; for one senses the present, recollects the past, and hopes for the future. Therefore our recollections are pleasant, not only when they recall things which when present were agreeable, but also some things which were not, if their consequence subsequently proves honorable or good; whence the saying:
"Truly it is pleasant to remember toil after one has escaped it,"
and,
"When a man has suffered much and accomplished much, he afterwards takes pleasure even in his sorrows when he recalls them."
The reason of this is that even to be free from evil is pleasant. Things which we hope for are pleasant, when their presence seems likely to afford us great pleasure or advantage, without the accompaniment of pain. In a word, all things that afford pleasure by their presence as a rule also afford pleasure when we hope for or remember them. Wherefore even resentment is pleasant, as Homer said of anger that it is
"Far sweeter than dripping honey;"
for no one feels resentment against those whom vengeance clearly cannot overtake, or those who are far more powerful than he is; against such, men feel either no resentment or at any rate less.

Most of our desires are accompanied by a feeling of pleasure, for the recollection of a past or the hope of a future pleasure creates a certain pleasurable enjoyment; thus, those suffering from fever and tormented by thirst enjoy the remembrance of having drunk and the hope that they will drink again. The lovesick always take pleasure in talking, writing, or composing verses about the beloved; for it seems to them that in all this recollection makes the object of their affection perceptible. Love always begins in this manner, when men are happy not only in the presence of the beloved, but also in his absence when they recall him to mind. This is why, even when his absence is painful, there is a certain amount of pleasure even in mourning and lamentation; for the pain is due to his absence, but there is pleasure in remembering and, as it were, seeing him and recalling his actions and personality. Wherefore it was rightly said by the poet;
"Thus he spake, and excited in all a desire of weeping."
And revenge is pleasant; for if it is painful to be unsuccessful, it is pleasant to succeed. Now, those who are resentful are pained beyond measure when they fail to secure revenge, while the hope of it delights them. Victory is pleasant, not only to those who love to conquer, but to all; for there is produced an idea of superiority, which all with more or less eagerness desire. And since victory is pleasant, competitive and disputatious amusements must be so too, for victories are often gained in them; among these we may include games with knuckle-bones, ball-games, dicing, and draughts. It is the same with serious sports; for some become pleasant when one is familiar with them, while others are so from the outset, such

as the chase and every description of outdoor sport; for rivalry implies victory. It follows from this that practice in the law courts and disputation are pleasant to those who are familiar with them and well qualified. Honor and good repute are among the most pleasant things, because every one imagines that he possesses the qualities of a worthy man, and still more when those whom he believes to be trustworthy say that he does. Such are neighbors rather than those who live at a distance; intimate friends and fellow-citizens rather than those who are unknown; contemporaries rather than those who come later; the sensible rather than the senseless; the many rather than the few; for such persons are more likely to be trustworthy than their opposites. As for those for whom men feel great contempt, such as children and animals, they pay no heed to their respect or esteem, or, if they do, it is not for the sake of their esteem, but for some other reason.

A friend also is among pleasant things, for it is pleasant to love—for no one loves wine unless he finds pleasure in it—just as it is pleasant to be loved; for in this case also a man has an impression that he is really endowed with good qualities, a thing desired by all who perceive it; and to be loved is to be cherished for one's own sake. And it is pleasant to be admired, because of the mere honor. Flattery and the flatterer are pleasant, the latter being a sham admirer and friend. It is pleasant to do the same things often; for that which is familiar is, as we said, pleasant. Change also is pleasant, since change is in the order of nature; for perpetual sameness creates an excess of the normal condition; whence it was said:

"Change in all things is sweet."

This is why what we only see at intervals, whether men or things, is pleasant; for there is a change from the present, and at the same time it is rare. And learning and admiring are as a rule pleasant; for admiring implies the desire to learn, so that what causes admiration is to be desired, and learning implies a return to the normal. It is pleasant to bestow and to receive benefits; the latter is the attainment of what we desire, the former the possession of more than sufficient means, both of them things that men desire. Since it is pleasant to do good, it must also be pleasant for men to set their neighbors on their feet, and to supply their deficiencies. And since learning and admiring are pleasant, all things connected with them must also be pleasant; for instance, a work of imitation, such as painting, sculpture, poetry, and all that is well imitated, even if the object of imitation is not pleasant; for it is not this that causes pleasure or the reverse, but the inference that the imitation and the object imitated are identical, so that the result is that we learn something. The same may be said of sudden changes and narrow escapes from danger; for all these things excite wonder. And since that which is in accordance with nature is pleasant, and things which are akin are akin in accordance with nature, all

things akin and like are for the most part pleasant to each other, as man to man; horse to horse, youth to youth. This is the origin of the proverbs:
"The old have charms for the old, the young for the young,"
"Like to like,"
"Beast knows beast,"
"Birds of a feather flock together,"
and all similar sayings.
And since things which are akin and like are always pleasant to one another, and every man in the highest degree feels this in regard to himself, it must needs be that all men are more or less selfish; for it is in himself above all that such conditions are to be found. Since, then, all men are selfish, it follows that all find pleasure in what is their own, such as their works and words. That is why men as a rule are fond of those who flatter and love them, of honor, and of children; for the last are their own work. It is also pleasant to supply what is wanting, for then it becomes our work. And since it is most pleasant to command, it is also pleasant to be regarded as wise for practical wisdom is commanding, and philosophy consists in the knowledge of many things that excite wonder. Further, since men are generally ambitious, it follows that it is also agreeable to find fault with our neighbors. And if a man thinks he excels in anything, he likes to devote his time to it; as Euripides says:
"And allotting the best part of each day to that in which he happens to surpass himself, he presses eagerly towards it."
Similarly, since amusement, every kind of relaxation, and laughter are pleasant, ridiculous things—men, words, or deeds—must also be pleasant. The ridiculous has been discussed separately in the Poetics. Let this suffice for things that are pleasant; those that are painful will be obvious from the contraries of these.

## Chapter 12

Such are the motives of injustice; let us now state the frame of mind of those who commit it, and who are the sufferers from it. Men do wrong when they think that it can be done and that it can be done by them; when they think that their action will either be undiscovered, or if discovered will remain unpunished; or if it is punished, that the punishment will be less than the profit to themselves or to those for whom they care. As for the kind of things which seem possible or impossible, we will discuss them later, for these topics are common to all kinds of rhetoric. Now men who commit wrong think they are most likely to be able to do so with impunity, if they are eloquent, business-like, experienced in judicial trials, if they have many friends, and if they are wealthy. They think there is the greatest chance of their being able to do so, if they themselves belong to the above classes; if not, if they have friends, servants, or accomplices who do; for thanks to these qualities they are able to commit wrong and to escape discovery and punishment. Similarly, if they are friends of those who are being wronged, or of the judges; for friends are not on their guard against being wronged and, besides, they prefer reconciliation to taking proceedings; and judges favor those whom they are fond of, and either let them off altogether or inflict a small penalty.

Those are likely to remain undetected whose qualities are out of keeping with the charges, for instance, if a man wanting in physical strength were accused of assault and battery, or a poor and an ugly man of adultery. Also, if the acts are done quite openly and in sight of all; for they are not guarded against, because no one would think them possible. Also, if they are so great and of such a nature that no one would even be likely to attempt them, for these also are not guarded against; for all guard against ordinary ailments and wrongs, but no one takes precautions against those ailments from which no one has ever yet suffered. And those who have either no enemy at all or many; the former hope to escape notice because they are not watched, the latter do escape because they would not be thought likely to attack those who are on their guard and because they can defend themselves by the plea that they would never have attempted it. And, those who have ways or places of concealment for stolen property, or abundant opportunities of disposing of it. And those who, even if they do not remain undetected, can get the trial set aside or put off, or corrupt the judges. And those who, if a fine be imposed, can get payment in full set aside or put off for a long time, or those who, owing to poverty, have nothing to lose. And in cases where the profit is certain, large, or immediate, while the punishment is small, uncertain, or remote. And where there can be no punishment equal to the advantages, as seems to be the case in a tyranny. And when the unjust acts are real gains and the only punishment is disgrace; and when, on the contrary, the unjust acts tend to our credit, for instance, if one avenges father or mother, as was the case with Zeno, while the punishment only involves loss of money, exile, or something of the kind. For men do wrong from both these motives and in both these conditions of mind; but the persons are not the same, and their characters are exactly opposite. And those who have often been undetected or have escaped punishment; and those who have often been unsuccessful; for in such cases, as in actual warfare, there are always men ready to return to the fight. And all who hope for pleasure and profit at once, while the pain and the loss come later; such are the intemperate, intemperance being concerned with all things that men long for. And when, on the contrary, the pain or the loss is immediate, while the pleasure and the profit are later and more lasting; for temperate and wiser men pursue such aims. And those who may possibly be thought to have acted by chance or from necessity, from some natural impulse or from habit, in a word, to have committed an error rather than a crime. And those who hope to obtain indulgence; and all those who are in need, which is of two kinds; for men either need what is necessary, as the poor, or what is superfluous, as the wealthy. And those who are highly esteemed or held in great contempt; the former will not be suspected, the latter no more than they are already.

In such a frame of mind men attempt to do wrong, and the objects of their wrongdoing are men and circumstances of the following kind. Those who possess what they themselves lack, things either necessary, or superfluous, or enjoyable; both those who are far off and those who are near, for in the one case the gain is speedy, in the other reprisals are slow, as if, for instance, Greeks were to plunder Carthaginians. And those who never take precautions and are never on their guard, but are confiding; for all these are easily taken unawares. And those who are indolent; for it requires a man who takes pains to prosecute. And those who are bashful; for they are not likely to fight about money. And those who have often been wronged but have not prosecuted, being, as the proverb says, "Mysian booty." And those who have never, or those who have often, suffered wrong; for both are off their guard, the one because they have never yet been attacked, the others because they do not expect to be attacked again. And those who have been slandered, or are easy to slander; for such men neither care to go to law, for fear of the judges, nor, if they do, can they convince them; to this class belong those who are exposed to hatred or envy. And those against whom the wrongdoer can pretend that either their ancestors, or themselves, or their friends, have either committed, or intended to commit, wrong either against himself, or his ancestors, or those for whom he has great regard; for, as the proverb says, "evil-doing only needs an excuse." And both enemies and friends; for it is easy to injure the latter, and pleasant to injure the former. And those who are friendless. And those who are unskilled in speech or action; for either they make no attempt to prosecute, or come to terms, or accomplish nothing. And those to whom it is no advantage to waste time waiting for the verdict or damages, such as strangers or husbandmen; for they are ready to compromise on easy terms and to drop proceedings. And those who have committed numerous wrongs, or such as those from which they themselves are suffering; for it seems almost an act of justice that a man should suffer a wrong such as he had been accustomed to make others suffer; if, for instance, one were to assault a man who was in the habit of outraging others. And those who have already injured us, or intended, or intend, or are about to do so; for in such a case vengeance is both pleasant and honorable, and seems to be almost an act of justice. And those whom we wrong in order to ingratiate ourselves with our friends, or persons whom we admire or love, or our masters, in a word, those by whom our life is ruled. And those in reference to whom there is a chance of obtaining merciful consideration. And those against whom we have a complaint, or with whom we have had a previous difference, as Callippus acted in the matter of Dion; for in such cases it seems almost an act of justice. And those who are going to be attacked by others, if we do not attack first, since it is no longer possible to deliberate; thus, Aenesidemus is said to have sent the prize in the game of cottabus to Gelon, who, having reduced a town to slavery, had anticipated him by doing what he had intended to do himself. And those to whom, after having injured them, we shall be enabled to do many acts of justice, in the idea that it will he easy to repair the wrong; as Jason the Thessalian said one should sometimes commit injustice, in order to be able also to do justice often.

Men are ready to commit wrongs which all or many are in the habit of committing, for they hope to be pardoned for their offences. They steal objects that are easy to conceal; such are things that are quickly consumed, as eatables; things which can easily be changed in form or color or composition; things for which there are many convenient hiding-places, such as those that are easy to carry or stow away in a corner; those of which a thief already possesses a considerable number exactly similar or hard to distinguish. Or they commit wrongs which the victims are ashamed to disclose, such as outrages upon the women of their family, upon themselves, or upon their children. And all those wrongs in regard to which appeal to the law would create the appearance of litigiousness; such are wrongs which are unimportant or venial. These are nearly all the dispositions which induce men to commit wrong, the nature and motive of the wrongs, and the kind of persons who are the victims of wrong.

# Chapter 13

Let us now classify just and unjust actions generally, starting from what follows. Justice and injustice have been defined in reference to laws and persons in two ways. Now there are two kinds of laws, particular and general. By particular laws I mean those established by each people in reference to themselves, which again are divided into written and unwritten; by general laws I mean those based upon nature. In fact, there is a general idea of just and unjust in accordance with nature, as all men in a manner divine, even if there is neither communication nor agreement between them. This is what Antigone in Sophocles evidently means, when she declares that it is just, though forbidden, to bury Polynices, as being naturally just:

"For neither to-day nor yesterday, but from all eternity, these statutes live and no man knoweth whence they came."
And as Empedocles says in regard to not killing that which has life, for this is not right for some and wrong for others,
"But a universal precept, which extends without a break throughout the wide-ruling sky and the boundless earth."
Alcidamas also speaks of this precept in his Messeniacus. . . . And in relation to persons, there is a twofold division of law; for what one ought to do or ought not to do is concerned with the community generally, or one of its members.
Therefore there are two kinds of just and unjust acts, since they can be committed against a definite individual or against the community; he who commits adultery or an assault is guilty of wrong against a definite individual, he who refuses to serve in the army of wrong against the State. All kinds of wrong acts having been thus distinguished, some of which affect the State, others one or several individuals, let us repeat the definition of being wronged, and then go on to the rest. Being wronged is to suffer injustice at the hands of one who voluntarily inflicts it, for it has been established that injustice is a voluntary act. And since the man who suffers injustice necessarily sustains injury and that against his will, it is evident from what has been said in what the injuries consist; for things good and bad have already been distinguished in themselves, and it has been said that voluntary acts are all such as are committed with knowledge of the case. Hence it necessarily follows that all accusations concern the State or the individual, the accused having acted either ignorantly and against his will, or voluntarily and with knowledge, and in the latter case with malice aforethought or from passion. We will speak of anger when we come to treat of the passions, and we have already stated in what circumstances and with what dispositions men act with deliberate purpose.
But since a man, while admitting the fact, often denies the description of the charge or the point on which it turns—for instance, admits that he took something, but did not steal it; that he was the first to strike, but committed no outrage; that he had relations, but did not commit adultery, with a woman; or that he stole something but was not guilty of sacrilege, since the object in question was not consecrated; or that he trespassed, but not on public land; or that he held converse with the enemy, but was not guilty of treason—for this reason it will be necessary that a definition should be given of theft, outrage, or adultery, in order that, if we desire to prove that an offence has or has not been committed, we may be able to put the case in a true light. In all such instances the question at issue is to know whether the supposed offender is a wrongdoer and a worthless person, or not; for vice and wrongdoing consist in the moral purpose, and

such terms as outrage and theft further indicate purpose; for if a man has struck, it does not in all cases follow that he has committed an outrage, but only if he has struck with a certain object, for instance, to bring disrepute upon the other or to please himself. Again, if a man has taken something by stealth, it is by no means certain that he has committed theft, but only if he has taken it to injure another or to get something for himself. It is the same in all other cases as in these.

We have said that there are two kinds of just and unjust actions (for some are written, but others are unwritten), and have spoken of those concerning which the laws are explicit; of those that are unwritten there are two kinds. One kind arises from an excess of virtue or vice, which is followed by praise or blame, honor or dishonor, and rewards; for instance, to be grateful to a benefactor, to render good for good, to help one's friends, and the like; the other kind contains what is omitted in the special written law. For that which is equitable seems to be just, and equity is justice that goes beyond the written law. These omissions are sometimes involuntary, sometimes voluntary, on the part of the legislators; involuntary when it may have escaped their notice, voluntary when, being unable to define for all cases, they are obliged to make a universal statement, which is not applicable to all, but only to most, cases; and whenever it is difficult to give a definition owing to the infinite number of cases, as, for instance, the size and kind of an iron instrument used in wounding; for life would not be long enough to reckon all the possibilities. If then no exact definition is possible, but legislation is necessary, one must have recourse to general terms; so that, if a man wearing a ring lifts up his hand to strike or actually strikes, according to the written law he is guilty of wrongdoing, but in reality he is not; and this is a case for equity.

If then our definition of equity is correct, it is easy to see what things and persons are equitable or not. Actions which should be leniently treated are cases for equity; errors, wrong acts, and misfortunes, must not be thought deserving of the same penalty. Misfortunes are all such things as are unexpected and not vicious; errors are not unexpected, but are not vicious; wrong acts are such as might be expected and vicious, for acts committed through desire arise from vice. And it is equitable to pardon human weaknesses, and to look, not to the law but to the legislator; not to the letter of the law but to the intention of the legislator; not to the action itself, but to the moral purpose; not to the part, but to the whole; not to what a man is now, but to what he has been, always or generally; to remember good rather than ill treatment, and benefits received rather than those conferred; to bear injury with patience; to be willing to appeal to the judgement of reason rather than to violence; to prefer arbitration to the law court, for the arbitrator keeps equity in view, whereas the dicast looks only to the law, and the reason why arbitrators were appointed was that equity might prevail. Let this manner of defining equity suffice.

## Chapter 14

Wrong acts are greater in proportion to the injustice from which they spring. For this reason the most trifling are sometimes the greatest, as in the charge brought by Callistratus against Melanopus that he had fraudulently kept back three consecrated half-obols from the temple-builders; whereas, in the case of just actions, it is quite the contrary. The reason is that the greater potentially inheres in the less; for he who has stolen three consecrated half-obols will commit any wrong whatever. Wrong acts are judged greater sometimes in this way, sometimes by the extent of the injury done. A wrong act is greater when there is no adequate punishment for it, but all are insufficient; when there is no remedy, because it is difficult if not impossible to repair it; and when the person injured cannot obtain legal satisfaction, since it is irremediable; for justice and punishment are kinds of remedies. And if the sufferer, having been wronged, has inflicted some terrible injury upon himself, the guilty person deserves greater punishment; wherefore Sophocles, when pleading on behalf of Euctemon, who had committed suicide after the outrage he had suffered, declared that he would not assess the punishment at less than the victim had assessed it for himself. A wrong act is also greater when it is unprecedented, or the first of its kind, or when committed with the aid of few accomplices; and when it has been frequently committed; or when because of it new prohibitions and penalties have been sought and found: thus, at Argos the citizen owing to whom a new law has been passed, is punished, as well as those on whose account a new prison had to be built. The crime is greater, the more brutal it is; or when it has been for a long time premeditated; when the recital of it inspires terror rather than pity. Rhetorical tricks of the following kind may be used:—the statement that the accused person has swept away or violated several principles of justice, for example, oaths, pledges of friendship, plighted word, the sanctity of marriage; for this amounts to heaping crime upon crime. Wrong acts are greater when committed in the very place where wrongdoers themselves are sentenced, as is done by false witnesses; for where would a man not commit wrong, if he does so in a court of justice? They are also greater when accompanied by the greatest disgrace; when committed against one who has been the guilty person's benefactor, for in that case, the wrongdoer is guilty of wrong twice over, in that he not only does wrong, but does not return good for good. So too, again, when a man offends against the unwritten laws of right, for there is greater merit in doing right without being compelled; now the written laws involve compulsion, the unwritten do not. Looked at in another way, wrongdoing is greater, if it violates the written laws; for a man who commits wrongs that alarm him and involve punishment, will be ready to commit wrong for which he will not be punished. Let this suffice for the treatment of the greater or less degree of wrongdoing.

# Chapter 15

Following on what we have just spoken of, we have now briefly to run over what are called the inartificial proofs, for these properly belong to forensic oratory. These proofs are five in number: laws, witnesses, contracts, torture, oaths. Let us first then speak of the laws, and state what use should be made of them when exhorting or dissuading, accusing or defending. For it is evident that, if the written law is counter to our case, we must have recourse to the general law and equity, as more in accordance with justice; and we must argue that, when the dicast takes an oath to decide to the best of his judgement, he means that he will not abide rigorously by the written laws; that equity is ever constant and never changes, even as the general law, which is based on nature, whereas the written laws often vary (this is why Antigone in Sophocles justifies herself for having buried Polynices contrary to the law of Creon, but not contrary to the unwritten law: "For this law is not of now or yesterday, but is eternal . . . this I was not likely [to infringe through fear of the pride] of any man);"
and further, that justice is real and expedient, but not that which only appears just; nor the written law either, because it does not do the work of the law; that the judge is like an assayer of silver, whose duty is to distinguish spurious from genuine justice; that it is the part of a better man to make use of and abide by the unwritten rather than the written law. Again, it is necessary to see whether the law is contradictory to another approved law or to itself; for instance, one law enacts that all contracts should be binding, while another forbids making contracts contrary to the law. If the meaning of the law is equivocal, we must turn it about, and see in which way it is to be interpreted so as to suit the application of justice or expediency, and have recourse to that. If the conditions which led to the enactment of the law are now obsolete, while the law itself remains, one must endeavor to make this clear and to combat the law by this argument. But if the written law favors our case, we must say that the oath of the dicast "to decide to the best of his judgement" does not justify him in deciding contrary to the law, but is only intended to relieve him from the charge of perjury, if he is ignorant of the meaning of the law; that no one chooses that which is good absolutely, but that which is good for himself;

that there is no difference between not using the laws and their not being enacted; that in the other arts there is no advantage in trying to be wiser than the physician, for an error on his part does not do so much harm as the habit of disobeying the authority; that to seek to be wiser than the laws is just what is forbidden in the most approved laws. Thus much for the laws.

Witnesses are of two kinds, ancient and recent; of the latter some share the risk of the trial, others are outside it. By ancient I mean the poets and men of repute whose judgements are known to all; for instance, the Athenians, in the matter of Salamis, appealed to Homer as a witness, and recently the inhabitants of Tenedos to Periander of Corinth against the Sigeans. Cleophon also made use of the elegiacs of Solon against Critias, to prove that his family had long been notorious for licentiousness, otherwise Solon would never have written:

"Bid me the fair-haired Critias listen to his father."

One should appeal to such witnesses for the past, but also to interpreters of oracles for the future; thus, for instance, Themistocles interpreted the wooden wall to mean that they must fight at sea. Further, proverbs, as stated, are evidence; for instance, if one man advises another not to make a friend of an old man, he can appeal to the proverb, "Never do good to an old man." And if he advises another to kill the children, after having killed the fathers, he can say,

"Foolish is he who, having killed the father, suffers the children to live."

By recent witnesses I mean all well-known persons who have given a decision on any point, for their decisions are useful to those who are arguing about similar cases. Thus for instance, Eubulus, when attacking Chares in the law courts, made use of what Plato said against Archibius, namely, "that the open confession of wickedness had increased in the city." And those who share the risk of the trial, if they are thought to be perjurers. Such witnesses only serve to establish whether an act has taken place or not, whether it is or is not the case; but if it is a question of the quality of the act, for instance, whether it is just or unjust, expedient or inexpedient, they are not competent witnesses; but witnesses from a distance are very trustworthy even in regard to this. But ancient witnesses are the most trustworthy of all, for they cannot be corrupted. In regard to the confirmation of evidence, when a man has no witnesses, he can say that the decision should be given in accordance with probabilities, and that this is the meaning of the oath "according to the best of one's judgement"; that probabilities cannot be bribed to deceive, and that they cannot be convicted of bearing false witness. But if a man has witnesses and his adversary has none, he can say that probabilities incur no responsibility, and that there would have been no need of evidence, if an investigation according to the arguments were sufficient. Evidence partly concerns ourselves, partly our adversary, as to the fact itself or moral character; so that it is evident that one never need lack useful evidence. For, if we have no evidence as to the fact itself, neither in confirmation of our own case nor against our opponent, it will always be possible to obtain some evidence as to character that will establish either our own respectability or the worthlessness of our opponent. As for all the other questions relative to a witness, whether he is a friend, an enemy, or neutral, of good or bad or middling reputation, and for all other differences of this kind, we must have recourse to the same topics as those from which we derive our enthymemes.

As for contracts, argument may be used to the extent of magnifying or minimizing their importance, of proving that they do or do not deserve credit. If we have them on our side, we must try to prove them worthy of credit and authoritative; but if they are on the side of our opponent, we must do the opposite. In view of rendering them worthy or unworthy of credit, the method of procedure is exactly the same as in the case of witnesses; for contracts are trustworthy according to the character of their signatories or depositaries. When the existence of the contract is admitted, if it is in our favor, we must strengthen it by asserting that the contract is a law, special and partial; and it is not the contracts that make the law authoritative, but it is the laws that give force to legal contracts. And in a general sense the law itself is a kind of contract, so that whoever disobeys or subverts a contract, subverts the laws. Further, most ordinary and all voluntary transactions are carried out according to contract; so that if you destroy the authority of contracts, the mutual intercourse of men is destroyed. All other arguments suitable to the occasion are easy to see. But if the contract is against us and in favor of our opponents, in the first place those arguments are suitable which we should oppose to the law if it were against us; that it would be strange if, while we consider ourselves entitled to refuse to obey ill-made laws, whose authors have erred, we should be obliged to consider ourselves always bound by contracts. Or, that the judge is the dispenser of justice; so that it is not the contents of the contract that he has to consider, but what is juster. Further, that one cannot alter justice either by fraud or compulsion, for it is based upon nature, whereas contracts may be entered into under both conditions. In addition to this, we must examine whether the contract is contrary to any written law of our own or foreign countries, or to any general law, or to other previous or subsequent contracts. For either the latter are valid and the former not, or the former are right and the latter fraudulent; we may put it in whichever way it seems fit. We must also consider the question of expediency—whether the contract is in any way opposed to the interest of the judges. There are a number of other arguments of the same kind, which are equally easy to discern.

Torture is a kind of evidence, which appears trustworthy, because a sort of compulsion is attached to it. Nor is it difficult to see what may be said concerning it, and by what arguments, if it is in our favor, we can exaggerate its importance by asserting that it is the only true kind of evidence; but if it is against us and in favor of our opponent, we can destroy its value by telling the truth about all kinds of torture generally; for those under compulsion are as likely to give false evidence as true, some being ready to endure everything rather than tell the truth, while others are equally ready to make false charges against others, in the hope of being sooner released from torture. It is also necessary to be able to quote actual examples of the kind with which the judges are acquainted. It may also be said that evidence given under torture is not true; for many thick-witted and thick-skinned persons, and those who are stout-hearted heroically hold out under sufferings, while the cowardly and cautious, before they see the sufferings before them, are bold enough; wherefore evidence from torture may be considered utterly untrustworthy.

As to oaths four divisions may be made; for either we tender an oath and accept it, or we do neither, or one without the other, and in the last case we either tender but do not accept, or accept but do not tender. Besides this, one may consider whether the oath has already been taken by us or by the other party. If you do not tender the oath to the adversary, it is because men readily perjure themselves, and because, after he has taken the oath, he will refuse to repay the money, while, if he does not take the oath, you think that the dicasts will condemn him; and also because the risk incurred in leaving the decision to the dicasts is preferable, for you have confidence in them, but not in your adversary. If you refuse to take the oath yourself, you may argue that the oath is only taken with a view to money; that, if you had been a scoundrel, you would have taken it at once, for it is better to be a scoundrel for something than for nothing; that, if you take it, you will win your case, if not, you will probably lose it; consequently, your refusal to take it is due to moral excellence, not to fear of committing perjury. And the apophthegm of Xenophanes is apposite—that "it is unfair for an impious man to challenge a pious one," for it is the same as a strong man challenging a weak one to hit or be hit. If you accept the oath, you may say that you have confidence in yourself, but not in your opponent, and, reversing the apophthegm of Xenophanes, that the only fair way is that the impious man should tender the oath and the pious man take it; and that it would be monstrous to refuse to take the oath yourself, while demanding that the judges should take it before giving their verdict. But if you tender the oath, you may say that it is an act of piety to be willing to leave the matter to the gods; that your opponent has no need to look for other judges, for you allow him to make the decision himself; and that it would be ridiculous that he should be unwilling to take an oath in cases where he demands that the dicasts should take one.

Now, since we have shown how we must deal with each case individually, it is clear how we must deal with them when taken two and two; for instance, if we wish to take the oath but not to tender it, to tender it but not to take it, to accept and tender it, or to do neither the one nor the other. For such cases, and similarly the arguments, must be a combination of those already mentioned. And if we have already taken an oath which contradicts the present one, we may argue that it is not perjury; for whereas wrongdoing is voluntary, and perjury is wrongdoing, what is done in error or under compulsion is involuntary. Here we must draw the conclusion that perjury consists in the intention, not in what is said. But if the opponent has taken such an oath, we may say that one who does not abide by what be has sworn subverts everything, for this is the reason why the dicasts take an oath before applying the laws; and [we may make this appeal]: "They demand that you abide by your oath as judges, while they themselves do not abide by theirs." Further, we should employ all means of amplification. Let this suffice for the inartificial proofs.

# Book II

## Chapter 1

Such then are the materials which we must employ in exhorting and dissuading, praising and blaming, accusing and defending, and such are the opinions and propositions that are useful to produce conviction in these circumstances; for they are the subject and source of enthymemes, which are specially suitable to each class (so to say) of speeches. But since the object of Rhetoric is judgement—for judgements are pronounced in deliberative rhetoric and judicial proceedings are a judgement—it is not only necessary to consider how to make the speech itself demonstrative and convincing, but also that the speaker should show himself to be of a certain character and should know how to put the judge into a certain frame of mind. For it makes a great difference with regard to producing conviction—especially in demonstrative, and, next to this, in forensic oratory—that the speaker should show himself to be possessed of certain qualities and that his hearers should think that he is disposed in a certain way towards them; and further, that they themselves should be disposed in a certain way towards him. In deliberative oratory, it is more useful that the orator should appear to be of a certain character, in forensic, that the hearer should be disposed in a certain way; for opinions vary, according as men love or hate, are wrathful or mild, and things appear either altogether different, or different in degree; for when a man is favorably disposed towards one on whom he is passing judgement, he either thinks that the accused has committed no wrong at all or that his offence is trifling; but if he hates him, the reverse is the case. And if a man desires anything and has good hopes of getting it, if what is to come is pleasant, he thinks that it is sure to come to pass and will be good; but if a man is unemotional or not hopeful it is quite the reverse.
For the orator to produce conviction three qualities are necessary; for, independently of demonstrations, the things which induce belief are three in number. These qualities are good sense, virtue, and goodwill; for speakers are wrong both in what they say and in the advice they give, because they lack either all three or one of them. For either through want of sense they form incorrect opinions, or, if their opinions are correct, through viciousness they do not say what they think, or, if they are sensible and good, they lack goodwill; wherefore it may happen that they do not give the best advice, although they know what it is. These qualities are all

that are necessary, so that the speaker who appears to possess all three will necessarily convince his hearers. The means whereby he may appear sensible and good must be inferred from the classification of the virtues; for to make himself appear such he would employ the same means as he would in the case of others. We must now speak of goodwill and friendship in our discussion of the emotions.

The emotions are all those affections which cause men to change their opinion in regard to their judgements, and are accompanied by pleasure and pain; such are anger, pity, fear, and all similar emotions and their contraries. And each of them must be divided under three heads; for instance, in regard to anger, the disposition of mind which makes men angry, the persons with whom they are usually angry, and the occasions which give rise to anger. For if we knew one or even two of these heads, but not all three, it would be impossible to arouse that emotion. The same applies to the rest. Just as, then, we have given a list of propositions in what we have previously said, we will do the same here and divide the emotions in the same manner.

# Chapter 2

Let us then define anger as a longing, accompanied by pain, for a real or apparent revenge for a real or apparent slight, affecting a man himself or one of his friends, when such a slight is undeserved. If this definition is correct, the angry man must always be angry with a particular individual (for instance, with Cleon, but not with men generally), and because this individual has done, or was on the point of doing, something against him or one of his friends; and lastly, anger is always accompanied by a certain pleasure, due to the hope of revenge to come. For it is pleasant to think that one will obtain what one aims at; now, no one aims at what is obviously impossible of attainment by him, and the angry man aims at what is possible for himself. Wherefore it has been well said of anger, that
"Far sweeter than dripping honey down the throat it spreads in men's hearts."
for it is accompanied by a certain pleasure, for this reason first, and also because men dwell upon the thought of revenge, and the vision that rises before us produces the same pleasure as one seen in dreams.

Slighting is an actualization of opinion in regard to something which appears valueless; for things which are really bad or good, or tend to become so, we consider worthy of attention, but those which are of no importance or trifling we ignore. Now there are three kinds of slight: disdain, spitefulness, and insult. For he who disdains, slights, since men disdain those things which they consider valueless and slight what is of no account. And the spiteful man appears to show disdain; for spitefulness consists in placing obstacles in the way of another's wishes, not in order that any advantage may accrue to him who spites, but to prevent any accruing to the other. Since then he does not act in this manner from self-interest, it is a slight; for it is evident that he has no idea that the other is likely to hurt him, for in that case he would be afraid of him instead of slighting him; nor that he will be of any use to him worth speaking of, for in that case his thought would be how to become his friend.

Similarly, he who insults another also slights him; for insult consists in causing injury or annoyance whereby the sufferer is disgraced, not to obtain any other advantage for oneself besides the performance of the act, but for one's own pleasure; for retaliation is not insult, but punishment. The cause of the pleasure felt by those who insult is the idea that, in ill-treating others, they are more fully showing superiority. That is why the young and the wealthy are given to insults; for they think that, in committing them, they are showing their superiority. Dishonor is characteristic of insult; and one who dishonors another slights him; for that which is worthless has no value, either as good or evil. Hence Achilles in his wrath exclaims:

"He has dishonored me, since he keeps the prize he has taken for himself," and

"[has treated me] like a dishonored vagrant,"

as if being angry for these reasons. Now men think that they have a right to be highly esteemed by those who are inferior to them in birth, power, and virtue, and generally, in whatever similar respect a man is far superior to another; for example, the rich man to the poor man in the matter of money, the eloquent to the incompetent speaker in the matter of oratory, the governor to the governed, and the man who thinks himself worthy to rule to one who is only fit to be ruled. Wherefore it has been said:

"Great is the wrath of kings cherished by Zeus,"
and
"Yet it may be that even afterwards he cherishes his resentment,"

for kings are resentful in consideration of their superior rank. Further, men are angry at slights from those by whom they think they have a right to expect to be well treated; such are those on whom they have conferred or are conferring benefits, either themselves, or some one else for them, or one of their friends; and all those whom they desire, or did desire, to benefit.

It is now evident from these considerations what is the disposition of those who are angry, with whom they are angry, and for what reasons. Men are angry when they are pained, because one who is pained aims at something; if then anyone directly opposes him in anything, as, for instance, prevents him from drinking when thirsty, or not directly, but seems to be doing just the same; and if anyone goes against him or refuses to assist him, or troubles him in any other way when he is in this frame of mind, he is angry with all such persons. Wherefore the sick, the necessitous, [those at war], the lovesick, the thirsty, in a word, all who desire something and cannot obtain it, are prone to anger and easily excited, especially against those who make light of their present condition; for instance, the sick man is easily provoked in regard to his illness, the necessitous in regard to his poverty, the warrior in regard to warlike affairs, the lover in regard to love affairs, and so with all the rest; for the passion present in his mind in each case paves the way for his anger. Again, men are angry when the event is contrary to their expectation, for the more unexpected a thing is, the more it pains; just as they are overjoyed if, contrary to expectation, what they desire comes to pass. From this it is obvious what are the seasons, times, states of mind, and conditions of age in which we are easily moved to anger; and what are the various times, places, and reasons, which make us more prone to anger in proportion as we are subject to their influence. Such then are the dispositions of those who are easily roused to anger. As to the objects of their anger, men are angry with those who ridicule, mock, and scoff at them, for this is an insult. And with those who injure them in ways that are indications of insult. But these acts must be of such a kind that they are neither retaliatory nor advantageous to those who commit them; for if they are, they then appear due to gratuitous insult. And men are angry with those who speak ill of or despise things which they themselves consider of the greatest importance; for instance, if a man speaks contemptuously of philosophy or of personal beauty in the presence of those who pride themselves upon them; and so in all other cases. But they are far more angry if they suspect that they do not possess these qualities, either not at all, or not to any great extent, or when others do not think they possess them. For when they feel strongly that they do possess those qualities which are the subject of mockery, they pay no heed to it. And they are more angry with those who are their friends than with those who are not, for they think that they have a right to be treated well by them rather than ill. And they are angry with those who have been in the habit of honoring and treating them with respect, if they no longer behave so towards them; for they think that they are being treated with contempt by them, otherwise they would treat them as before. And with those who do not return their kindnesses nor requite them in full; and with those who oppose them, if they are inferiors; for all such appear to treat them with contempt, the latter as if they regarded them as inferiors, the former as if they had received kindnesses from inferiors.

And they are more angry with those who are of no account, if they slight them; for anger at a slight was assumed to be felt at those who ought not to behave in such a manner; for inferiors ought not to slight their superiors. And they are angry with friends, if they neither speak well of nor treat them well, and in an even greater degree, if they do the opposite. And if they fail to perceive that they want something from them, as Plexippus in Antiphon's tragedy reproached Meleager; for failure to perceive this is a sign of slight; since, when we care for people, these things are noticed. And they are angry with those who rejoice, or in a general way are cheerful when they are unfortunate; for this is an indication of enmity or slight. And with those who do not care if they pain them; whence they are angry with those who bring bad news. And with those who listen to the tale of their faults, or look on them with indifference, for they resemble slighters or enemies; for friends sympathize and all men are pained to see their own faults exposed. And further, with those who slight them before five classes of persons: namely, their rivals, those whom they admire, those by whom they would like to be admired, those whom they respect, or those who respect them; when anyone slights them before these, their anger is greater. They are also angry with those who slight such persons as it would be disgraceful for them not to defend, for instance, parents, children, wives, and dependents. And with those who are ungrateful, for the slight is contrary to all sense of obligation. And with those who employ irony, when they themselves are in earnest; for irony shows contempt. And with those who do good to others, but not to them; for not to think them worthy of what they bestow upon all others also shows contempt. Forgetfulness also is a cause of anger, such as forgetting names, although it is a mere trifle, since even forgetfulness seems a sign of slight; for it is caused by indifference, and indifference is a slight. We have thus stated at one and the same time the frame of mind and the reasons which make men angry, and the objects of their anger. It is evident then that it will be necessary for the speaker, by his eloquence, to put the hearers into the frame of mind of those who are inclined to anger, and to show that his opponents are responsible for things which rouse men to anger and are people of the kind with whom men are angry.

## Chapter 3

And since becoming angry is the opposite of becoming mild, and anger of mildness, we must determine the state of mind which makes men mild, towards whom they become mild, and the reasons which make them so. Let us then define making mild as the quieting and appeasing of anger. If then men are angry with those who slight them, and slight is voluntary, it is evident that they are mild towards those who do none of these things, or do them involuntarily, or at least appear to be such; and towards those who intended the opposite of what they have done, and all who behave in the same way to themselves, for no one is likely to slight himself. And towards those who admit and are sorry for a slight; for finding as it were satisfaction in the pain the offenders feel at what they have done, men cease to be angry. Evidence of this may be seen in the punishment of slaves; for we punish more severely those who contradict us and deny their offence, but cease to be angry with those who admit that they are justly punished. The reason is that to deny what is evident is disrespect, and disrespect is slight and contempt; anyhow, we show no respect for those for whom we entertain a profound contempt. Men also are mild towards those who humble themselves before them and do not contradict them, for they seem to recognize that they are inferior; now, those who are inferior are afraid, and no one who is afraid slights another. Even the behavior of dogs proves that anger ceases towards those who humble themselves, for they do not bite those who sit down. And men are mild towards those who are serious with them when they are serious, for they think they are being treated seriously, not with contempt. And towards those who have rendered them greater services. And towards those who want something and deprecate their anger, for they are humbler. And towards those who refrain from insulting, mocking, or slighting anyone, or any virtuous man, or those who resemble themselves. And generally speaking, one can determine the reasons that make for mildness by their opposites. Thus, men are mild towards those whom they fear or respect, as long as they feel so towards them, for it is impossible to be afraid and angry at the same time. And against those who have acted in anger they either feel no anger or in a less degree, for they do not seem to have acted from a desire to slight. For no one slights another when angry, since slight is free from pain, but anger is accompanied by it. And men are not angry with those who usually show respect for them.

It is also evident that those are mild whose condition is contrary to that which excites anger, as when laughing, in sport, at a feast, in prosperity, in success, in abundance, and, in general, in freedom from pain, in pleasure which does not imply insult, or in virtuous hope. Further, those whose anger is of long standing and not in its full flush, for time appeases anger. Again, vengeance previously taken upon one person appeases anger against another, even though it be greater. Wherefore Philocrates, when someone asked him why he did not justify himself when the people were angry with him, made the judicious reply, "Not yet." "When then?" "When I see someone accused of the same offence"; for men grow mild when they have exhausted their anger upon another, as happened in the case of Ergophilus. For although the Athenians were more indignant with him than with Callisthenes, they acquitted him, because they had condemned Callicrates to death on the previous day. Men also grow mild towards those

whom they pity; and if an offender has suffered greater evil than those who are angry would have inflicted, for they have an idea that they have as it were obtained reparation. And if they think that they themselves are wrong and deserve what they suffer, for anger is not aroused against what is just; they no longer think that they are being treated otherwise than they should be, which, as we have said, is the essence of anger. Wherefore we should inflict a preliminary verbal chastisement, for even slaves are less indignant at punishment of this kind. And men are milder if they think that those punished will never know that the punishment comes from them in requital for their own wrongs; for anger has to do with the individual, as is clear from our definition. Wherefore it is justly said by the poet:
"Tell him that it is Odysseus, sacker of cities,"
as if Polyphemus would not have been punished, had he remained ignorant who had blinded him and for what. So that men are not angry either with any others who cannot know who punishes them, or with the dead, since they have paid the last penalty and can feel neither pain nor anything else, which is the aim of those who are angry. So then, in regard to Hector, Homer, when desirous of restraining the anger of Achilles against a dead man, well says:
"For it is senseless clay that he outrages in his wrath."
It is evident, then, that men must have recourse to these topics when they desire to appease their audience, putting them into the frame of mind required and representing those with whom they are angry as either formidable or deserving of respect, or as having rendered them great services, or acted involuntarily, or as exceedingly grieved at what they have done.

## Chapter 4

Let us now state who are the persons that men love or hate, and why, after we have defined love and loving. Let loving, then, be defined as wishing for anyone the things which we believe to be good, for his sake but not for our own, and procuring them for him as far as lies in our power. A friend is one who loves and is loved in return, and those who think their relationship is of this character consider themselves friends. This being granted, it necessarily follows that he is a friend who shares our joy in good fortune and our sorrow in affliction, for our own sake and not for any other reason. For all men rejoice when what they desire comes to pass and are pained when the contrary happens, so that pain and pleasure are indications of their wish. And those are friends who have the same ideas of good and bad, and love and hate the same persons, since they necessarily wish the same things; wherefore one who wishes for another what he wishes for himself seems to be the other's friend.

We also like those who have done good either to us or to those whom we hold dear, if the services are important, or are cordially rendered, or under certain circumstances, and for our sake only; and all those whom we think desirous of doing us good. And those who are friends of our friends and who like those whom we like, and those who are liked by those who are liked by us; and those whose enemies are ours, those who hate those whom we ourselves hate, and those who are hated by those who are hated by us; for all such persons have the same idea as ourselves of what is good, so that they wish what is good for us, which, as we said, is the characteristic of a friend. Further, we like those who are ready to help others in the matter of money or personal safety; wherefore men honor those who are liberal and courageous and just. And such we consider those who do not live upon others; the sort of men who live by their exertions, and among them agriculturists, and, beyond all others, those who work with their own hands. And the self-controlled, because they are not likely to commit injustice; and those who are not busybodies, for the same reason. And those with whom we wish to be friends, if they also seem to wish it; such are those who excel in virtue and enjoy a good reputation, either generally, or amongst the best, or amongst those who are admired by us or by whom we are admired. Further, those who are agreeable to live or spend the time with; such are those who are good-tempered and not given to carping at our errors, neither quarrelsome nor contentious, for all such persons are pugnacious, and the wishes of the pugnacious appear to be opposed to ours.

And those are liked who are clever at making or taking a joke, for each has the same end in view as his neighbor, being able to take a joke and return it in good taste. And those who praise our good qualities, especially those which we ourselves are afraid we do not possess; those who are neat in their personal appearance and dress, and clean-living; those who do not make our errors or the benefits they have conferred a matter of reproach, for both these are inclined to be censorious; those who bear no malice and do not cherish the memory of their wrongs, but are easily appeased; for we think that they will be to ourselves such as we suppose them to be to others; and those who are neither given to slander, or eager to know the faults of their neighbors nor our own, but only the good qualities; for this is the way in which the good man acts. And those who do not oppose us when we are angry or occupied, for such persons are pugnacious; and those who show any good feeling towards us; for instance, if they admire us, think us good men, and take pleasure in our company, especially those who are so disposed towards us in regard to things for which we particularly desire to be either admired or to be thought worthy or agreeable. And we like those

who resemble us and have the same tastes, provided their interests do not clash with ours and that they do not gain their living in the same way; for then it becomes a case of
"Potter [being jealous] of potter."
And those who desire the same things, provided it is possible for us to share them; otherwise the same thing would happen again. And those with whom we are on such terms that we do not blush before them for faults merely condemned by public opinion, provided that this is not due to contempt; and those before whom we do blush for faults that are really bad. And those whose rivals we are, or by whom we wish to be emulated, but not envied,—these we either like or wish to be friends with them. And those whom we are ready to assist in obtaining what is good, provided greater evil does not result for ourselves. And those who show equal fondness for friends, whether absent or present; wherefore all men like those who show such feeling for the dead.

In a word, men like those who are strongly attached to their friends and do not leave them in the lurch; for among good men they chiefly like those who are good friends. And those who do not dissemble with them; such are those who do not fear to mention even their faults. (For, as we have said, before friends we do not blush for faults merely condemned by public opinion; if then he who blushes for such faults is not a friend, he who does not is likely to be one). And men like those who are not formidable, and in whom they have confidence; for no one likes one whom he fears. Companionship, intimacy, kinship, and similar relations are species of friendship. Things that create friendship are doing a favor, and doing it unasked, and not making it public after doing it; for then it seems to have been rendered for the sake of the friend, and not for any other reason.

As for enmity and hatred, it is evident that they must be examined in the light of their contraries. The causes which produce enmity are anger, spitefulness, slander. Anger arises from acts committed against us, enmity even from those that are not; for if we imagine a man to be of such and such a character, we hate him. Anger has always an individual as its object, for instance Callias or Socrates, whereas hatred applies to classes; for instance, every one hates a thief or informer. Anger is curable by time, hatred not; the aim of anger is pain, of hatred evil; for the angry man wishes to see what happens; to one who hates it does not matter. Now, the things which cause pain are all perceptible, while things which are especially bad, such as injustice or folly, are least perceptible; for the presence of vice causes no pain. Anger is accompanied by pain, but hatred not; for he who is angry suffers pain, but he who hates does not. One who is angry might feel compassion in many cases, but one who hates, never; for the former wishes that the object of his anger should suffer in his turn, the latter, that he should perish. It is evident, then, from what we have just said, that it is possible to prove that men are enemies or friends, or to make them such if they are not; to refute those who pretend that they are, and when they oppose us through anger or enmity, to bring them over to whichever side may be preferred. The things and persons that men fear and in what frame of mind, will be evident from the following considerations.

## Chapter 5

Let fear be defined as a painful or troubled feeling caused by the impression of an imminent evil that causes destruction or pain; for men do not fear all evils, for instance, becoming unjust or slow-witted, but only such as involve great pain or destruction, and only if they appear to be not far off but near at hand and threatening, for men do not fear things that are very remote; all know that they have to die, but as death is not near at hand, they are indifferent. If then this is fear, all things must be fearful that appear to have great power of destroying or inflicting injuries that tend to produce great pain. That is why even the signs of such misfortunes are fearful, for the fearful thing itself appears to be near at hand, and danger is the approach of anything fearful. Such signs are the enmity and anger of those able to injure us in any way; for it is evident that they have the wish, so that they are not far from doing so. And injustice possessed of power is fearful, for the unjust man is unjust through deliberate inclination. And outraged virtue when it has power, for it is evident that it always desires satisfaction, whenever it is outraged, and now it has the power. And fear felt by those able to injure us in any way, for such as these also must be ready to act. And since most men are rather bad than good and the slaves of gain and cowardly in time of danger, being at the mercy of another is generally fearful, so that one who has committed a crime has reason to fear his accomplices as likely to denounce or leave him in the lurch. And those who are able to ill-treat others are to be feared by those who can be so treated; for as a rule men do wrong whenever they can. Those who have been, or think they are being, wronged, are also to be feared, for they are ever on the look out for an opportunity. And those who have committed some wrong, when they have the power, since they are afraid of retaliation, which was assumed to be something to be feared. And those who are our rivals for the same things, whenever it is impossible to share them, for men are always contending with such persons. And those who are feared by those who are stronger than we are, for they would be better able to injure us, if they could injure those stronger than ourselves and those whom those who are stronger than ourselves are afraid of, for the same reason. And those who have overthrown those who are stronger than us and those who attack those who are weaker, for they are either already to be feared, or will be, when they have grown stronger.

And among those whom we have wronged, or are our enemies or rivals, we should fear not the hot-tempered or outspoken, but those who are mild, dissemblers, and thorough rascals; for it is uncertain whether they are on the point of acting, so that one never knows whether they are far from it. All things that are to be feared are more so when, after an error has once been committed, it is impossible to repair it, either because it is absolutely impossible, or no longer in our power, but in that of our opponents; also when there is no possibility of help or it is not easy to obtain. In a word, all things are to be feared which, when they happen, or are on the point of happening, to others, excite compassion. These are, so to say, nearly all the most important things which are to be feared and which men fear. Let us now state the frame of mind which leads men to fear.

If then fear is accompanied by the expectation that we are going to suffer some fatal misfortune, it is evident that none of those who think that they will suffer nothing at all is afraid either of those things which he does not think will happen to him, or of those from whom he does not expect them, or at a time when he does not think them likely to happen. It therefore needs be that those who think they are likely to suffer anything should be afraid, either of the persons at whose hands they expect it, or of certain things, and at certain times. Those who either are, or seem to be, highly prosperous do not think they are likely to suffer anything; wherefore they are insolent, contemptuous, and rash, and what makes them such is wealth, strength, a number of friends, power. It is the same with those who think that they have already suffered all possible ills and are coldly indifferent to the future, like those who are being beaten to death; for it is a necessary incentive to fear that there should remain some hope of being saved from the cause of their distress. A sign of this is that fear makes men deliberate, whereas no one deliberates about things that are hopeless. So that whenever it is preferable that the audience should feel afraid, it is necessary to make them think they are likely to suffer, by reminding them that others greater than they have suffered, and showing that their equals are suffering or have suffered, and that at the hands of those from whom they did not expect it, in such a manner and at times when they did not think it likely.

Now, since we have made clear what fear and fearful things are, and the frame of mind in each case which makes men fear, one can see from this what confidence is, what are the things that give it, and the frame of mind of those who possess it; for confidence is the contrary of fear and that which gives confidence of that which causes fear, so that the hope of what is salutary is accompanied by an impression that it is quite near at hand, while the things to be feared are either non-existent or far off. Confidence is inspired by the remoteness of fearful things, or by the nearness of things that justify it. If remedies are possible, if there are means of help, either great or numerous, or both; if we have neither committed nor suffered wrong if we have no rivals at all, or only such as are powerless, or, if they have power, are our friends, or have either done us good or have received it from us; if those whose interests are the same as ours are more numerous, or stronger, or both. We feel confidence in the following states of mind: if we believe that we have often succeeded and have not suffered, or if we have often been in danger and escaped it; for men are unaffected by fear in two ways, either because they have never been tested or have means of help; thus, in dangers at sea, those who have never experienced a storm and those who have means of help as the result of experience have confidence as to the future. We are also reassured, when a thing does not inspire fear in our equals, our inferiors, or those to whom we think ourselves superior; and we think ourselves superior to those whom we have conquered, either themselves or their superiors or equals. And if we think we possess more or more considerable advantages, such as make their possessors formidable; such are abundance of money, strength of body, friends, territory, military equipments, either all or the most important. And if we have never done wrong to anyone, or only to a few, or not to such as are to be feared; and, generally, if it is well with us in regard to the gods, especially as to intimations from signs and oracles, and everything else of the kind; for anger inspires confidence, and it is the wrong that we suffer and not that which we inflict upon others that causes anger, and the gods are supposed to assist those who are wronged. Lastly, we feel confidence when, at the beginning of any undertaking, we do not expect disaster either in the present or future, or hope for success. Such are the things that inspire fear or confidence.

## Chapter 6

What are the things of which men are ashamed or the contrary, and before whom, and in what frame of mind, will be clear from the following considerations. Let shame then be defined as a kind of pain or uneasiness in respect of misdeeds, past, present, or future, which seem to tend to bring dishonor; and shamelessness as contempt and indifference in regard to these same things. If this definition of shame is correct, it follows that we are ashamed of all such misdeeds as seem to be disgraceful, either for ourselves or for those whom we care for. Such are all those that are due to vice, such as throwing away one's shield or taking to flight, for this is due to cowardice; or withholding a deposit, for this is due to injustice. And illicit relations with any persons, at forbidden places or times, for this is due to licentiousness. And making profit out of what is petty or disgraceful, or out of the weak, such as the indigent or dead; whence the proverb, "to rob even a corpse," for this is due to base love of gain and stinginess. And to refuse assistance in money matters when we are able to render it, or to give less than we can; to accept assistance from those less able to afford it than ourselves; to borrow when anyone seems likely to ask for a loan, to ask for a loan from one who wants his money back, and asking for repayment from one who wants to borrow; to praise in order to seem to be asking for a loan, and when you have failed to obtain it to keep on asking; for all these are signs of stinginess. And to praise people when they are present, to overpraise their good qualities and to palliate the bad, to show excessive grief at another's grief when present, and all similar actions; for they are signs of flattery.

And not to submit to toils, which those put up with who are older or live luxuriously or hold higher positions, or, generally speaking, are less fitted to do so; for all these are signs of effeminacy. To accept favors from another and often, and then to throw them in his teeth; for all these things are signs of littleness and abasement of soul. And to speak at great length about oneself and to make all kinds of professions, and to take the credit for what another has done; for this is a sign of boastfulness. Similarly, in regard to each of all the other vices of character, the acts resulting from them, their signs, and the things which resemble them, all these are disgraceful, and should make us ashamed. It is also shameful not to have a share in the honorable things which all men, or all who resemble us, or the majority of them, have a share in. By those who resemble us I mean those of the same race, of the same city, of the same age, of the same family, and, generally speaking, those who are on an equality; for then it is disgraceful not to have a share, for instance, in education and other things, to the same extent. All these things are the more disgraceful, if the fault appears to be our own; for they are at once seen to be due rather to natural depravity if we ourselves are the cause of past, present, or future defects. And we are ashamed when we suffer or have suffered or are likely to suffer things which tend to ignominy and reproach; such are prostituting one's person or performing disgraceful actions, including unnatural lust. And of these actions those that promote licentiousness are disgraceful, whether voluntary or involuntary (the latter being those that are done under compulsion), since meek endurance and the absence of resistance are the result of unmanliness or cowardice.

These and similar things are those of which men are ashamed. And since shame is an impression about dishonor, and that for its own sake and not for its results; and since no one heeds the opinion of others except on account of those who hold it, it follows that men feel shame before those whom they esteem. Now men esteem those who admire them and those whom they admire, those by whom they wish to be admired, those whose rivals they are, and whose opinion they do not despise. They desire to be admired by those, and admire those who possess anything good that is greatly esteemed, or from whom they urgently require something which it is in their power to give, as is the case with lovers. And they are rivals of those who are like them; and they give heed to the men of practical wisdom as likely to be truthful; such are the older and well educated. They are also more ashamed of things that are done before their eyes and in broad daylight; whence the proverb, The eyes are the abode of shame. That is why they feel more ashamed before those who are likely to be always with them or who keep watch upon them, because in both cases they are under the eyes of others.

Men are also ashamed before those who are not open to the same accusations, for it is evident that their feelings are contrary. And before those who are not indulgent towards those who appear to err; for a man is supposed not to reproach others with what he does himself, so it is clear that what he reproaches them with is what he does not do himself. And before those who are fond of gossiping generally; for not to gossip about the fault of another amounts to not regarding it as a fault at all. Now those who are inclined to gossip are those who have suffered wrong, because they always have their eyes upon us; and slanderers, because, if they traduce the innocent, still more will they traduce the guilty. And before those who spend their time in looking for their neighbors' faults, for instance, mockers and comic poets; for they are also in a manner slanderers and gossips. And before those from whom they have never asked anything in vain, for they feel as if they were greatly esteemed. For this reason they feel ashamed before those who ask them for something for the first time, as never yet having lost their good opinion. Such are those who have recently sought their friendship (for they have only seen what is best in them, which is the point of the answer of Euripides to the Syracusans), or old acquaintances who know nothing against us. And men are ashamed not only of the disgraceful things we have spoken of, but also of indications of them, for instance, not only of sensual pleasures, but also of the indications of them; and not only of doing, but also of saying disgraceful things. Similarly, men are ashamed not only before those who have been mentioned, but also before those who will reveal their faults to them, such as their servants or friends. In a word, they are not ashamed either before those whose opinion in regard to the truth they greatly despise—for instance, no one feels shame before children or animals—or of the same things before those who are known to them and those who are not; before the former, they are ashamed of things that appear really disgraceful, before strangers, of those which are only condemned by convention.

Men are likely to feel shame in the following situations; first, if there are any who are so related to them as those before whom we said that they feel shame. These, as we pointed out, are those who are admired by them or who admire them, or by whom they wish to be admired, or from whom they need some service, which they will not obtain if they lose their reputation. These, again, are either persons who directly see what is going on (just as Cydias, when haranguing the people about the allotment of the territory of Samos, begged the Athenians to picture to themselves that the Greeks were standing round them and would not only hear, but also see what they were going to decree); or neighbors; or those likely to be aware of what they say or do. That is why men do not like, when unfortunate, to be seen by those who were once their rivals, for rivalry presumes admiration. Men also feel shame when they are connected with actions or things which entail disgrace, for which either they themselves, or their ancestors, or any others with whom they are closely connected are responsible. In a word, men feel shame for those whom they themselves respect; such are those mentioned and those who have any relation to them, for instance, whose teachers or advisers they have been; similarly, when they are in rivalry with others who are like them; for there are many things which they either do or do not do owing to the feeling of shame which these men inspire. And they are more likely to be ashamed when they have to be seen and to associate openly with those who are aware of their disgrace. Wherefore the tragic poet Antiphon, when he was about to be flogged to death by order of Dionysius, seeing that those who were to die with him covered their faces as they passed through the gates, said, "Why cover your faces? Is it because you are afraid that one of the crowd should see you tomorrow?" Let this account of shame suffice; as for shamelessness, it is evident that we shall be able to obtain ample knowledge of it from the contrary arguments.

## Chapter 7

The persons towards whom men feel benevolent, and for what reasons, and in what frame of mind, will be clear when we have defined what favor is. Let it then be taken to be the feeling in accordance with which one who has it is said to render a service to one who needs it, not in return for something nor in the interest of him who renders it, but in that of the recipient. And the favor will be great if the recipient is in pressing need, or if the service or the times and circumstances are important or difficult, or if the benefactor is the only one, or the first who has rendered it, or has done so in the highest degree. By needs I mean longings, especially for things the failure to obtain which is accompanied by pain; such are the desires, for instance, love; also those which arise in bodily sufferings and dangers, for when a man is in pain or danger he desires something. That is why those who help a man who is poor or an exile, even if the service be ever so small, are regarded with favor owing to the urgency and occasion of the need; for instance, the man who gave the mat to another in the Lyceum. It is necessary then, if possible, that the service should be in the same direction; if not, that it should apply to cases of similar or greater need.

Since then it is evident on what occasions, for what reasons, and in what frame of mind a feeling of benevolence arises, it is clear that we must derive our arguments from this—to show that the one side either has been, or still is, in such pain or need, and that the other has rendered, or is rendering, such a service in such a time of need. It is evident also by what means it is possible to make out that there is no favor at all, or that those who render it are not actuated by benevolence; for it can either be said that they do, or have done so, for their own sake, in which case there is no favor; or that it was mere chance; or that they acted under compulsion; or that they were making a return, not a gift, whether they knew it or not; for in both cases it is an equivalent return, so that in this case also there is no favor. And the action must be considered in reference to all the categories; for if there is a favor it is so because of substance, quantity, quality, time, or place. And it denotes lack of goodwill, if persons have not rendered a smaller service, or if they have rendered similar, equal, or greater services to our enemies; for it is evident that they do not act for our sake in this case either. Or if the service was insignificant, and rendered by one who knew it; for no one admits that he has need of what is insignificant.

## Chapter 8

Let this suffice for benevolence and the opposite. We will now state what things and persons excite pity, and the state of mind of those who feel it. Let pity then be a kind of pain excited by the sight of evil, deadly or painful, which befalls one who does not deserve it; an evil which one might expect to come upon himself or one of his friends, and when it seems near. For it is evident that one who is likely to feel pity must be such as to think that he, or one of his friends, is liable to suffer some evil, and such an evil as has been stated in the definition, or one similar, or nearly similar. Wherefore neither those who are utterly ruined, are capable of pity, for they think they have nothing more to suffer, since they have exhausted suffering; nor those who think themselves supremely fortunate, who rather are insolent. For if they think that all good things are theirs, it is clear that they think that they cannot possibly suffer evil, and this is one of the good things. Now those persons who think they are likely to suffer are those who have already suffered and escaped; the advanced in age, by reason of their wisdom and experience; and the weak, and those who are rather more timid; and the educated, for they reckon rightly; and those who have parents, children, or wives, for these are part of them and likely to suffer the evils of which we have spoken; and those who are not influenced by any courageous emotion, such as anger or confidence, for these emotions do not take thought of the future and those who are not in a wantonly insolent frame of mind, for they also take no thought of future suffering; but it is those who are between the two extremes that feel pity. Those who are not in great fear; for those who are panic-stricken are incapable of pity, because they are preoccupied with their own emotion. And men feel pity if they think that some persons are virtuous; for he who thinks that no one is will think that all deserve misfortune. And, generally speaking, a man is moved to pity when he is so affected that he remembers that such evils have happened, or expects that they may happen, either to himself or to one of his friends.

We have stated the frame of mind which leads men to pity; and the things which arouse this feeling are clearly shown by the definition. They are all painful and distressing things that are also destructive, and all that are ruinous; and all evils of which fortune is the cause, if they are great. Things distressing and destructive are various kinds of death, personal ill-treatment and injuries, old age, disease, and lack of food. The evils for which fortune is responsible are lack of friends, or few friends (wherefore it is pitiable to be torn away from friends and intimates), ugliness, weakness, mutilation; if some misfortune comes to pass from a quarter whence one might have reasonably expected something good; and if this happens often; and if good fortune does not come until a man has already suffered, as when the presents from the Great King were not dispatched to Diopithes until he was dead. Those also are to be pitied to whom no good has ever accrued, or who are unable to enjoy it when it has.

These and the like things, then, excite pity. The persons men pity are those whom they know, provided they are not too closely connected with them for if they are, they feel the same as if they themselves were likely to suffer. This is why Amasis is said not to have wept when his son was led to execution, but did weep at the sight of a friend reduced to beggary, for the latter excited pity, the former terror. The terrible is different from the pitiable, for it drives out pity, and often serves to produce the opposite feeling. Further, the nearness of the terrible makes men pity. Men also pity those who resemble them in age, character, habits, position, or family; for all such relations make a man more likely to think that their misfortune may befall him as well. For, in general, here also we may conclude that all that men fear in regard to themselves excites their pity when others are the victims. And since sufferings are pitiable when they appear close at hand, while those that are past or future, ten thousand years backwards or forwards, either do not excite pity at all or only in a less degree, because men neither expect the one nor remember the other, it follows that those who contribute to the effect by gestures, voice, dress, and dramatic action generally, are more pitiable; for they make the evil appear close at hand, setting it before our eyes as either future or past. And disasters that have just happened or are soon about to happen excite more pity for the same reason. Pity is also aroused by signs and actions, such as the dress of those who have suffered, and all such objects, and the words and everything else that concerns those who are actually suffering, for instance, at the point of death. And when men show themselves undaunted at such critical times it is specially pitiable; for all these things, because they come immediately under our observation, increase the feeling of pity, both because the sufferer does not seem to deserve his fate, and because the suffering is before our eyes.

## Chapter 9

Now what is called indignation is the antithesis to pity; for the being pained at undeserved good fortune is in a manner contrary to being pained at undeserved bad fortune and arises from the same character. And both emotions show good character, for if we sympathize with and pity those who suffer undeservedly, we ought to be indignant with those who prosper undeservedly; for that which happens beyond a man's deserts is unjust, wherefore we attribute this feeling even to gods. It would seem that envy also is similarly opposed to pity, as being akin to or identical with indignation, although it is really different; envy also is indeed a disturbing pain and directed against good fortune, but not that of one who does not deserve it, but of one who is our equal and like. Now, all who feel envy and indignation must have this in common, that they are disturbed, not because they think that any harm will happen to themselves, but on account of their neighbor; for it will cease to be indignation and envy, but will be fear, if the pain and disturbance arise from the idea that harm may come to themselves from another's good fortune. And it is evident that these feelings will be accompanied by opposite feelings; for he who is pained at the sight of those who are undeservedly unfortunate will rejoice or will at least not be pained at the sight of those who are deservedly so; for instance, no good man would be pained at seeing parricides or assassins punished; we should rather rejoice at their lot, and at that of men who are deservedly fortunate; for both these are just and cause the worthy man to rejoice, because he cannot help hoping that what has happened to his like may also happen to himself. And all these feelings arise from the same character and their contraries from the contrary; for he who is malicious is also envious, since, if the envious man is pained at another's possession or acquisition of good fortune, he is bound to rejoice at the destruction or non-acquisition of the same. Wherefore all these emotions are a hindrance to pity, although they differ for the reasons stated; so that they are all equally useful for preventing any feeling of pity.

Let us then first speak of indignation, the persons with whom men feel indignant, for what reasons, and in what frame of mind; and then proceed to the rest of the emotions. What we have just said will make matters clear. For if indignation is being pained at the sight of good fortune that is apparently undeserved, in the first place it is clear that it is not possible to feel indignation at all things; for no one will be indignant with a man who is just or courageous, or may acquire any virtue (for one does not feel pity in the case of opposites of those qualities), but men are indignant at wealth, power, in a word, at all the advantages of which good men are worthy. [And those who possess natural advantages, such as noble birth, beauty, and all such things.] And since that which is old seems closely to resemble that which is natural, it follows that, if two parties have the same good, men are more indignant with the one who has recently acquired it and owes his prosperity to it; for the newly rich cause more annoyance than those who have long possessed or inherited wealth. The same applies to offices of state, power, numerous friends, virtuous children, and any other advantages of the kind. And if these advantages bring them some other advantage, men are equally indignant; for in this case also the newly rich who attain to office owing to their wealth cause more annoyance than those who have long been wealthy; and similarly in all other cases of the same kind. The reason is that the latter seem to possess what belongs to them, the former not; for that which all along shows itself in the same light suggests a reality, so that the former seem to possess what is not theirs. And since every kind of good is not suitable to the first comer, but a certain proportion and suitability are necessary (as for instance beautiful weapons are not suitable to the just but to the courageous man, and distinguished marriages not to the newly rich but to the nobly born), if a virtuous man does not obtain what is suitable to him, we feel indignant. Similarly, if the inferior contends with the superior, especially among those engaged in the same pursuit,—whence the saying of the poet,

"He avoided battle with Ajax, son of Telamon, for Zeus was indignant with him, when he would fight with a better man;"

or, if the pursuit is not the same, wherever the inferior contends with the superior in anything whatever, as for instance, the musician with the just man; for justice is better than music.

From this it is clear, then, with whom men are indignant and for what reasons; they are these or of such a kind. Men are prone to indignation, first, if they happen to deserve or possess the greatest advantages, for it is not just that those who do not resemble them should be deemed worthy of the same advantages; secondly, if they happen to be virtuous and worthy, for they both judge correctly and hate what is unjust. And those who are ambitious and long for certain positions, especially if they are those which others, although unworthy, have obtained. And, in general, those who think themselves worthy of advantages of which they consider others unworthy, are inclined to be indignant with the latter and because of these advantages. This is why the servile and worthless and unambitious are not inclined to indignation; for there is nothing of which they think themselves worthy. It is evident from this what kind of men they are whose ill fortunes, calamities, and lack of success must make us rejoice or at least feel no pain; for the opposites are clear from what has been said. If then the speaker puts the judges into such a frame of mind and proves that those who claim our pity (and the reasons why they do so) are unworthy to obtain it and deserve that it should be refused them, then pity will be impossible.

## Chapter 10

It is equally clear for what reason, and of whom, and in what frame of mind, men are envious, if envy is a kind of pain at the sight of good fortune in regard to the goods mentioned; in the case of those like themselves; and not for the sake of a man getting anything, but because of others possessing it. For those men will be envious who have, or seem to have, others "like" them. I mean like in birth, relationship, age, moral habit, reputation, and possessions. And those will be envious who possess all but one of these advantages; that is why those who attempt great things and succeed are envious, because they think that every one is trying to deprive them of their own. And those who are honored for some special reason, especially for wisdom or happiness. And the ambitious are more envious than the unambitious. And those who are wise in their own conceit, for they are ambitious of a reputation for wisdom; and, in general, those who wish to be distinguished in anything are envious in regard to it. And the little-minded, because everything appears to them to be great.
The advantages which excite envy have already been stated. Nearly all the actions or possessions which make men desire glory or honor and long for fame, and the favors of fortune, create envy, especially when men long for them themselves, or think that they have a right to them, or the possession of which makes them slightly superior or slightly inferior.

And it is evident whom men envy, for it has just been stated by implication. They envy those who are near them in time, place, age, and reputation, whence it was said,
"Kinship knows how to envy also;"
and those with whom they are in rivalry, who are those just spoken of; for no man tries to rival those who lived ten thousand years ago, or are about to be born, or are already dead; nor those who live near the Pillars of Hercules; nor those who, in his own opinion or in that of others, are either far inferior or superior to him; and the people and things which one envies are on the same footing. And since men strive for honor with those who are competitors, or rivals in love, in short, with those who aim at the same things, they are bound to feel most envious of these; whence the saying,
"Potter [being jealous] of potter."
And those who have succeeded with difficulty or have failed envy those whose success has been rapid. And those whose possessions or successes are a reproach to themselves, and these, too, are those near or like them; for it is clear that it is their own fault that they do not obtain the same advantage, so that this pains and causes envy. And those who either have or have acquired what was naturally theirs or what they had once acquired; this is why an older man is envious of a younger one. Those who have spent much envy those who have only spent little to obtain the same thing. And it is clear at what things and persons the envious rejoice, and in what frame of mind; for, as when they do not possess certain things, they are pained, so when they do possess them, they will rejoice in the opposite circumstances. So that if the judges are brought into that frame of mind, and those who claim their pity or any other boon are such as we have stated, it is plain that they will not obtain pity from those with whom the decision rests.

## Chapter 11

The frame of mind in which men feel emulation, what things and persons give rise to it, will be clear from the following considerations. Let us assume that emulation is a feeling of pain at the evident presence of highly valued goods, which are possible for us to obtain, in the possession of those who naturally resemble us—pain not due to the fact that another possesses them, but to the fact that we ourselves do not. Emulation therefore is virtuous and characteristic of virtuous men, whereas envy is base and characteristic of base men; for the one, owing to emulation, fits himself to obtain such goods, while the object of the other, owing to envy, is to prevent his neighbor possessing them. Necessarily, then, those are emulous who hold that they have a claim to goods that they do not possess;

for no one claims what seems impossible. Hence the young and high-minded are emulous. And so are those who possess such advantages as are worthy of honorable men, which include wealth, a number of friends, positions of office, and all similar things. For, believing it their duty to be good, because such goods naturally belong to those who are good, they strive to preserve them. And those are emulous, whom others think worthy of them. Honors obtained by ancestors, kinsfolk, intimates, nation, or city make men emulous in regard to such honors; for they think that these honors really belong to them and that they are worthy of them. And if highly valued goods are the object of emulation, it necessarily follows that the virtues must be such and all things that are useful and beneficial to the rest of mankind, for benefactors and virtuous men are honored; to these we may add all the goods which our neighbors can enjoy with us, such as wealth and beauty, rather than health.

It is also evident who are the objects of emulation; for they are those who possess these or similar goods, such as have already been spoken of, for instance, courage, wisdom, authority; for those in authority, such as generals, orators, and all who have similar powers, can do good to many. And those whom many desire to be like, or to be their acquaintances or friends; those whom many or ourselves admire; those who are praised or eulogized either by poets or by prose writers. The opposite characters we despise; for contempt is the opposite of emulation, and the idea of emulation of the idea of contempt. And those who are in a condition which makes them emulate, or be emulated by, others, must be inclined to despise those persons (and for that reason) who suffer from defects contrary to the good things which excite emulation. That is why we often despise those who are fortunate, whenever their good fortune is not accompanied by highly valued goods. The means of producing and destroying the various emotions in men, from which the methods of persuasion that concern them are derived, have now been stated.

## Chapter 12

Let us now describe the nature of the characters of men according to their emotions, habits, ages, and fortunes. By the emotions I mean anger, desire, and the like, of which we have already spoken; by habits virtues and vices, of which also we have previously spoken, as well as the kind of things men individually and deliberately choose and practise. The ages are youth, the prime of life, and old age. By fortune I mean noble birth, wealth, power, and their contraries, and, in general, good or bad fortune.

The young, as to character, are ready to desire and to carry out what they desire. Of the bodily desires they chiefly obey those of sensual pleasure and these they are unable to control. Changeable in their desires and soon tiring of them, they desire with extreme ardor, but soon cool; for their will, like the hunger and thirst of the sick, is keen rather than strong. They are passionate, hot-tempered, and carried away by impulse, and unable to control their passion; for owing to their ambition they cannot endure to be slighted, and become indignant when they think they are being wronged. They are ambitious of honor, but more so of victory; for youth desires superiority, and victory is a kind of superiority. And their desire for both these is greater than their desire for money, to which they attach only the slightest value, because they have never yet experienced want, as Pittacus said in his pithy remark on Amphiaraus. They are not ill-natured but simple-natured, because they have never yet witnessed much depravity; confiding, because they have as yet not been often deceived; full of hope, for they are naturally as hot-blooded as those who are drunken with wine, and besides they have not yet experienced many failures. For the most part they live in hope, for hope is concerned with the future as memory is with the past. For the young the future is long, the past short; for in the morning of life it is not possible for them to remember anything, but they have everything to hope; which makes them easy to deceive, for they readily hope. And they are more courageous, for they are full of passion and hope, and the former of these prevents them fearing, while the latter inspires them with confidence, for no one fears when angry, and hope of some advantage inspires confidence. And they are bashful, for as yet they fail to conceive of other things that are noble, but have been educated solely by convention. They are high-minded, for they have not yet been humbled by life nor have they experienced the force of necessity; further, there is high-mindedness in thinking oneself worthy of great things, a feeling which belongs to one who is full of hope.

In their actions, they prefer the noble to the useful; their life is guided by their character rather than by calculation, for the latter aims at the useful, virtue at the noble. At this age more than any other they are fond of their friends and companions because they take pleasure in living in company and as yet judge nothing by expediency, not even their friends. All their errors are due to excess and vehemence and their neglect of the maxim of Chilon, for they do everything to excess, love, hate, and everything else. And they think they know everything, and confidently affirm it, and this is the cause of their excess in everything. If they do wrong, it is due to insolence, not to wickedness. And they are inclined to pity, because they think all men are virtuous and better than themselves; for they measure their neighbors by their own inoffensiveness, so that they think that they suffer undeservedly. And they are fond of laughter, and therefore witty; for wit is cultured insolence. Such then is the character of the young.

# Chapter 13

Older men and those who have passed their prime have in most cases characters opposite to those of the young. For, owing to their having lived many years and having been more often deceived by others or made more mistakes themselves, and since most human things turn out badly, they are positive about nothing, and in everything they show an excessive lack of energy. They always "think," but "know" nothing; and in their hesitation they always add "perhaps," or "maybe"; all their statements are of this kind, never unqualified. They are malicious; for malice consists in looking upon the worse side of everything. Further, they are always suspicious owing to mistrust, and mistrustful owing to experience. And neither their love nor their hatred is strong for the same reasons; but, according to the precept of Bias, they love as if they would one day hate, and hate as if they would one day love. And they are little-minded, because they have been humbled by life; for they desire nothing great or uncommon, but only the necessaries of life. They are not generous, for property is one of these necessaries, and at the same time, they know from experience how hard it is to get and how easy to lose. And they are cowardly and inclined to anticipate evil, for their state of mind is the opposite of that of the young; they are chilled, whereas the young are hot, so that old age paves the way for cowardice, for fear is a kind of chill. And they are fond of life, especially in their last days, because desire is directed towards that which is absent and men especially desire what they lack. And they are unduly selfish, for this also is littleness of mind. And they live not for the noble, but for the useful, more than they ought, because they are selfish; for the useful is a good for the individual, whereas the noble is good absolutely.

And they are rather shameless than modest; for since they do not care for the noble so much as for the useful, they pay little attention to what people think. And they are little given to hope owing to their experience, for things that happen are mostly bad and at all events generally turn out for the worse, and also owing to their cowardice. They live in memory rather than in hope; for the life that remains to them is short, but that which is past is long, and hope belongs to the future, memory to the past. This is the reason of their loquacity; for they are incessantly talking of the past, because they take pleasure in recollection. Their outbursts of anger are violent, but feeble; of their desires some have ceased, while others are weak, so that they neither feel them nor act in accordance with them, but only from motives of gain. Hence men of this age are regarded as self-controlled, for their desires have slackened, and they are slaves to gain. In their manner of life there is more calculation than moral character, for calculation is concerned with that which is useful, moral character with virtue. If they commit acts of injustice it is due to vice rather than to insolence. The old, like the young, are inclined to pity, but not for the same reason; the latter show pity from humanity, the former from weakness, because they think that they are on the point of suffering all kinds of misfortunes, and this is one of the reasons that incline men to pity. That is why the old are querulous, and neither witty nor fond of laughter; for a querulous disposition is the opposite of a love of laughter. Such are the characters of the young and older men. Wherefore, since all men are willing to listen to speeches which harmonize with their own character and to speakers who resemble them, it is easy to see what language we must employ so that both ourselves and our speeches may appear to be of such and such a character.

## Chapter 14

It is evident that the character of those in the prime of life will be the mean between that of the other two, if the excess in each case be removed. At this age, men are neither over-confident, which would show rashness, nor too fearful, but preserving a right attitude in regard to both, neither trusting nor distrusting all, but judging rather in accordance with actual facts. Their rule of conduct is neither the noble nor the useful alone, but both at once. They are neither parsimonious nor prodigal, but preserve the due mean. It is the same in regard to passion and desire. Their self-control is combined with courage and their courage with self-control, whereas in the young and old these qualities are found separately; for the young are courageous but without self-control, the old are self-controlled but cowardly. Speaking generally, all the advantages that youth and old age possess separately, those in the prime of life possess combined; and all cases of excess or defect in the other two are replaced by due moderation and fitness. The body is most fully developed from thirty to thirty-five years of age, the mind at about forty-nine. Let this suffice for youth, old age, and the prime of life, and the characters which belong to each.

## Chapter 15

Let us next speak of the goods that are due to fortune, all those, at least, which produce certain characters in men. A characteristic of noble birth is that he who possesses it is more ambitious; for all men, when they start with any good, are accustomed to heap it up, and noble birth is a heritage of honor from one's ancestors. Such men are prone to look down even upon those who are as important as their ancestors, because the same things are more honorable and inspire greater vanity when remote than when they are recent. The idea of noble birth refers to excellence of race, that of noble character to not degenerating from the family type, a quality not as a rule found in those of noble birth, most of whom are good for nothing. For in the generations of men there is a kind of crop as in the fruits of the field; sometimes, if the race is good, for a certain period men out of the common are born in it, and then it deteriorates. Highly gifted families often degenerate into maniacs, as, for example, the descendants of Alcibiades and the elder Dionysius; those that are stable into fools and dullards, like the descendants of Cimon, Pericles, and Socrates.

## Chapter 16

The characters which accompany wealth are plain for all to see. The wealthy are insolent and arrogant, being mentally affected by the acquisition of wealth, for they seem to think that they possess all good things; for wealth is a kind of standard of value of everything else, so that everything seems purchasable by it. They are luxurious and swaggerers, luxurious because of their luxury and the display of their prosperity, swaggerers and ill-mannered because all men are accustomed to devote their attention to what they like and admire, and the rich suppose that what they themselves are emulous of is the object of all other men's emulation. At the same time this feeling is not unreasonable; for those who have need of the wealthy are many in number. Hence the answer of Simonides to the wife of Hiero concerning the wise and the rich, when she asked which was preferable, to be wise or to be rich. "Rich," he answered, "for we see the wise spending their time at the doors of the rich." And the rich think they are worthy to rule, because they believe they possess that which makes them so. In a word, the character of the rich man is that of a fool favored by fortune. At the same time there is a difference between the character of the newly rich and of those whose wealth is of long standing, because the former have the vices of wealth in a greater degree and more; for, so to say, they have not been educated to the use of wealth. Their unjust acts are not due to malice, but partly to insolence, partly to incontinence, which tends to make them commit assault and battery and adultery.

## Chapter 17

In regard to power, nearly all the characters to which it gives rise are equally clear; for power, compared with wealth, exhibits partly identical, and partly superior characteristics. Thus, the powerful are more ambitious and more manly in character than the rich, since they aim at the performance of deeds which their power gives them the opportunity of carrying out. And they are more energetic; for being obliged to look after their power, they are always on the watch. And they are dignified rather than heavily pompous; for their rank renders them more conspicuous, so that they avoid excess; and this dignity is a mild and decent pomposity. And their wrongdoings are never petty, but great.

Good fortune in its divisions exhibits characters corresponding to those which have just been mentioned; for those which appear to be the most important kinds of good fortune tend in their direction; further, good fortune furnishes advantages over others in the blessing of children and bodily goods. Now, although men are more arrogant and thoughtless owing to good fortune, it is accompanied by a most precious quality. Fortunate men stand in a certain relation to the divinity and love the gods, having confidence in them owing to the benefits they have received from fortune. We have spoken of the characters associated with different ages and fortunes; the opposite characters to those described, for instance, of the poor, of the unfortunate, and of the weak, are obvious from their opposites.

## Chapter 18

Now the employment of persuasive speeches is directed towards a judgement; for when a thing is known and judged, there is no longer any need of argument. And there is judgement, whether a speaker addresses himself to a single individual and makes use of his speech to exhort or dissuade, as those do who give advice or try to persuade, for this single individual is equally a judge, since, speaking generally, he who has to be persuaded is a judge; if the speaker is arguing against an opponent or against some theory, it is just the same, for it is necessary to make use of speech to destroy the opposing arguments, against which he speaks as if they were the actual opponent; and similarly in epideictic speeches, for the speech is put together with reference to the spectator as if he were a judge. Generally speaking, however, only he who decides questions at issue in civil controversies is a judge in the proper sense of the word, for in judicial cases the point at issue is the state of the case, in deliberative the subjects of deliberation. We have already spoken of the characters of forms of government in treating of deliberative rhetoric, so that it has been determined how and by what means we must make our speeches conform to those characters.

Now, since each kind of Rhetoric, as was said, has its own special end, and in regard to all of them we have gathered popular opinions and premises whence men derive their proofs in deliberative, epideictic, and judicial speeches, and, further, we have determined the special rules according to which it is possible to make our speeches ethical, it only remains to discuss the topics common to the three kinds of rhetoric. For all orators are obliged, in their speeches, also to make use of the topic of the possible and impossible, and to endeavor to show, some of them that a thing will happen, others that it has happened. Further, the topic of magnitude is common to all kinds of Rhetoric, for all men employ extenuation or amplification whether deliberating, praising or blaming, accusing or defending. When these topics have been determined, we will endeavor to say what we can in general about enthymemes and examples, in order that, when we have added what remains, we may carry out what we proposed at the outset. Now, of the commonplaces amplification is most appropriate to epideictic rhetoric, as has been stated; the past to forensic, since things past are the subject of judgement; and the possible and future to deliberative.

## Chapter 19

Let us first speak of the possible and the impossible. If of two contrary things it is possible that one should exist or come into existence, then it would seem that the other is equally possible; for instance, if a man can be cured, he can also be ill; for the potentiality of contraries, qua contraries, is the same. Similarly, if of two like things the one is possible, so also is the other. And if the harder of two things is possible, so also is the easier. And if it is possible for a thing to be made excellent or beautiful, it is possible for it to be made in general; for it is harder for a beautiful house to be made than a mere house. Again, if the beginning is possible, so also is the end; for no impossible thing comes, or begins to come, into existence; for instance, that the diameter of a square should be commensurable with the side of a square is neither possible nor could be possible. And when the end is possible, so also is the beginning; for all things arise from a beginning. And if that which is subsequent in being or generation can come into being, so then can that which is antecedent; for instance, if a man can come into being, so can a child, for the child is antecedent; and similarly, if a child can come into being, so can a man, for the child is a beginning. And things which we love or desire naturally are possible; for as a rule no one loves the impossible or desires it. And those things which form the subject of sciences or arts can also exist and come into existence. And so with all those things, the productive principles of which reside in those things which we can control by force or persuasion, when they depend upon those whose superiors, masters, or friends we are. And if the parts are possible, so also is the whole; and if the whole is possible, so also are the parts, speaking generally; for instance, if the front, toe-cap, and upper leather, can be made, then shoes can be made, and if shoes, then the above parts. And if the whole genus is among things possible to be made, so is the species, and if the species, so the genus; for example, if a vessel can be built, so can a trireme, if a trireme can, so can a vessel. If of two naturally corresponding things one is possible, so also is the other; for instance, if the double is possible, so is the half, if the half, so the double. If a thing can be made without art or preparation, much the more can it be made with the help of art and carefulness. Whence it was said by Agathon: "And moreover we have to do some things by art, while others fall to our lot by compulsion or chance."

And if a thing is possible for those who are inferior, or weaker, or less intelligent, it will be still more so for those whose qualities are the opposite; as Isocrates said, it would be very strange if he were unable by himself to find out what Euthynus had learnt [with the help of others]. As for the impossible, it is clear that there is a supply of arguments to be derived from the opposite of what has been said about the possible.

The question whether a thing has or has not happened must be considered from the following points of view. In the first place, if that which is naturally less likely has happened, then that which is more likely will most probably have happened. If that which usually happens afterwards has happened, then that which precedes must also have happened; for instance, if a man has forgotten a thing, he must once have learnt it. If a man was able and wished to do a thing, he has done it; for all men do a thing, when they are able and resolve to do it, for nothing hinders them. Further, if a man wished to do it and there was no external obstacle; if he was able to do it and was in a state of anger; if he was able and desired to do it; for men as a rule, whenever they can, do those things which they long for, the vicious owing to want of self-control, the virtuous because they desire what is good. And if anything was on the point of being done, it most probably was done; for it is likely that one who was on the point of doing something has carried it out. And if all the natural antecedents or causes of a thing have happened; for instance, if it has lightened, it has also thundered; and if a man has already attempted a crime, he has also committed it. And if all the natural consequences or motives of actions have happened, then the antecedent or the cause has happened; for instance, if it has thundered, it has also lightened, and if a man has committed a crime, he has also attempted it. Of all these things some are so related necessarily, others only as a general rule. To establish that a thing has not happened, it is evident that our argument must be derived from the opposite of what has been said.

In regard to the future, it is clear that one can argue in the same way; for if we are able and wish to do a thing, it will be done; and so too will those things which desire, anger, and reasoning urge us to do, if we have the power. For this reason also, if a man has an eager desire, or intention, of doing a thing, it will probably be done; since, as a rule, things that are about to happen are more likely to happen than those which are not. And if all the natural antecedents have happened; for instance, if the sky is cloudy, it will probably rain. And if one thing has been done with a view to another, it is probable that the latter will also be done; for instance, if a foundation has been laid, a house will probably be built.

What we have previously said clearly shows the nature of the greatness and smallness of things, of the greater and less, and of things great and small generally. For, when treating of deliberative rhetoric, we spoke of greatness of goods, and of the greater and less generally. Therefore, since in each branch of Rhetoric the end set before it is a good, such as the expedient, the noble, or the just, it is evident that all must take the materials of amplification from these. To make any further inquiry as to magnitude and superiority absolutely would be waste of words; for the particular has more authority than the general for practical purposes. Let this suffice for the possible and impossible; for the question whether a thing has happened, or will happen, or not; and for the greatness or smallness of things.

## Chapter 20

It remains to speak of the proofs common to all branches of Rhetoric, since the particular proofs have been discussed. These common proofs are of two kinds, example and enthymeme (for the maxim is part of an enthymeme). Let us then first speak of the example; for the example resembles induction, and induction is a beginning.

There are two kinds of examples; namely, one which consists in relating things that have happened before, and another in inventing them oneself. The latter are subdivided into comparisons or fables, such as those of Aesop and the Libyan. It would be an instance of the historical kind of example, if one were to say that it is necessary to make preparations against the Great King and not to allow him to subdue Egypt; for Darius did not cross over to Greece until he had obtained possession of Egypt; but as soon as he had done so, he did. Again, Xerxes did not attack us until he had obtained possession of that country, but when he had, he crossed over; consequently, if the present Great King shall do the same, he will cross over, wherefore it must not be allowed. Comparison is illustrated by the sayings of Socrates; for instance, if one were to say that magistrates should not be chosen by lot, for this would be the same as choosing as representative athletes not those competent to contend, but those on whom the lot falls; or as choosing any of the sailors as the man who should take the helm, as if it were right that the choice should be decided by lot, not by a man's knowledge.

A fable, to give an example, is that of Stesichorus concerning Phalaris, or that of Aesop on behalf of the demagogue. For Stesichorus, when the people of Himera had chosen Phalaris dictator and were on the point of giving him a body-guard, after many arguments related a fable to them: "A horse was in sole occupation of a meadow. A stag having come and done much damage to the pasture, the horse, wishing to avenge himself on the stag, asked a man whether he could help him to punish the stag. The man consented, on condition that the horse submitted to the bit and allowed him to mount him javelins in hand. The horse agreed to the terms and the man mounted him, but instead of obtaining vengeance on the stag, the horse from that time became the man's slave. So then," said he, "do you take care lest, in your desire to avenge yourselves on the enemy, you be treated like the horse. You already have the bit, since you have chosen a dictator; if you give him a body-guard and allow him to mount you, you will at once be the slaves of Phalaris." Aesop, when defending at Samos a demagogue who was being tried for his life, related the following anecdote. "A fox, while crossing a river, was driven into a ravine. Being unable to get out, she was for a long time in sore distress, and a number of dog-fleas clung to her skin. A hedgehog, wandering about, saw her and, moved with compassion, asked her if he should remove the fleas. The fox refused and when the hedgehog asked the reason, she answered: 'They are already full of me and draw little blood; but if you take them away, others will come that are hungry and will drain what remains to me.' You in like manner, O Samians, will suffer no more harm from this man, for he is wealthy; but if you put him to death, others will come who are poor, who will steal and squander your public funds." Fables are suitable for public speaking, and they have this advantage that, while it is difficult to find similar things that have really happened in the past, it is easier to invent fables; for they must be invented, like comparisons, if a man is capable of seizing the analogy; and this is easy if one studies philosophy. Thus, while the lessons conveyed by fables are easier to provide, those derived from facts are more useful for deliberative oratory, because as a rule the future resembles the past.

If we have no enthymemes, we must employ examples as demonstrative proofs, for conviction is produced by these; but if we have them, examples must be used as evidence and as a kind of epilogue to the enthymemes. For if they stand first, they resemble induction, and induction is not suitable to rhetorical speeches except in very few cases; if they stand last they resemble evidence, and a witness is in every case likely to induce belief. Wherefore also it is necessary to quote a number of examples if they are put first, but one alone is sufficient if they are put last; for even a single trustworthy witness is of use. We have thus stated how many kinds of examples there are, and how and when they should be made use of.

# Chapter 21

In regard to the use of maxims, it will most readily be evident on what subjects, and on what occasions, and by whom it is appropriate that maxims should be employed in speeches, after a maxim has been defined. Now, a maxim is a statement, not however concerning particulars, as, for instance, what sort of a man Iphicrates was, but general; it does not even deal with all general things, as for instance that the straight is the opposite of the crooked, but with the objects of human actions, and with what should be chosen or avoided with reference to them. And as the enthymeme is, we may say, the syllogism dealing with such things, maxims are the premises or conclusions of enthymemes without the syllogism. For example:
"No man who is sensible ought to have his children taught to be excessively clever,"
is a maxim; but when the why and the wherefore are added, the whole makes an enthymeme; for instance,
"for, not to speak of the charge of idleness brought against them, they earn jealous hostility from the citizens."
Another example:
"There is no man who is happy in everything;"
or,
"There is no man who is really free."
The latter is a maxim, but taken with the next verse it is an enthymeme:
"for he is the slave of either wealth or fortune."
Now, if a maxim is what we have stated, it follows that maxims are of four kinds; for they are either accompanied by an epilogue or not. Now all those that state anything that is contrary to the general opinion or is a matter of dispute, need demonstrative proof; but those that do not, need no epilogue, either because they are already known, as, for instance,
"Health is a most excellent thing for a man, at least in our opinion,"
for this is generally agreed; or because, no sooner are they uttered than they are clear to those who consider them, for instance,
"He is no lover who does not love always."
As for the maxims that are accompanied by an epilogue, some form part of an enthymeme, as
"No one who is sensible, etc.,"

while others are enthymematic, but are not part of an enthymeme; and these are most highly esteemed. Such are those maxims in which the reason of what is said is apparent: for instance,
"Being a mortal, do not nourish immortal wrath;"
to say that one should not always nourish immortal wrath is a maxim, but the addition "being a mortal" states the reason. It is the same with
"A mortal should have mortal, not immortal thoughts."
It is evident, therefore, from what has been said, how many kinds of maxims there are, and to what it is appropriate to apply them in each case. For in the case of matters of dispute or what is contrary to the general opinion, the epilogue is necessary; but either the epilogue may be put first and the conclusion used as a maxim, as, for example, if one were to say, "As for me, since one ought neither to be the object of jealousy nor to be idle, I say that children ought not to be educated"; or put the maxim first and append the epilogue. In all cases where the statements made, although not paradoxical, are obscure, the reason should be added as concisely as possible. In such cases Laconic apophthegms and riddling sayings are suitable; as, for instance, to say what Stesichorus said to the Locrians, that they ought not to be insolent, lest their cicadas should be forced to chirp from the ground. The use of maxims is suitable for one who is advanced in years, and in regard to things in which one has experience; since the use of maxims before such an age is unseemly, as also is story-telling; and to speak about things of which one has no experience shows foolishness and lack of education. A sufficient proof of this is that rustics especially are fond of coining maxims and ready to make display of them.
To express in general terms what is not general is especially suitable in complaint or exaggeration, and then either at the beginning or after the demonstration. One should even make use of common and frequently quoted maxims, if they are useful; for because they are common, they seem to be true, since all as it were acknowledge them as such; for instance, one who is exhorting his soldiers to brave danger before having sacrificed may say,
"The best of omens is to defend one's country,"
and if they are inferior in numbers,
"The chances of war are the same for both,"
and if advising them to destroy the children of the enemy even though they are innocent of wrong,
"Foolish is he who, having slain the father, suffers the children to live."
Further, some proverbs are also maxims; for example, "An Attic neighbor." Maxims should also be used even when contrary to the most popular sayings, such as "Know thyself" and "Nothing in excess," either when one's character is thereby likely to appear better, or if they are expressed in the language of passion. It would be an instance of the latter if a man in a rage

were to say, "It is not true that a man should know himself; at any rate, such a man as this, if he had known himself, would never have claimed the chief command." And one's character would appear better, if one were to say that it is not right, as men say, to love as if one were bound to hate, but rather to hate as if one were bound to love. The moral purpose also should be made clear by the language, or else one should add the reason; for example, either by saying "that it is right to love, not as men say, but as if one were going to love for ever, for the other kind of love would imply treachery"; or thus, "The maxim does not please me, for the true friend should love as if he were going to love for ever. Nor do I approve the maxim 'Nothing in excess,' for one cannot hate the wicked too much." Further, maxims are of great assistance to speakers, first, because of the vulgarity of the hearers, who are pleased if an orator, speaking generally, hits upon the opinions which they specially hold. What I mean will be clear from the following, and also how one should hunt for maxims. The maxim, as we have said, is a statement of the general; accordingly, the hearers are pleased to hear stated in general terms the opinion which they have already specially formed. For instance, a man who happened to have bad neighbors or children would welcome any one's statement that nothing is more troublesome than neighbors or more stupid than to beget children. Wherefore the speaker should endeavor to guess how his hearers formed their preconceived opinions and what they are, and then express himself in general terms in regard to them. This is one of the advantages of the use of maxims, but another is greater; for it makes speeches ethical. Speeches have this character, in which the moral purpose is clear. And this is the effect of all maxims, because he who employs them in a general manner declares his moral preferences; if then the maxims are good, they show the speaker also to be a man of good character. Let this suffice for what we had to say concerning maxims, their nature, how many kinds of them there are, the way they should be used, and what their advantages are.

## Chapter 22

Let us now speak of enthymemes in general and the manner of looking for them, and next of their topics; for each of these things is different in kind. We have already said that the enthymeme is a kind of syllogism, what makes it so, and in what it differs from the dialectic syllogisms; for the conclusion must neither be drawn from too far back nor should it include all the steps of the argument. In the first case its length causes obscurity, in the second, it is simply a waste of words, because it states much that is obvious. It is this that makes the ignorant more persuasive than the educated in the presence of crowds; as the poets say, "the ignorant are more skilled at speaking before a mob." For the educated use commonplaces and generalities, whereas the ignorant speak of what they know and of what more nearly concerns the audience. Wherefore one must not argue from all possible opinions, but only from such as are definite and admitted, for instance, either by the judges themselves or by those of whose judgement they approve. Further, it should be clear that this is the opinion of all or most of the hearers; and again, conclusions should not be drawn from necessary premises alone, but also from those which are only true as a rule.

First of all, then, it must be understood that, in regard to the subject of our speech or reasoning, whether it be political or of any other kind, it is necessary to be also acquainted with the elements of the question, either entirely or in part; for if you know none of these things, you will have nothing from which to draw a conclusion. I should like to know, for instance, how we are to give advice to the Athenians as to making war or not, if we do not know in what their strength consists, whether it is naval, military, or both, how great it is, their sources of revenue, their friends and enemies, and further, what wars they have already waged, with what success, and all similar things? Again, how could we praise them, if we did not know of the naval engagement at Salamis or the battle of Marathon, or what they did for the Heraclidae, and other similar things? for men always base their praise upon what really are, or are thought to be, glorious deeds. Similarly, they base their censure upon actions that are contrary to these, examining whether those censured have really, or seem to have, committed them; for example, that the Athenians subjugated the Greeks, and reduced to slavery the Aeginetans and Potidaeans who had fought with distinction on their side against the barbarians, and all such acts, and whatever other similar offences may have been committed by them. Similarly, in accusation and defence, speakers argue from an examination of the circumstances of the case. It makes no difference in doing this, whether it is a question of Athenians or Lacedaemonians, of a man or a god. For, when advising Achilles, praising or censuring, accusing or defending him, we must grasp all that really belongs, or appears to belong to him, in order that we may praise or censure in accordance with this, if there is anything noble or disgraceful; defend or accuse, if there is anything just or unjust; advise, if there is anything expedient or harmful. And similarly in regard to any subject whatever. For instance, in regard to justice, whether it is good or not, we must consider the question in the light of what is inherent in justice or the good.

Therefore, since it is evident that all men follow this procedure in demonstration, whether they reason strictly or loosely—since they do not derive their arguments from all things indiscriminately, but from what is inherent in each particular subject, and reason makes it clear that it is impossible to prove anything in any other way—it is evidently necessary, as has been stated in the Topics, to have first on each subject a selection of premises about probabilities and what is most suitable. As for those to be used in sudden emergencies, the same method of inquiry must be adopted; we must look, not at what is indefinite but at what is inherent in the subject treated of in the speech, marking off as many facts as possible, particularly those intimately connected with the subject; for the more facts one has, the easier it is to demonstrate, and the more closely connected they are with the subject, the more suitable are they and less common. By common I mean, for instance, praising Achilles because he is a man, or one of the demigods, or because he went on the expedition against Troy; for this is applicable to many others as well, so that such praise is no more suited to Achilles than to Diomedes. By particular I mean what belongs to Achilles, but to no one else; for instance, to have slain Hector, the bravest of the Trojans, and Cycnus, who prevented all the Greeks from disembarking, being invulnerable; to have gone to the war when very young, and without having taken the oath; and all such things.

One method of selection then, and this the first, is the topical. Let us now speak of the elements of enthymemes (by element and topic of enthymeme I mean the same thing). But let us first make some necessary remarks. There are two kinds of enthymemes, the one demonstrative, which proves that a thing is or is not, and the other refutative, the two differing like refutation and syllogism in Dialectic. The demonstrative enthymeme draws conclusions from admitted premises, the refutative draws conclusions disputed by the adversary. We know nearly all the general heads of each of the special topics that are useful or necessary; for the propositions relating to each have been selected, so that we have in like manner already established all the topics from which enthymemes may be derived on the subject of good or bad, fair or foul, just or unjust, characters, emotions, and habits.
Let us now endeavor to find topics about enthymemes in general in another way, noting in passing those which are refutative and those which are demonstrative, and those of apparent enthymemes, which are not really enthymemes, since they are not syllogisms. After this has been made clear, we will settle the question of solutions and objections, and whence they must be derived to refute enthymemes.

## Chapter 23

One topic of demonstrative enthymemes is derived from opposites; for it is necessary to consider whether one opposite is predicable of the other, as a means of destroying an argument, if it is not, as a means of constructing one, if it is; for instance, self-control is good, for lack of self-control is harmful; or as in the Messeniacus,

"If the war is responsible for the present evils, one must repair them with the aid of peace."

And,

"For if it is unfair to be angry with those who have done wrong unintentionally, it is not fitting to feel beholden to one who is forced to do us good."

Or,

"If men are in the habit of gaining credit for false statements, you must also admit the contrary, that men often disbelieve what is true."

Another topic is derived from similar inflections, for in like manner the derivatives must either be predicable of the subject or not; for instance, that the just is not entirely good, for in that case good would be predicable of anything that happens justly; but to be justly put to death is not desirable.

Another topic is derived from relative terms. For if to have done rightly or justly may be predicated of one, then to have suffered similarly may be predicated of the other; there is the same relation between having ordered and having carried out, as Diomedon the tax-gatherer said about the taxes, "If selling is not disgraceful for you, neither is buying disgraceful for us." And if rightly or justly can be predicated of the sufferer, it can equally be predicated of the one who inflicts suffering; if of the latter, then also of the former. However, in this there is room for a fallacy. For if a man has suffered justly, he has suffered justly, but perhaps not at your hands. Wherefore one must consider separately whether the sufferer deserves to suffer, and whether he who inflicts suffering is the right person to do so, and then make use of the argument either way; for sometimes there is a difference in such a case, and nothing prevents [its being argued], as in the Alcmaeon of Theodectes:

"And did no one of mortals loathe thy mother?"

Alcmaeon replied: "We must make a division before we examine the matter." And when Alphesiboea asked "How?", he rejoined, "Their decision was that she should die, but that it was not for me to kill her."

Another example may be found in the trial of Demosthenes and those who slew Nicanor. For since it was decided that they had justly slain him, it was thought that he had been justly put to death. Again, in the case of the man who was murdered at Thebes, when the defendants demanded that the judges should decide whether the murdered man deserved to die, since a man who deserved it could be put to death without injustice.

Another topic is derived from the more and less. For instance, if not even the gods know everything, hardly can men; for this amounts to saying that

if a predicate, which is more probably affirmable of one thing, does not belong to it, it is clear that it does not belong to another of which it is less probably affirmable. And to say that a man who beats his father also beats his neighbors, is an instance of the rule that, if the less exists, the more also exists. Either of these arguments may be used, according as it is necessary to prove either that a predicate is affirmable or that it is not. Further, if there is no question of greater or less; whence it was said,
"Thy father deserves to be pitied for having lost his children; is not Oeneus then equally to be pitied for having lost an illustrious offspring?"
Other instances are: if Theseus did no wrong, neither did Alexander (Paris); if the sons of Tyndareus did no wrong, neither did Alexander; and if Hector did no wrong in slaying Patroclus, neither did Alexander in slaying Achilles; if no other professional men are contemptible, then neither are philosophers; if generals are not despised because they are frequently defeated, neither are the sophists; or, if it behoves a private citizen to take care of your reputation, it is your duty to take care of that of Greece.
Another topic is derived from the consideration of time. Thus Iphicrates, in his speech against Harmodius, says: "If, before accomplishing anything, I had demanded the statue from you in the event of my success, you would have granted it; will you then refuse it, now that I have succeeded? Do not therefore make a promise when you expect something, and break it when you have received it." Again, to persuade the Thebans to allow Philip to pass through their territory into Attica, they were told that "if he had made this request before helping them against the Phocians, they would have promised; it would be absurd, therefore, if they refused to let him through now, because he had thrown away his opportunity and had trusted them."
Another topic consists in turning upon the opponent what has been said against ourselves; and this is an excellent method. For instance, in the Teucer . . . and Iphicrates employed it against Aristophon, when he asked him whether he would have betrayed the fleet for a bribe; when Aristophon said no, "Then," retorted Iphicrates, "if you, Aristophon, would not have betrayed it, would I, Iphicrates, have done so?" But the opponent must be a man who seems the more likely to have committed a crime; otherwise, it would appear ridiculous, if anyone were to make use of such an argument in reference to such an opponent, for instance, as Aristides; it should only be used to discredit the accuser. For in general the accuser aspires to be better than the defendant; accordingly, it must always be shown that this is not the case. And generally, it is ridiculous for a man to reproach others for what he does or would do himself, or to encourage others to do what he does not or would not do himself.
Another topic is derived from definition. For instance, that the daimonion is nothing else than a god or the work of a god; but he who thinks it to be

the work of a god necessarily thinks that gods exist. When Iphicrates desired to prove that the best man is the noblest, he declared that there was nothing noble attaching to Harmodius and Aristogiton, before they did something noble; and, "I myself am more akin to them than you; at any rate, my deeds are more akin to theirs than yours." And as it is said in the Alexander that it would be generally admitted that men of disorderly passions are not satisfied with the enjoyment of one woman's person alone. Also, the reason why Socrates refused to visit Archelaus, declaring that it was disgraceful not to be in a position to return a favor as well as an injury. In all these cases, it is by definition and the knowledge of what the thing is in itself that conclusions are drawn upon the subject in question. Another topic is derived from the different significations of a word, as explained in the Topics, where the correct use of these terms has been discussed.

Another, from division. For example, "There are always three motives for wrongdoing; two are excluded from consideration as impossible; as for the third, not even the accusers assert it."

Another, from induction. For instance, from the case of the woman of Peparethus, it is argued that in matters of parentage women always discern the truth; similarly, at Athens, when Mantias the orator was litigating with his son, the mother declared the truth; and again, at Thebes, when Ismenias and Stilbon were disputing about a child, Dodonis declared that Ismenias was its father, Thettaliscus being accordingly recognized as the son of Ismenias. There is another instance in the "law" of Theodectes: "If we do not entrust our own horses to those who have neglected the horses of others, or our ships to those who have upset the ships of others; then, if this is so in all cases, we must not entrust our own safety to those who have failed to preserve the safety of others." Similarly, in order to prove that men of talent are everywhere honored, Alcidamas said: "The Parians honored Archilochus, in spite of his evil-speaking; the Chians Homer, although he had rendered no public services; the Mytilenaeans Sappho, although she was a woman; the Lacedaemonians, by no means a people fond of learning, elected Chilon one of their senators; the Italiotes honored Pythagoras, and the Lampsacenes buried Anaxagoras, although he was a foreigner, and still hold him in honor... The Athenians were happy as long as they lived under the laws of Solon, and the Lacedaemonians under those of Lycurgus; and at Thebes, as soon as those who had the conduct of affairs became philosophers, the city flourished."

Another topic is that from a previous judgement in regard to the same or a similar or contrary matter, if possible when the judgement was unanimous or the same at all times; if not, when it was at least that of the majority, or of the wise, either all or most, or of the good; or of the judges themselves or of those whose judgement they accept, or of those whose judgement it is not possible to contradict, for instance, those in authority, or of those whose judgement it is unseemly to contradict, for instance, the gods, a father, or instructors; as Autocles said in his attack on Mixidemides, "If the awful goddesses were content to stand their trial before the Areopagus, should not Mixidemides?" Or Sappho, "Death is an evil; the gods have so decided, for otherwise they would die." Or as Aristippus, when in his opinion Plato had expressed himself too presumptuously, said, "Our friend at any rate never spoke like that," referring to Socrates. Hegesippus, after having first consulted the oracle at Olympia, asked the god at Delphi whether his opinion was the same as his father's, meaning that it would be disgraceful to contradict him. Helen was a virtuous woman, wrote Isocrates, because Theseus so judged; the same applies to Alexander (Paris), whom the goddesses chose before others. Evagoras was virtuous, as Isocrates says, for at any rate Conon in his misfortune, passing over everyone else, sought his assistance.

Another topic is that from enumerating the parts, as in the Topics: What kind of movement is the soul? for it must be this or that. There is an instance of this in the Socrates of Theodectes: "What holy place has he profaned? Which of the gods recognized by the city has he neglected to honor?"

Again, since in most human affairs the same thing is accompanied by some bad or good result, another topic consists in employing the consequence to exhort or dissuade, accuse or defend, praise or blame. For instance, education is attended by the evil of being envied, and by the good of being wise; therefore we should not be educated, for we should avoid being envied; nay rather, we should be educated, for we should be wise. This topic is identical with the "Art" of Callippus, when you have also included the topic of the possible and the others which have been mentioned.

Another topic may be employed when it is necessary to exhort or dissuade in regard to two opposites, and one has to employ the method previously stated in the case of both. But there is this difference, that in the former case things of any kind whatever are opposed, in the latter opposites. For instance, a priestess refused to allow her son to speak in public; "For if," said she, "you say what is just, men will hate you; if you say what is unjust, the gods will." On the other hand, "you should speak in public; for if you say what is just, the gods will love you, if you say what is unjust, men will." This is the same as the proverb, "To buy the swamp with the salt"; and retorting a dilemma on its proposer takes place when, two things being opposite, good and evil follow on each, the good and evil being opposite like the things themselves.

Again, since men do not praise the same things in public and in secret, but in public chiefly praise what is just and beautiful, and in secret rather wish for what is expedient, another topic consists in endeavoring to infer its opposite from one or other of these statements. This topic is the most weighty of those that deal with paradox.

Another topic is derived from analogy in things. For instance, Iphicrates, when they tried to force his son to perform public services because he was tall, although under the legal age, said: "If you consider tall boys men, you must vote that short men are boys." Similarly, Theodectes in his "law," says: "Since you bestow the rights of citizenship upon mercenaries such as Strabax and Charidemus on account of their merits, will you not banish those of them who have wrought such irreparable misfortunes?"

Another topic consists in concluding the identity of antecedents from the identity of results. Thus Xenophanes said: "There is as much impiety in asserting that the gods are born as in saying that they die; for either way the result is that at some time or other they did not exist." And, generally speaking, one may always regard as identical the results produced by one or other of any two things: "You are about to decide, not about Isocrates alone, but about education generally, whether it is right to study philosophy." And, "to give earth and water is slavery," and "to be included in the common peace implies obeying orders." Of two alternatives, you should take that which is useful.

Another topic is derived from the fact that the same men do not always choose the same thing before and after, but the contrary. The following enthymeme is an example: "If, when in exile, we fought to return to our country [it would be monstrous] if, now that we have returned, we were to return to exile to avoid fighting"! This amounts to saying that at one time they preferred to hold their ground at the price of fighting; at another, not to fight at the price of not remaining.

Another topic consists in maintaining that the cause of something which is or has been is something which would generally, or possibly might, be the cause of it; for example, if one were to make a present of something to another, in order to cause him pain by depriving him of it. Whence it has been said:

"It is not from benevolence that the deity bestows great blessings upon many, but in order that they may suffer more striking calamities."

And these verses from the Meleager of Antiphon:

"Not in order to slay the monster, but that they may be witnesses to Greece of the valor of Meleager."

And the following remark from the Ajax of Theodectes, that Diomedes chose Odysseus before all others, not to do him honor, but that his companion might be his inferior; for this may have been the reason.

Another topic common to forensic and deliberative rhetoric consists in examining what is hortatory and dissuasive, and the reasons which make men act or not. Now, these are the reasons which, if they exist, determine us to act, if not, not; for instance, if a thing is possible, easy, or useful to ourselves or our friends, or injurious and prejudicial to our enemies, or if the penalty is less than the profit. From these grounds we exhort, and dissuade from their contraries. It is on the same grounds that we accuse and defend; for what dissuades serves for defence, what persuades, for accusation. This topic comprises the whole "Art" of Pamphilus and Callippus.

Another topic is derived from things which are thought to happen but are incredible, because it would never have been thought so, if they had not happened or almost happened. And further, these things are even more likely to be true; for we only believe in that which is, or that which is probable: if then a thing is incredible and not probable, it will be true; for it is not because it is probable and credible that we think it true. Thus, Androcles of Pitthus, speaking against the law, being shouted at when he said "the laws need a law to correct them," went on, "and fishes need salt, although it is neither probable nor credible that they should, being brought up in brine; similarly, pressed olives need oil, although it is incredible that what produces oil should itself need oil."

Another topic, appropriate to refutation, consists in examining contradictories, whether in dates, actions, or words, first, separately in the case of the adversary, for instance, "he says that he loves you, and yet he conspired with the Thirty;" next, separately in your own case, "he says that I am litigious, but he cannot prove that I have ever brought an action against anyone"; lastly, separately in the case of your adversary and yourself together: "he has never yet lent anything, but I have ransomed many of you."

Another topic, when men or things have been attacked by slander, in reality or in appearance, consists in stating the reason for the false opinion; for there must be a reason for the supposition of guilt. For example, a woman embraced her son in a manner that suggested she had illicit relations with him, but when the reason was explained, the slander was quashed. Again, in the Ajax of Theodectes, Odysseus explains to Ajax why, although really more courageous than Ajax, he is not considered to be so.

Another topic is derived from the cause. If the cause exists, the effect exists; if the cause does not exist, the effect does not exist; for the effect exists with the cause, and without cause there is nothing. For example, Leodamas, when defending himself against the accusation of Thrasybulus that his name had been posted in the Acropolis but that he had erased it in the time of the Thirty, declared that it was impossible, for the Thirty would have had more confidence in him if his hatred against the people had been graven on the stone.

Another topic consists in examining whether there was or is another better course than that which is advised, or is being, or has been, carried out. For it is evident that, if this has not been done, a person has not committed a certain action; because no one, purposely or knowingly, chooses what is bad. However, this argument may be false; for often it is not until later that it becomes clear what was the better course, which previously was uncertain.

Another topic, when something contrary to what has already been done is on the point of being done, consists in examining them together. For instance, when the people of Elea asked Xenophanes if they ought to sacrifice and sing dirges to Leucothea, or not, he advised them that, if they believed her to be a goddess they ought not to sing dirges, but if they believed her to be a mortal, they ought not to sacrifice to her.

Another topic consists in making use of errors committed, for purposes of accusation or defence. For instance, in the Medea of Carcinus, some accuse Medea of having killed her children,—at any rate, they had disappeared; for she had made the mistake of sending them out of the way. Medea herself pleads that she would have slain, not her children, but her husband Jason; for it would have been a mistake on her part not to have done this, if she had done the other. This topic and kind of enthymeme is the subject of the whole of the first "Art" of Theodorus.

Another topic is derived from the meaning of a name. For instance, Sophocles says,

"Certainly thou art iron, like thy name."

This topic is also commonly employed in praising the gods. Conon used to call Thrasybulus "the man bold in counsel," and Herodicus said of Thrasymachus, "Thou art ever bold in fight," and of Polus, "Thou art ever Polus (colt) by name and colt by nature," and of Draco the legislator that his laws were not those of a man, but of a dragon, so severe were they. Hecuba in Euripides speaks thus of Aphro-dite:

"And rightly does the name of the goddess begin like the word aphro-syne (folly);"

and Chaeremon of Pentheus,

"Pentheus named after his unhappy future."

Enthymemes that serve to refute are more popular than those that serve to demonstrate, because the former is a conclusion of opposites in a small compass, and things in juxtaposition are always clearer to the audience. But of all syllogisms, whether refutative or demonstrative, those are specially applauded, the result of which the hearers foresee as soon as they are begun, and not because they are superficial (for as they listen they congratulate themselves on anticipating the conclusion); and also those which the hearers are only so little behind that they understand what they mean as soon as they are delivered.

# Chapter 24

But as it is possible that some syllogisms may be real, and others not real but only apparent, there must also be real and apparent enthymemes, since the enthymeme is a kind of syllogism.

Now, of the topics of apparent enthymemes one is that of diction, which is of two kinds. The first, as in Dialectic, consists in ending with a conclusion syllogistically expressed, although there has been no syllogistic process, "therefore it is neither this nor that," "so it must be this or that"; and similarly in rhetorical arguments a concise and antithetical statement is supposed to be an enthymeme; for such a style appears to contain a real enthymeme. This fallacy appears to be the result of the form of expression. For the purpose of using the diction to create an impression of syllogistic reasoning it is useful to state the heads of several syllogisms: "He saved some, avenged others, and freed the Greeks"; for each of these propositions has been proved by others, but their union appears to furnish a fresh conclusion.

The second kind of fallacy of diction is homonymy. For instance, if one were to say that the mouse is an important animal, since from it is derived the most honored of all religious festivals, namely, the mysteries; or if, in praising the dog, one were to include the dog in heaven (Sirius), or Pan, because Pindar said,

"O blessed one, whom the Olympians call dog of the Great Mother, taking every form,"

or were to say that the dog is an honorable animal, since to be without a dog is most dishonorable. And to say that Hermes is the most sociable of the gods, because he alone is called common; and that words are most excellent, since good men are considered worthy, not of riches but of consideration; for λόγου ἄξιος has a double meaning.

Another fallacy consists in combining what is divided or dividing what is combined. For since a thing which is not the same as another often appears to be the same, one may adopt the more convenient alternative. Such was the argument of Euthydemus, to prove, for example, that a man knows that there is a trireme in the Piraeus, because he knows the existence of two things, the Piraeus and the trireme; or that, when one knows the letters, one also knows the word made of them, for word and letters are the same thing. Further, since twice so much is unwholesome, one may argue that neither is the original amount wholesome; for it would be absurd that two halves separately should be good, but bad combined. In this way the argument may be used for refutation, in another way for demonstration, if one were to say, one good thing cannot make two bad things. But the whole topic is fallacious. Again, one may quote what Polycrates said of

Thrasybulus, that he deposed thirty tyrants, for here he combines them; or the example of the fallacy of division in the Orestes of Theodectes: "It is just that a woman who has killed her husband" should be put to death, and that the son should avenge the father; and this in fact is what has been done. But if they are combined, perhaps the act ceases to be just. The same might also be classed as an example of the fallacy of omission; for the name of the one who should put the woman to death is not mentioned.

Another topic is that of constructing or destroying by exaggeration, which takes place when the speaker, without having proved that any crime has actually been committed, exaggerates the supposed fact; for it makes it appear either that the accused is not guilty, when he himself exaggerates it, or that he is guilty, when it is the accuser who is in a rage. Therefore there is no enthymeme; for the hearer falsely concludes that the accused is guilty or not, although neither has been proved.

Another fallacy is that of the sign, for this argument also is illogical. For instance, if one were to say that those who love one another are useful to States, since the love of Harmodius and Aristogiton overthrew the tyrant Hipparchus; or that Dionysius is a thief, because he is a rascal; for here again the argument is inconclusive; not every rascal is a thief although every thief is a rascal.

Another fallacy is derived from accident; for instance, when Polycrates says of the mice, that, they rendered great service by gnawing the bowstrings. Or if one were to say that nothing is more honorable than to be invited to a dinner, for because he was not invited Achilles was angry with the Achaeans at Tenedos; whereas he was really angry because he had been treated with disrespect, but this was an accident due to his not having been invited.

Another fallacy is that of the Consequence. For instance, in the Alexander (Paris) it is said that Paris was high-minded, because he despised the companionship of the common herd and dwelt on Ida by himself; for because the high-minded are of this character, Paris also might be thought high-minded. Or, since a man pays attention to dress and roams about at night, he is a libertine, because libertines are of this character. Similarly, the poor sing and dance in the temples, exiles can live where they please; and since these things belong to those who are apparently happy, those to whom they belong may also be thought happy. But there is a difference in conditions; wherefore this topic also falls under the head of omission.

Another fallacy consists of taking what is not the cause for the cause, as when a thing has happened at the same time as, or after, another; for it is believed that what happens after is produced by the other, especially by politicians. Thus, Demades declared that the policy of Demosthenes was the cause of all the evils that happened, since it was followed by the war.

Another fallacy is the omission of when and how. For instance, Alexander (Paris) had a right to carry off Helen, for the choice of a husband had been given her by her father. But (this was a fallacy), for it was not, as might be thought, for all time, but only for the first time; for the father's authority only lasts till then. Or, if one should say that it is wanton outrage to beat a free man; for this is not always the case, but only when the assailant gives the first blow.

Further, as in sophistical disputations, an apparent syllogism arises as the result of considering a thing first absolutely, and then not absolutely, but only in a particular case. For instance, in Dialectic, it is argued that that which is not is, for that which is not is that which is not; also, that the unknown can be known, for it can be known of the unknown that it is unknown. Similarly, in Rhetoric, an apparent enthymeme may arise from that which is not absolutely probable but only in particular cases. But this is not to be understood absolutely, as Agathon says:

"One might perhaps say that this very thing is probable, that many things happen to men that are not probable;"

for that which is contrary to probability nevertheless does happen, so that that which is contrary to probability is probable. If this is so, that which is improbable will be probable. But not absolutely; but as, in the case of sophistical disputations, the argument becomes fallacious when the circumstances, reference, and manner are not added, so here it will become so owing to the probability being not probable absolutely but only in particular cases.

The "Art" of Corax is composed of this topic. For if a man is not likely to be guilty of what he is accused of, for instance if, being weak, he is accused of assault and battery, his defence will be that the crime is not probable; but if he is likely to be guilty, for instance, if he is strong, it may be argued again that the crime is not probable, for the very reason that it was bound to appear so. It is the same in all other cases; for a man must either be likely to have committed a crime or not. Here, both the alternatives appear equally probable, but the one is really so, the other not probable absolutely, but only in the conditions mentioned. And this is what "making the worse appear the better argument" means. Wherefore men were justly disgusted with the promise of Protagoras; for it is a lie, not a real but an apparent probability, not found in any art except Rhetoric and Sophistic. So much for real or apparent enthymemes.

## Chapter 25

Next to what has been said we must speak of refutation. An argument may be refuted either by a counter-syllogism or by bringing an objection. It is clear that the same topics may furnish counter-syllogisms; for syllogisms are derived from probable materials and many probabilities are contrary to one another. An objection is brought, as shown in the Topics, in four ways: it may be derived either from itself, or from what is similar, or from what is contrary, or from what has been decided. In the first case, if for instance the enthymeme was intended to prove that love is good, two objections might be made; either the general statement that all want is bad, or in particular, that Caunian love would not have become proverbial, unless some forms of love had been bad. An objection from what is contrary is brought if, for instance, the enthymeme is that the good man does good to all his friends; it may be objected: But the bad man does not do harm [to all his friends]. An objection from what is similar is brought, if the enthymeme is that those who have been injured always hate, by arguing that those who have been benefited do not always love. The fourth kind of objection is derived from the former decisions of well-known men. For instance, if the enthymeme is that one should make allowance for those who are drunk, for their offence is the result of ignorance, it may be objected that Pittacus then is unworthy of commendation, otherwise he would not have laid down severer punishment for a man who commits an offence when drunk.

Now the material of enthymemes is derived from four sources—probabilities, examples, necessary signs, and signs. Conclusions are drawn from probabilities, when based upon things which most commonly occur or seem to occur; from examples, when they are the result of induction from one or more similar cases, and when one assumes the general and then concludes the particular by an example; from necessary signs, when based upon that which is necessary and ever exists; from signs, when their material is the general or the particular, whether true or not. Now, the probable being not what occurs invariably but only for the most part, it is evident that enthymemes of this character can always be refuted by bringing an objection. But the objection is often only apparent, not real; for he who brings the objection endeavors to show, not that the argument is not probable, but that it is not necessary. Wherefore, by the employment of this fallacy, the defendant always has an advantage over the accuser. For since the latter always bases his proof upon probabilities, and it is not the same thing to show that an argument is not probable as to show that it is not necessary, and that which is only true for the most part is always liable to objection (otherwise it would not be probable, but constant and necessary),—then the judge thinks, if the refutation is made in this manner, either that the argument is not probable, or that it is not for him to decide, being deceived by the fallacy, as we have just indicated. For his judgement must not rest upon necessary arguments alone, but also upon probabilities; for this is what is meant by deciding according to the best of one's judgement. It is therefore not enough to refute an argument by showing that it is not necessary; it must also be shown that it is not probable. This will be attained if the objection itself is specially based upon what happens generally. This may take place in two ways, from consideration either of the time or of the facts. The strongest objections are those in which both are combined; for a thing is more probable, the greater the number of similar cases.

Signs and enthymemes based upon signs, even if true, may be refuted in the manner previously stated; for it is clear from the Analytics that no sign can furnish a logical conclusion. As for enthymemes derived from examples, they may be refuted in the same manner as probabilities. For if we have a single fact that contradicts the opponent's example, the argument is refuted as not being necessary, even though examples, more in number and of more common occurrence, are otherwise; but if the majority and greater frequency of examples is on the side of the opponent, we must contend either that the present example is not similar to those cited by him, or that the thing did not take place in the same way, or that there is some difference. But necessary signs and the enthymemes derived from them cannot be refuted on the ground of not furnishing a logical conclusion, as is clear from the Analytics; the only thing that remains is to prove that the thing alleged is non-existent. But if it is evident that it is true and that it is a necessary sign, the argument at once becomes irrefutable; for, by means of demonstration, everything at once becomes clear.

# Chapter 26

Amplification and depreciation are not elements of enthymeme (for I regard element and topic as identical), since element (or topic) is a head under which several enthymemes are included, but they are enthymemes which serve to show that a thing is great or small, just as others serve to show that it is good or bad, just or unjust, or anything else. All these are the materials of syllogisms and enthymemes; so that if none of these is a topic of enthymeme, neither is amplification or depreciation. Nor are enthymemes by which arguments are refuted of a different kind from those by which they are established; for it is clear that demonstration or bringing an objection is the means of refutation. By the first the contrary of the adversary's conclusion is demonstrated; for instance, if he has shown that a thing has happened, his opponent shows that it has not; if he has shown that a thing has not happened, he shows that it has. This, therefore, will not be the difference between them; for both employ the same arguments; they bring forward enthymemes to show that the thing is or that it is not. And the objection is not an enthymeme, but, as I said in the

Topics, it is stating an opinion which is intended to make it clear that the adversary's syllogism is not logical, or that he has assumed some false premise. Now, since there are three things in regard to speech, to which special attention should be devoted, let what has been said suffice for examples, maxims, enthymemes, and what concerns the intelligence generally; for the sources of a supply of arguments and the means of refuting them. It only remains to speak of style and arrangement.

# Book III

## Chapter 1

There are three things which require special attention in regard to speech: first, the sources of proofs; secondly, style; and thirdly, the arrangement of the parts of the speech. We have already spoken of proofs and stated that they are three in number, what is their nature, and why there are only three; for in all cases persuasion is the result either of the judges themselves being affected in a certain manner, or because they consider the speakers to be of a certain character, or because something has been demonstrated. We have also stated the sources from which enthymemes should be derived—some of them being special, the others general commonplaces. We have therefore next to speak of style; for it is not sufficient to know what one ought to say, but one must also know how to say it, and this largely contributes to making the speech appear of a certain character. In the first place, following the natural order, we investigated that which first presented itself—what gives things themselves their persuasiveness; in the second place, their arrangement by style; and in the third place, delivery, which is of the greatest importance but has not yet been treated of by anyone. In fact, it only made its appearance late in tragedy and rhapsody, for at first the poets themselves acted their tragedies. It is clear, therefore, that there is something of the sort in rhetoric as well as in poetry, and it has been dealt with by Glaucon of Teos among others. Now delivery is a matter of voice, as to the mode in which it should be used for each particular emotion; when it should be loud, when low, when intermediate; and how the tones, that is, shrill, deep, and intermediate, should be used; and what rhythms are adapted to each subject. For there are three qualities that are considered,—volume, harmony, rhythm. Those who use these properly nearly always carry off the prizes in dramatic contests, and as at the present day actors have greater influence on the stage than the poets, it is the same In political contests, owing to the corruptness of our forms of government. But no treatise has yet been composed on delivery, since the matter of style itself only lately came into notice; and rightly considered it is thought vulgar. But since the whole business of Rhetoric is to influence opinion, we must pay attention to it, not as being right, but necessary; for, as a matter of right, one should aim at nothing more in a speech than how to avoid exciting pain or pleasure. For justice should consist in fighting the case with the facts alone, so that everything else that is beside demonstration is superfluous; nevertheless, as we have just said, it is of great importance owing to the corruption of the hearer. However, in every system of instruction there is some slight necessity to pay attention to style; for it does make a difference, for the purpose of making a thing clear, to speak in this or that manner; still, the difference is not so very great, but all these things are mere outward show for pleasing the hearer; wherefore no one teaches geometry in this way.

Now, when delivery comes into fashion, it will have the same effect as acting. Some writers have attempted to say a few words about it, as Thrasymachus, in his Eleoi; and in fact, a gift for acting is a natural talent and depends less upon art, but in regard to style it is artificial. Wherefore people who excel in this in their turn obtain prizes, just as orators who excel in delivery; for written speeches owe their effect not so much to the sense as to the style.

The poets, as was natural, were the first to give an impulse to style; for words are imitations, and the voice also, which of all our parts is best adapted for imitation, was ready to hand; thus the arts of the rhapsodists, actors, and others, were fashioned. And as the poets, although their utterances were devoid of sense, appeared to have gained their reputation through their style, it was a poetical style that first came into being, as that of Gorgias. Even now the majority of the uneducated think that such persons express themselves most beautifully, whereas this is not the case, for the style of prose is not the same as that of poetry. And the result proves it; for even the writers of tragedies do not employ it in the same manner, but as they have changed from the tetrametric to the iambic meter, because the latter, of all other meters, most nearly resembles prose, they have in like manner discarded all such words as differ from those of ordinary conversation, with which the early poets used to adorn their writings, and which even now are employed by the writers of hexameters. It is therefore ridiculous to imitate those who no longer employ that manner of writing. Consequently, it is evident that we need not enter too precisely into all questions of style, but only those which concern such a style as we are discussing. As for the other kind of style, it has already been treated in the Poetics.

## Chapter 2

Let this suffice for the consideration of these points. In regard to style, one of its chief merits may be defined as perspicuity. This is shown by the fact that the speech, if it does not make the meaning clear, will not perform its proper function; neither must it be mean, nor above the dignity of the subject, but appropriate to it; for the poetic style may be is not mean, but it is not appropriate to prose. Of nouns and verbs it is the proper ones that make style perspicuous; all the others which have been spoken of in the Poetics elevate and make it ornate; for departure from the ordinary makes it appear more dignified. In this respect men feel the same in regard to style as in regard to foreigners and fellow-citizens. Wherefore we should give our language a "foreign air"; for men admire what is remote, and that which excites admiration is pleasant. In poetry many things conduce to this and there it is appropriate; for the subjects and persons spoken of are more out of the common. But in prose such methods are appropriate in much fewer instances, for the subject is less elevated; and even in poetry, if fine language were used by a slave or a very young man, or about quite unimportant matters, it would be hardly becoming; for even here due proportion consists in contraction and amplification as the subject requires. Wherefore those who practise this artifice must conceal it and avoid the appearance of speaking artificially instead of naturally; for that which is natural persuades, but the artificial does not. For men become suspicious of one whom they think to be laying a trap for them, as they are of mixed wines. Such was the case with the voice of Theodorus as contrasted with that of the rest of the actors; for his seemed to be the voice of the speaker, that of the others the voice of someone else. Art is cleverly concealed when the speaker chooses his words from ordinary language and puts them together like Euripides, who was the first to show the way. Nouns and verbs being the components of speech, and nouns being of the different kinds which have been considered in the Poetics, of these we should use strange, compound, or coined words only rarely and in few places. We will state later in what places they should be used; the reason for this has already been mentioned, namely, that it involves too great a departure from suitable language. Proper and appropriate words and metaphors are alone to be employed in the style of prose; this is shown by the fact that no one employs anything but these. For all use metaphors in conversation, as well as proper and appropriate words; wherefore it is clear that, if a speaker manages well, there will be some thing "foreign" about his speech, while possibly the art may not be detected, and his meaning will be clear. And this, as we have said, is the chief merit of rhetorical language. (In regard to nouns, homonyms are most useful to the sophist, for it is by their aid that he employs captious arguments, and synonyms to the poet. Instances of words that are both proper and synonymous are "going" and "walking": for these two words are proper and have the same meaning.)

It has already been stated, as we have said, in the Poetics, what each of these things is, how many kinds of metaphor there are, and that it is most important both in poetry and in prose. But the orator must devote the greater attention to them in prose, since the latter has fewer resources

than verse. It is metaphor above all that gives perspicuity, pleasure, and a foreign air, and it cannot be learnt from anyone else; but we must make use of metaphors and epithets that are appropriate. This will be secured by observing due proportion; otherwise there will be a lack of propriety, because it is when placed in juxtaposition that contraries are most evident. We must consider, as a red cloak suits a young man, what suits an old one; for the same garment is not suitable for both. And if we wish to ornament our subject, we must derive our metaphor from the better species under the same genus; if to depreciate it, from the worse. Thus, to say (for you have two opposites belonging to the same genus) that the man who begs prays, or that the man who prays begs (for both are forms of asking) is an instance of doing this; as, when Iphicrates called Callias a mendicant priest instead of a torch-bearer, Callias replied that Iphicrates himself could not be initiated, otherwise he would not have called him mendicant priest but torch-bearer; both titles indeed have to do with a divinity, but the one is honorable, the other dishonorable. And some call actors flatterers of Dionysus, whereas they call themselves "artists." Both these names are metaphors, but the one is a term of abuse, the other the contrary. Similarly, pirates now call themselves purveyors; and so it is allowable to say that the man who has committed a crime has "made a mistake," that the man who has "made a mistake" is "guilty of crime", and that one who has committed a theft has either "taken" or "ravaged." The saying in the Telephus of Euripides,
"Ruling over the oar and having landed in Mysia,"
is inappropriate, because the word ruling exceeds the dignity of the subject, and so the artifice can be seen. Forms of words also are faulty, if they do not express an agreeable sound; for instance, Dionysius the Brazen in his elegiacs speaks of poetry as
"the scream of Calliope;"
both are sounds, but the metaphor is bad, because the sounds have no meaning.
Further, metaphors must not be far-fetched, but we must give names to things that have none by deriving the metaphor from what is akin and of the same kind, so that, as soon as it is uttered, it is clearly seen to be akin, as in the famous enigma,
"I saw a man who glued bronze with fire upon another."
There was no name for what took place, but as in both cases there is a kind of application, he called the application of the cupping-glass gluing. And, generally speaking, clever enigmas furnish good metaphors; for metaphor is a kind of enigma, so that it is clear that the transference is clever. Metaphors should also be derived from things that are beautiful, the beauty of a word consisting, as Licymnius says, in its sound or sense, and its ugliness in the same. There is a third condition, which refutes the

sophistical argument; for it is not the case, as Bryson said, that no one ever uses foul language, if the meaning is the same whether this or that word is used; this is false; for one word is more proper than another, more of a likeness, and better suited to putting the matter before the eyes. Further, this word or that does not signify a thing under the same conditions; thus for this reason also it must be admitted that one word is fairer or fouler than the other. Both, indeed, signify what is fair or foul, but not qua fair or foul; or if they do, it is in a greater or less degree. Metaphors therefore should be derived from what is beautiful either in sound, or in signification, or to sight, or to some other sense. For it does make a difference, for instance, whether one says "rosy-fingered morn," rather than "purple-fingered," or, what is still worse, "red-fingered."

As for epithets, they may be applied from what is vile or disgraceful, for instance, "the matricide," or from what is more honorable, for instance, "the avenger of his father." When the winner in a mule-race offered Simonides a small sum, he refused to write an ode, as if he thought it beneath him to write on half-asses; but when he gave him a sufficient amount, he wrote,

"Hail, daughters of storm-footed steeds!"

and yet they were also the daughters of asses. Further, the use of diminutives amounts to the same. It is the diminutive which makes the good and the bad appear less, as Aristophanes in the Babylonians jestingly uses "goldlet, cloaklet, affrontlet, diseaselet" instead of "gold, cloak, affront, disease." But one must be careful to observe the due mean in their use as well as in that of epithets.

## Chapter 3

Frigidity of style arises from four causes: first, the use of compound words, as when Lycophron speaks of the "many-faced sky of the mighty-topped earth," "narrow-passaged shore"; and Gorgias of "a begging-poet flatterer," "those who commit perjury and those who swear right solemnly." And as Alcidamas says, "the soul full of anger and the face fire-colored," "he thought that their zeal would be end-accomplishing," "he made persuasive words end-accomplishing," and "the azure-colored floor of the sea," for all these appear poetical because they are compound.

This is one cause of frigidity; another is the use of strange words; as Lycophron calls Xerxes "a monster of a man," Sciron "a human scourge"; and Alcidamas says "plaything in poetry," "the audaciousness of nature," "whetted with unmitigated wrath of thought."

A third cause is the use of epithets that are either long or unseasonable or too crowded; thus, in poetry it is appropriate to speak of white milk, but in prose it is less so; and if epithets are employed to excess, they reveal the art and make it evident that it is poetry. And yet such may be used to a certain extent, since it removes the style from the ordinary and gives a "foreign" air. But one must aim at the mean, for neglect to do so does more harm than speaking at random; for a random style lacks merit, but excess is vicious. That is why the style of Alcidamas appears frigid; for he uses epithets not as a seasoning but as a regular dish, so crowded, so long, and so glaring are they. For instance, he does not say "sweat" but "damp sweat"; not "to the Isthmian games" but "to the solemn assembly of the Isthmian games"; not "laws", but "the laws, the rulers of states"; not "running", but "with a race-like impulse of the soul"; not "museum", but "having taken up the museum of nature"; and "the scowling anxiety of the soul"; "creator", not "of favor", but "all-popular favor"; and "dispenser of the pleasure of the hearers"; "he hid," not "with branches," but "with the branches of the forest"; "he covered," not "his body," but "the nakedness of his body." He also calls desire "counter-initiative of the soul"—an expression which is at once compound and an epithet, so that it becomes poetry—and "the excess of his depravity so beyond all bounds." Hence those who employ poetic language by their lack of taste make the style ridiculous and frigid, and such idle chatter produces obscurity; for when words are piled upon one who already knows, it destroys perspicuity by a cloud of verbiage. People use compound words, when a thing has no name and the word is easy to combine, as χρονοτριβεῖν, to pass time; but if the practice is abused, the style becomes entirely poetical. This is why compound words are especially employed by dithyrambic poets, who are full of noise; strange words by epic poets, for they imply dignity and self-assertion; metaphor to writers of iambics, who now employ them, as we have stated.

The fourth cause of frigidity of style is to be found in metaphors; for metaphors also are inappropriate, some because they are ridiculous—for the comic poets also employ them—others because they are too dignified and somewhat tragic; and if they are farfetched, they are obscure, as when Gorgias says: "Affairs pale and bloodless"; "you have sown shame and reaped misfortune"; for this is too much like poetry. And as Alcidamas calls philosophy "a bulwark of the laws," and the Odyssey "a beautiful mirror of human life," and "introducing no such plaything in poetry." All these expressions fail to produce persuasion, for the reasons stated. As for what Gorgias said to the swallow which, flying over his head, let fall her droppings upon him, it was in the best tragic style. He exclaimed, "Fie, for shame, Philomela!"; for there would have been nothing in this act disgraceful for a bird, whereas it would have been for a young lady. The reproach therefore was appropriate, addressing her as she was, not as she is.

## Chapter 4

The simile also is a metaphor; for there is very little difference. When the poet says of Achilles,
"he rushed on like a lion,"
it is a simile; if he says, "a lion, he rushed on," it is a metaphor; for because both are courageous, he transfers the sense and calls Achilles a lion. The simile is also useful in prose, but should be less frequently used, for there is something poetical about it. Similes must be used like metaphors, which only differ in the manner stated. The following are examples of similes. Androtion said of Idrieus that he was like curs just unchained; for as they attack and bite, so he when loosed from his bonds was dangerous. Again, Theodamas likened Archidamus to a Euxenus ignorant of geometry, by proportion; for Euxenus "will be Archidamus acquainted with geometry." Again, Plato in the Republic compares those who strip the dead to curs, which bite stones, but do not touch those who throw them; he also says that the people is like a ship's captain who is vigorous, but rather deaf; that poets' verses resemble those who are in the bloom of youth but lack beauty; for neither the one after they have lost their bloom, nor the others after they have been broken up, appear the same as before. Pericles said that the Samians were like children who cry while they accept the scraps. He also compared the Boeotians to holm-oaks; for just as these are beaten down by knocking against each other, so are the Boeotians by their civil strife. Demosthenes compared the people to passengers who are seasick. Democrates said that orators resembled nurses who gulp down the morsel and rub the babies' lips with the spittle. Antisthenes likened the skinny Cephisodotus to incense, for he also gives pleasure by wasting away. All such expressions may be used as similes or metaphors, so that all that are approved as metaphors will obviously also serve as similes which are metaphors without the details. But in all cases the metaphor from proportion should be reciprocal and applicable to either of the two things of the same genus; for instance, if the goblet is the shield of Dionysus, then the shield may properly be called the goblet of Ares.

## Chapter 5

Such then are the elements of speech. But purity, which is the foundation of style, depends upon five rules. First, connecting particles should be

introduced in their natural order, before or after, as they require; thus, μέν and ἐγὼ μέν require to be followed by δέ and ὁ δέ. Further, they should be made to correspond whilst the hearer still recollects; they should not be put too far apart, nor should a clause be introduced before the necessary connection; for this is rarely appropriate. For instance, "As for me, I, after he had told me—for Cleon came begging and praying—set out, taking them with me." For in this phrase several connecting words have been foisted in before the one which is to furnish the apodosis; and if the interval between "I" and "set out" is too great, the result is obscurity. The first rule therefore is to make a proper use of connecting particles; the second, to employ special, not generic terms. The third consists in avoiding ambiguous terms, unless you deliberately intend the opposite, like those who, having nothing to say, yet pretend to say something; such people accomplish this by the use of verse, after the manner of Empedocles. For the long circumlocution takes in the hearers, who find themselves affected like the majority of those who listen to the soothsayers. For when the latter utter their ambiguities, they also assent; for example,
"Croesus, by crossing the Halys, shall ruin a mighty dominion."
And as there is less chance of making a mistake when speaking generally, diviners express themselves in general terms on the question of fact; for, in playing odd or even, one is more likely to be right if he says "even" or "odd" than if he gives a definite number, and similarly one who says "it will be" than if he states "when." This is why soothsayers do not further define the exact time. All such ambiguities are alike, wherefore they should be avoided, except for some such reason. The fourth rule consists in keeping the genders distinct—masculine, feminine, and neuter, as laid down by Protagoras; these also must be properly introduced: "She, having come (fem.) and having conversed (fem.) with me, went away." The fifth rule consists in observing number, according as many, few, or one are referred to: "They, having come (pl.), began to beat (pl.) me."
Generally speaking, that which is written should be easy to read or easy to utter, which is the same thing. Now, this is not the case when there is a number of connecting particles, or when the punctuation is hard, as in the writings of Heraclitus. For it is hard, since it is uncertain to which word another belongs, whether to that which follows or that which precedes; for instance, at the beginning of his composition he says: "Of this reason which exists always men are ignorant," where it is uncertain whether "always" should go with "which exists" or with "are ignorant." Further, a solecism results from not appropriately connecting or joining two words with a word which is equally suitable to both. For instance, in speaking of "sound" and "color", the word "seeing" should not be used, for it is not suitable to both, whereas "perceiving" is. It also causes obscurity, if you do not say at the outset what you mean, when you intend to insert a number of details in

the middle; for instance, if you say: "I intended after having spoken to him thus and thus and in this way to set out" instead of "I intended to set out after having spoken to him," and then this or that happened, in this or that manner.

## Chapter 6

The following rules contribute to loftiness of style. Use of the description instead of the name of a thing; for instance, do not say "circle," but "a plane figure, all the points of which are equidistant from the center." But for the purpose of conciseness the reverse—use the name instead of the description. You should do the same to express anything foul or indecent; if the foulness is in the description, use the name; if in the name, the description. Use metaphors and epithets by way of illustration, taking care, however, to avoid what is too poetical. Use the plural for the singular, after the manner of the poets, who, although there is only one harbor, say "to Achaean harbors,"
and,
"Here are the many-leaved folds of the tablet."
You should avoid linking up, but each word should have its own article: τῆς γυναικὸς τῆς ἡμετέρας. But for conciseness, the reverse: τῆς ἡμετέρας γυναικός. Employ a connecting particle or for conciseness omit it, but avoid destroying the connection; for instance "having gone and having conversed with him," or, "having gone, I conversed with him." Also the practice of Antimachus is useful, that of describing a thing by the qualities it does not possess; thus, in speaking of the hill Teumessus, he says, "There is a little windswept hill;"
for in this way amplification may be carried on ad infinitum. This method may be applied to things good and bad, in whichever way it may be useful. Poets also make use of this in inventing words, as a melody "without strings" or "without the lyre"; for they employ epithets from negations, a course which is approved in proportional metaphors, as for instance, to say that the sound of the trumpet is a melody without the lyre.

## Chapter 7

Propriety of style will be obtained by the expression of emotion and character, and by proportion to the subject matter. Style is proportionate to the subject matter when neither weighty matters are treated offhand, nor trifling matters with dignity, and no embellishment is attached to an ordinary word; otherwise there is an appearance of comedy, as in the poetry of Cleophon, who used certain expressions that reminded one of saying "madam fig." Style expresses emotion, when a man speaks with anger of wanton outrage; with indignation and reserve, even in mentioning them, of things foul or impious; with admiration of things praiseworthy; with lowliness of things pitiable; and so in all other cases. Appropriate style also makes the fact appear credible; for the mind of the hearer is imposed upon under the impression that the speaker is speaking the truth, because, in such circumstances, his feelings are the same, so that he thinks (even if it is not the case as the speaker puts it) that things are as he represents them; and the hearer always sympathizes with one who speaks emotionally, even though he really says nothing. This is why speakers often confound their hearers by mere noise.

Character also may be expressed by the proof from signs, because to each class and habit there is an appropriate style. I mean class in reference to age—child, man, or old man; to sex—man or woman; to country—Lacedaemonian or Thessalian. I call habits those moral states which form a man's character in life; for not all habits do this. If then anyone uses the language appropriate to each habit, he will represent the character; for the uneducated man will not say the same things in the same way as the educated. But the hearers also are impressed in a certain way by a device employed ad nauseam by writers of speeches: "Who does not know?" "Everybody knows"; for the hearer agrees, because he is ashamed to appear not to share what is a matter of common knowledge.

The opportune or inopportune use of these devices applies to all kinds of Rhetoric. But whenever one has gone too far, the remedy may be found in the common piece of advice—that he should rebuke himself in advance; then the excess seems true, since the orator is obviously aware of what he is doing. Further, one ought not to make use of all kinds of correspondence together; for in this manner the hearer is deceived. I mean, for instance, if the language is harsh, the voice, features, and all things connected should not be equally harsh; otherwise what each really is becomes evident. But if you do this in one instance and not in another, the art escapes notice, although the result is the same. If mild sentiments are harshly expressed or harsh sentiments mildly, the speech lacks persuasiveness.

Compound words, a number of epithets, and "foreign" words especially, are appropriate to an emotional speaker; for when a man is enraged it is excusable for him to call an evil "high-as-heaven" or "stupendous." He may do the same when he has gripped his audience and filled it with enthusiasm, either by praise, blame, anger, or friendliness, as Isocrates does at the end of his Panegyricus: "Oh, the fame and the name!" and "In that they endured." For such is the language of enthusiastic orators, and it is clear that the hearers accept what they say in a sympathetic spirit.

Wherefore this style is appropriate to poetry; for there is something inspired in poetry. It should therefore be used either in this way or when speaking ironically, after the manner of Gorgias, or of Plato in the Phaedrus.

## Chapter 8

The form of diction should be neither metrical nor without rhythm. If it is metrical, it lacks persuasiveness, for it appears artificial, and at the same time it distracts the hearer's attention, since it sets him on the watch for the recurrence of such and such a cadence; just as, when the public criers ask, "Whom does the emancipated choose for his patron?" the children shout "Cleon." If it is without rhythm, it is unlimited, whereas it ought to be limited (but not by meter); for that which is unlimited is unpleasant and unknowable. Now all things are limited by number, and the number belonging to the form of diction is rhythm, of which the meters are divisions. Wherefore prose must be rhythmical, but not metrical, otherwise it will be a poem. Nor must this rhythm be rigorously carried out, but only up to a certain point.

Of the different rhythms the heroic is dignified, but lacking the harmony of ordinary conversation; the iambic is the language of the many, wherefore of all meters it is most used in common speech; but speech should be dignified and calculated to rouse the hearer. The trochaic is too much like the cordax; this is clear from the tetrameters, which form a tripping rhythm. There remains the paean, used by rhetoricians from the time of Thrasymachus, although they could not define it.

The paean is a third kind of rhythm closely related to those already mentioned; for its proportion is 3 to 2, that of the others 1 to 1 and 2 to 1, with both of which the paean, whose proportion is 1½ to 1, is connected. All the other meters then are to be disregarded for the reasons stated, and also because they are metrical; but the paean should be retained, because it is the only one of the rhythms mentioned which is not adapted to a metrical system, so that it is most likely to be undetected. At the present day one kind of paean alone is employed, at the beginning as well as at the end; the end, however, ought to differ from the beginning. Now there are two kinds of paeans, opposed to each other. The one is appropriate at the beginning, where in fact it is used. It begins with a long syllable and ends with three short:

"Δᾱλοˇγεˇνεˇς εἴτε Λυˇκιˇαν, ("O Delos-born, or it may be Lycia"),"
and
"Χρῡσεˇοˇκόˇμᾱ Ἕˉκαˇτεˇ παῖ Διόˇς ("Golden-haired far-darter, son of Zeus")."

The other on the contrary begins with three short syllables and ends with one long one:
"μετὰ δὲ γᾶν ὕδατά τ' ὠκεανὸν ἠφάνισε νύξ ("after earth and waters, night obscured ocean")."
This is a suitable ending, for the short syllable, being incomplete, mutilates the cadence. But the period should be broken off by a long syllable and the end should be clearly marked, not by the scribe nor by a punctuation mark, but by the rhythm itself. That the style should be rhythmical and not unrhythmical, and what rhythms and what arrangement of them make it of this character, has now been sufficiently shown.

# Chapter 9

The style must be either continuous and united by connecting particles, like the dithyrambic preludes, or periodic, like the antistrophes of the ancient poets. The continuous style is the ancient one; for example, "This is the exposition of the investigation of Herodotus of Thurii." It was formerly used by all, but now is used only by a few. By a continuous style I mean that which has no end in itself and only stops when the sense is complete. It is unpleasant, because it is endless, for all wish to have the end in sight. That explains why runners, just when they have reached the goal, lose their breath and strength, whereas before, when the end is in sight, they show no signs of fatigue. Such is the continuous style. The other style consists of periods, and by period I mean a sentence that has a beginning and end in itself and a magnitude that can be easily grasped. What is written in this style is pleasant and easy to learn, pleasant because it is the opposite of that which is unlimited, because the hearer at every moment thinks he is securing something for himself and that some conclusion has been reached; whereas it is unpleasant neither to foresee nor to get to the end of anything. It is easy to learn, because it can be easily retained in the memory. The reason is that the periodic style has number, which of all things is the easiest to remember; that explains why all learn verse with greater facility than prose, for it has number by which it can be measured. But the period must be completed with the sense and not stop short, as in the iambics of Sophocles,
"This is Calydon, territory of the land of Pelops;"
for by a division of this kind it is possible to suppose the contrary of the fact, as in the example, that Calydon is in Peloponnesus.
A period may be composed of clauses, or simple. The former is a complete sentence, distinct in its parts and easy to repeat in a breath, not divided like the period in the line of Sophocles above, but when it is taken as a whole. By clause I mean one of the two parts of this period, and by a simple

period one that consists of only one clause. But neither clauses nor periods should be curtailed or too long. If too short, they often make the hearer stumble; for when he is hurrying on towards the measure of which he already has a definite idea, if he is checked by the speaker stopping, a sort of stumble is bound to occur in consequence of the sudden stop. If too long, they leave the hearer behind, as those who do not turn till past the ordinary limit leave behind those who are walking with them. Similarly long periods assume the proportions of a speech and resemble dithyrambic preludes. This gives rise to what Democritus of Chios jokingly rebuked in Melanippides, who instead of antistrophes composed dithyrambic preludes:

"A man does harm to himself in doing harm to another, and a long prelude is most deadly to one who composes it;"

for these verses may be applied to those who employ long clauses. Again, if the clauses are too short, they do not make a period, so that the hearer himself is carried away headlong.

The clauses of the periodic style are divided or opposed; divided, as in the following sentence: "I have often wondered at those who gathered together the general assemblies and instituted the gymnastic contests"; opposed, in which, in each of the two clauses, one contrary is brought close to another, or the same word is coupled with both contraries; for instance, "They were useful to both, both those who stayed and those who followed; for the latter they gained in addition greater possessions than they had at home, for the former they left what was sufficient in their own country." Here "staying behind," "following," "sufficient," "more" are contraries. Again: "to those who need money and those who wish to enjoy it"; where "enjoying" is contrary to "acquiring." Again: "It often happens in these vicissitudes that the wise are unsuccessful, while fools succeed": "At once they were deemed worthy of the prize of valor and not long after won the command of the sea": "To sail over the mainland, to go by land over the sea, bridging over the Hellespont and digging through Athos": "And that, though citizens by nature, they were deprived of the rights of citizenship by law": "For some of them perished miserably, others saved themselves disgracefully": "Privately to employ barbarians as servants, but publicly to view with indifference many of the allies reduced to slavery": "Either to possess it while living or to leave it behind when dead." And what some one said against Pitholaus and Lycophron in the lawcourt: "These men, who used to sell you when they were at home, having come to you have bought you." All these passages are examples of antithesis. This kind of style is pleasing, because contraries are easily understood and even more so when placed side by side, and also because antithesis resembles a syllogism; for refutation is a bringing together of contraries.

Such then is the nature of antithesis; equality of clauses is parisosis; the similarity of the final syllables of each clause paromoiosis. This must take place at the beginning or end of the clauses. At the beginning the similarity is always shown in entire words; at the end, in the last syllables, or the inflections of one and the same word, or the repetition of the same word. For instance, at the beginning: Ἀγρὸν γὰρ ἔλαβεν ἀργὸν παρ' αὐτοῦ, "for he received from him land untilled"; "δωρητοί τ' ἐπέλοντο παράρρητοί τ' ἐπέεσσιν, "they were ready to accept gifts and to be persuaded by words;" "
at the end: ᾠήθησαν αὐτὸν παιδίον τετοκέναι, ἀλλ' αὐτοῦ αἴτιον γεγονέναι, "they thought that he was the father of a child, but that he was the cause of it"; ἐν πλείσταις δὲ φροντίσι καὶ ἐν ἐλαχίσταις ἐλπίσιν, "in the greatest anxiety and the smallest hopes." Inflections of the same word: ἄξιος δὲ σταθῆναι χαλκοῦς, οὐκ ἄξιος ὢν χαλκοῦ, "worthy of a bronze statue, not being worth a brass farthing." Repetition of a word: σὺ δ' αὐτὸν καὶ ζῶντα ἔλεγες κακῶς καὶ νῦν γράφεις κακῶς, "while he lived you spoke ill of him, now he is dead you write ill of him." Resemblance of one syllable: τί ἂν ἔπαθες δεινόν, εἰ ἄνδρ' εἶδες ἀργόν, "what ill would you have suffered, if you had seen an idle man?" All these figures may be found in the same sentence at once—antithesis, equality of clauses, and similarity of endings. In the Theodectea nearly all the beginnings of periods have been enumerated. There are also false antitheses, as in the verse of Epicharmus:

"τόκα μὲν ἐν τήνων ἐγὼν ἦν, τόκα δὲ παρὰ τήνοις ἐγών, "at one time I was in their house, at another I was with them." "

## Chapter 10

Having settled these questions, we must next state the sources of smart and popular sayings. They are produced either by natural genius or by practice; to show what they are is the function of this inquiry. Let us therefore begin by giving a full list of them, and let our starting-point be the following. Easy learning is naturally pleasant to all, and words mean something, so that all words which make us learn something are most pleasant. Now we do not know the meaning of strange words, and proper terms we know already. It is metaphor, therefore, that above all produces this effect; for when Homer calls old age stubble, he teaches and informs us through the genus; for both have lost their bloom. The similes of the poets also have the same effect; wherefore, if they are well constructed, an impression of smartness is produced. For the simile, as we have said, is a metaphor differing only by the addition of a word, wherefore it is less pleasant because it is longer; it does not say that this is that, so that the mind does not even examine this. Of necessity, therefore, all style and enthymemes that give us rapid information are smart. This is the reason why superficial enthymemes, meaning those that are obvious to all and need no mental effort, and those which, when stated, are not understood, are not popular, but only those which are understood the moment they are stated, or those of which the meaning, although not clear at first, comes a little later; for from the latter a kind of knowledge results, from the former neither the one nor the other.

In regard to the meaning of what is said, then, such enthymemes are popular. As to style, popularity of form is due to antithetical statement; for instance, "accounting the peace that all shared to be a war against their private interests," where "war" is opposed to "peace"; as to words, they are popular if they contain metaphor, provided it be neither strange, for then it is difficult to take in at a glance, nor superficial, for then it does not impress the hearer; further, if they set things "before the eyes"; for we ought to see what is being done rather than what is going to be done. We ought therefore to aim at three things—metaphor, antithesis, actuality.

Of the four kinds of metaphor the most popular are those based on proportion. Thus, Pericles said that the youth that had perished during the war had disappeared from the State as if the year had lost its springtime. Leptines, speaking of the Lacedaemonians, said that he would not let the Athenians stand by and see Greece deprived of one of her eyes. When Chares was eager to have his accounts for the Olynthian war examined, Cephisodotus indignantly exclaimed that, now he had the people by the throat, he was trying to get his accounts examined; on another occasion also he exhorted the Athenians to set out for Euboea without delay "and provision themselves there, like the decree of Miltiades." After the Athenians had made peace with Epidaurus and the maritime cities, Iphicrates indignantly declared "that they had deprived themselves of provisions for the war." Pitholaus called the Paralus "the bludgeon of the people," and Sestos "the corn-chest of the Piraeus." Pericles recommended that Aegina, "the eyesore of the Piraeus," should be removed. Moerocles, mentioning a very "respectable" person by name, declared that he was as much a scoundrel as himself; for whereas that honest man played the scoundrel at 33 per cent. he himself was satisfied with 10 per cent. And the iambic of Anaxandrides, on girls who were slow to marry,

"My daughters are "past the time" of marriage."

And the saying of Polyeuctus upon a certain paralytic named Speusippus, "that he could not keep quiet, although Fortune had bound him in a five-holed pillory of disease." Cephisodotus called the triremes "parti-colored mills," and [Diogenes] the Cynic used to say that the taverns were "the messes" of Attica. Aesion used to say that they had "drained" the State into Sicily, which is a metaphor and sets the thing before the eyes. His words "so that Greece uttered a cry" are also in a manner a metaphor and a vivid one. And again, as Cephisodotus bade the Athenians take care not to hold their "concourses" too often; and in the same way Isocrates, who spoke of those "who rush together" in the assemblies. And as Lysias says in his Funeral Oration, that it was right that Greece should cut her hair at the tomb of those who fell at Salamis, since her freedom was buried along with their valor. If the speaker had said that it was fitting that Greece should weep, her valor being buried with them, it would have been a metaphor and a vivid one, whereas "freedom" by the side of "valor" produces a kind of antithesis. And as Iphicrates said, "The path of my words leads through the center of the deeds of Chares"; here the metaphor is proportional and the words "through the center" create vividness. Also, to say that one "calls upon dangers to help against dangers" is a vivid metaphor. And Lycoleon on behalf of Chabrias said, "not even reverencing the suppliant attitude of his statue of bronze," a metaphor for the moment, not for all time, but still vivid; for when Chabrias is in danger, the statue intercedes for him, the inanimate becomes animate, the memorial of what he has done for the State. And "in every way studying poorness of spirit," for "studying" a thing implies to increase it. And that "reason is a light that God has kindled in the soul," for both the words reason and light make something clear. "For we do not put an end to wars, but put them off," for both ideas refer to the future—putting off and a peace of such a kind. And again, it is a metaphor to say that such a treaty is "a trophy far more splendid than those gained in war; for the latter are raised in memory of trifling advantages and a single favor of fortune, but the former commemorates the end of the whole war"; for both treaty and trophy are signs of victory. Again, that cities also render a heavy account to the censure of men; for rendering an account is a sort of just punishment.

## Chapter 11

We have said that smart sayings are derived from proportional metaphor and expressions which set things before the eyes. We must now explain the meaning of "before the eyes," and what must be done to produce this. I mean that things are set before the eyes by words that signify actuality. For instance, to say that a good man is "four-square" is a metaphor, for both these are complete, but the phrase does not express actuality, whereas "of one having the prime of his life in full bloom" does; similarly, "thee, like a sacred animal ranging at will" expresses actuality, and in
"Thereupon the Greeks shooting forward with their feet"
the word "shooting" contains both actuality and metaphor. And as Homer often, by making use of metaphor, speaks of inanimate things as if they

were animate; and it is to creating actuality in all such cases that his popularity is due, as in the following examples:
"Again the ruthless stone rolled down to the plain."
"The arrow flew."
"[The arrow] eager to fly [towards the crowd]."
"[The spears] were buried in the ground, longing to take their fill of flesh."
"The spear-point sped eagerly through his breast."
For in all these examples there is appearance of actuality, since the objects are represented as animate: "the shameless stone," "the eager spear-point," and the rest express actuality. Homer has attached these attributes by the employment of the proportional metaphor; for as the stone is to Sisyphus, so is the shameless one to the one who is shamelessly treated. In his popular similes also he proceeds in the same manner with inanimate things:
"Arched, foam-crested, some in front, others behind;"
for he gives movement and life to all, and actuality is movement.

As we have said before, metaphors should be drawn from objects which are proper to the object, but not too obvious; just as, for instance, in philosophy it needs sagacity to grasp the similarity in things that are apart. Thus Archytas said that there was no difference between an arbitrator and an altar, for the wronged betakes itself to one or the other. Similarly, if one were to say that an anchor and a pot-hook hung up were identical; for both are the same sort of thing, but they differ in this—that one is hung up above and the other below. And if one were to say "the cities have been reduced to the same level," this amounts to the same in the case of things far apart—the equality of "levelling" in regard to superficies and resources. Most smart sayings are derived from metaphor, and also from misleading the hearer beforehand. For it becomes more evident to him that he has learnt something, when the conclusion turns out contrary to his expectation, and the mind seems to say, "How true it is! but I missed it." And smart apophthegms arise from not meaning what one says, as in the apophthegm of Stesichorus, that "the grasshoppers will sing to themselves from the ground." And clever riddles are agreeable for the same reason; for something is learnt, and the expression is also metaphorical. And what Theodorus calls "novel expressions" arise when what follows is paradoxical, and, as he puts it, not in accordance with our previous expectation; just as humorists make use of slight changes in words. The same effect is produced by jokes that turn on a change of letter; for they are deceptive. These novelties occur in poetry as well as in prose; for instance, the following verse does not finish as the hearer expected:
"And he strode on, under his feet—chilblains,"

whereas the hearer thought he was going to say "sandals." This kind of joke must be clear from the moment of utterance. Jokes that turn on the word are produced, not by giving it the proper meaning, but by perverting it; for instance, when Theodorus said to Nicon, the player on the cithara, "you are troubled" (θράττει); for while pretending to say "something troubles you," he deceives us; for he means something else. Therefore the joke is only agreeable to one who understands the point; for if one does not know that Nicon is a Thracian, he will not see any joke in it. Similarly, "you wish to destroy him (πέρσαι)." Jokes of both these kinds must be suitably expressed. Similar instances are such witticisms as saying that "the empire of the sea" was not "the beginning of misfortunes" for the Athenians, for they benefited by it; or, with Isocrates, that "empire" was "the beginning of misfortunes for the city"; in both cases that which one would not have expected to be said is said, and recognized as true. For, in the second example, to say that "empire is empire" shows no cleverness, but this is not what he means, but something else; in the first, the ἀρχή which is negatived is used in a different sense. In all these cases, success is attained when a word is appropriately applied, either by homonym or by metaphor. For example, in the phrase Anaschetos (Bearable) is Unbearable, there is a contradiction of the homonym, which is only appropriate, if Anaschetus is an unbearable person. And, "Thou shalt not be more of a stranger than a stranger," or "not more than you should be," which is the same thing. And again,
"The stranger must not always be a stranger,"
for here too the word repeated is taken in a different sense. It is the same with the celebrated verse of Anaxandrides,
"It is noble to die before doing anything that deserves death;"
for this is the same as saying that "it is worthy to die when one does not deserve to die," or, that "it is worthy to die when one is not worthy of death," or, "when one does nothing that is worthy of death." Now the form of expression of these sayings is the same; but the more concisely and antithetically they are expressed, the greater is their popularity. The reason is that antithesis is more instructive and conciseness gives knowledge more rapidly. Further, in order that what is said may be true and not superficial, it must always either apply to a particular person or be suitably expressed; for it is possible for it to have one quality and not the other. For instance, "One ought to die guiltless of any offence," "The worthy man should take a worthy woman to wife." There is no smartness in either of these expressions, but there will be if both conditions are fulfilled: "It is worthy for a man to die, when he is not worthy of death." The more special qualities the expression possesses, the smarter it appears; for instance, if the words contain a metaphor, and a metaphor of a special kind, antithesis, and equality of clauses, and actuality.

Similes also, as said above, are always in a manner approved metaphors; since they always consist of two terms, like the proportional metaphor, as when we say, for instance, that the shield is the goblet of Ares, and the bow a lyre without strings. But such an expression is not simple, but when we call the bow a lyre, or the shield a goblet, it is. And similes may be formed as follows: a flute-player resembles an ape, a short-sighted man a spluttering lamp; for in both cases there is contraction. But they are excellent when there is a proportional metaphor; for it is possible to liken a shield to the goblet of Ares and a ruin to the rag of a house; to say that Niceratus is a Philoctetes bitten by Pratys, to use the simile of Thrasymachus, when he saw Niceratus, defeated by Pratys in a rhapsodic competition, still dirty with his hair uncut. It is herein that poets are especially condemned if they fail, but applauded if they succeed. I mean, for instance, when they introduce an answering clause:
"He carries his legs twisted like parsley,"
or again,
"Like Philammon punching the leather sack."
All such expressions are similes, and similes, as has been often said, are metaphors of a kind.
Proverbs also are metaphors from species to species. If a man, for instance, introduces into his house something from which he expects to benefit, but afterwards finds himself injured instead, it is as the Carpathian says of the hare; for both have experienced the same misfortunes. This is nearly all that can be said of the sources of smart sayings and the reasons which make them so.
Approved hyperboles are also metaphors. For instance, one may say of a man whose eye is all black and blue, "you would have thought he was a basket of mulberries," because the black eye is something purple, but the great quantity constitutes the hyperbole. Again, when one says "like this or that" there is a hyperbole differing only in the wording:
"Like Philammon punching the leather sack,"
or, "you would have thought that he was Philammon fighting the sack";
"Carrying his legs twisted like parsley,"
or, "you would have thought that he had no legs, but parsley, they being so twisted." There is something youthful about hyperboles; for they show vehemence. Wherefore those who are in a passion most frequently make use of them:
"Not even were he to offer me gifts as many in number as the sand and dust... but a daughter of Agamemnon, son of Atreus, I will not wed, not even if she rivalled golden Aphrodite in beauty, or Athene in accomplishments."
(Attic orators are especially fond of hyperbole.) Wherefore it is unbecoming for elderly people to make use of them.

# Chapter 12

But we must not lose sight of the fact that a different style is suitable to each kind of Rhetoric. That of written compositions is not the same as that of debate; nor, in the latter, is that of public speaking the same as that of the law courts. But it is necessary to be acquainted with both; for the one requires a knowledge of good Greek, while the other prevents the necessity of keeping silent when we wish to communicate something to others, which happens to those who do not know how to write. The style of written compositions is most precise, that of debate is most suitable for delivery. Of the latter there are two kinds, ethical and emotional; this is why actors are always running after plays of this character, and poets after suitable actors. However, poets whose works are only meant for reading are also popular, as Chaeremon, who is as precise as a writer of speeches, and Licymnius among dithyrambic poets. When compared, the speeches of writers appear meagre in public debates, while those of the rhetoricians, however well delivered, are amateurish when read. The reason is that they are only suitable to public debates; hence speeches suited for delivery, when delivery is absent, do not fulfil their proper function and appear silly. For instance, asyndeta and frequent repetition of the same word are rightly disapproved in written speech, but in public debate even rhetoricians make use of them, for they lend themselves to acting. (But one must vary the expression when one repeats the same thing, for this as it were paves the way for declamation: as, "This is he who robbed you, this is he who deceived you, this is he who at last attempted to betray you." This is what Philemon the actor did in The Old Man's Folly of Anaxandrides, when he says "Rhadamanthus and Palamedes," and when he repeats the word "I" in the prologue to The Pious. For unless such expressions are varied by action, it is a case of "the man who carries the beam" in the proverb.) It is the same with asyndeta: "I came, I met, I entreated." For here delivery is needed, and the words should not be pronounced with the same tone and character, as if there was only one clause. Further, asyndeta have a special characteristic; for in an equal space of time many things appear to be said, because the connecting particle makes many things one, so that, if it be removed, it is clear that the contrary will be the case, and that the one will become many. Therefore an asyndeton produces amplification: thus, in "I came, I conversed, I besought," the hearer seems to be surveying many things, all that the speaker said. This also is Homer's intention in the passage
"Nireus, again, from Syme . . .,
Nireus son of Aglaia . . .,
Nireus, the most beautiful . . . ;"

for it is necessary that one of whom much has been said should be often mentioned; if then the name is often mentioned, it seems as if much has been said; so that, by means of this fallacy, Homer has increased the reputation of Nireus, though he only mentions him in one passage; he has perpetuated his memory, though he never speaks of him again.

The deliberative style is exactly like a rough sketch, for the greater the crowd, the further off is the point of view; wherefore in both too much refinement is a superfluity and even a disadvantage. But the forensic style is more finished, and more so before a single judge, because there is least opportunity of employing rhetorical devices, since the mind more readily takes in at a glance what belongs to the subject and what is foreign to it; there is no discussion, so the judgement is clear. This is why the same orators do not excel in all these styles; where action is most effective, there the style is least finished, and this is a case in which voice, especially a loud one, is needed.

The epideictic style is especially suited to written compositions, for its function is reading; and next to it comes the forensic style. It is superfluous to make the further distinction that style should be pleasant or magnificent. Why so, any more than temperate, liberal, or anything else that indicates moral virtue? For it is evident that, if virtue of style has been correctly defined, what we have said will suffice to make it pleasant. For why, if not to please, need it be clear, not mean, but appropriate? If it be too diffuse, or too concise, it will not be clear; but it is plain that the mean is most suitable. What we have said will make the style pleasant, if it contains a happy mixture of proper and "foreign" words, of rhythm, and of persuasiveness resulting from propriety. This finishes what we had to say about style; of all the three kinds of Rhetoric in general, and of each of them in particular. It only remains to speak of arrangement.

## Chapter 13

A speech has two parts. It is necessary to state the subject, and then to prove it. Wherefore it is impossible to make a statement without proving it, or to prove it without first putting it forward; for both he who proves proves something, and he who puts something forward does so in order to prove it. The first of these parts is the statement of the case, the second the proof, a similar division to that of problem and demonstration. But the division now generally made is absurd; for narrative only belongs in a manner to forensic speech, but in epideictic or deliberative speech how is it possible that there should be narrative as it is defined, or a refutation; or an epilogue in demonstrative speeches? In deliberative speeches, again, exordium, comparison, and recapitulation are only admissible when there is a conflict of opinion. For both accusation and defence are often found in deliberative, but not qua deliberative speech. And further, the epilogue does not even belong to every forensic speech, for instance, when it is short, or the matter is easy to recollect; for in the epilogue what happens is that there is a reduction of length.

So then the necessary parts of a speech are the statement of the case and proof. These divisions are appropriate to every speech, and at the most the parts are four in number—exordium, statement, proof, epilogue; for refutation of an opponent is part of the proofs, and comparison is an amplification of one's own case, and therefore also part of the proofs; for he who does this proves something, whereas the exordium and the epilogue are merely aids to memory. Therefore, if we adopt all such divisions we shall be following Theodorus and his school, who distinguished narrative, additional narrative, and preliminary narrative, refutation and additional refutation. But one must only adopt a name to express a distinct species or a real difference; otherwise, it becomes empty and silly, like the terms introduced by Licymnius in his "Art," where he speaks of "being wafted along," "wandering from the subject," and "ramifications."

# Chapter 14

The exordium is the beginning of a speech, as the prologue in poetry and the prelude in flute-playing; for all these are beginnings, and as it were a paving the way for what follows. The prelude resembles the exordium of epideictic speeches; for as flute-players begin by playing whatever they can execute skilfully and attach it to the key-note, so also in epideictic speeches should be the composition of the exordium; the speaker should say at once whatever he likes, give the key-note and then attach the main subject. And all do this, an example being the exordium of the Helen of Isocrates; for the eristics and Helen have nothing in common. At the same time, even if the speaker wanders from the point, this is more appropriate than that the speech should be monotonous.

In epideictic speeches, the sources of the exordia are praise and blame, as Gorgias, in the Olympiacus, says, "Men of Greece, you are worthy to be admired by many," where he is praising those who instituted the solemn assemblies. Isocrates on the other hand blames them because they rewarded bodily excellences, but instituted no prize for men of wisdom. Exordia may also be derived from advice, for instance, one should honor the good, wherefore the speaker praises Aristides, or such as are neither famous nor worthless, but who, although they are good, remain obscure, as Alexander, son of Priam; for this is a piece of advice. Again, they may be

derived from forensic exordia, that is to say, from appeals to the hearer, if the subject treated is paradoxical, difficult, or commonly known, in order to obtain indulgence, like Choerilus:
"But now when all has been allotted."
These then are the sources of epideictic exordia—praise, blame, exhortation, dissuasion, appeals to the hearer. And these exordia may be either foreign or intimately connected with the speech.
As for the exordia of the forensic speech, it must be noted that they produce the same effect as dramatic prologues and epic exordia (for those of dithyrambs resemble epideictic exordia:
"For thee and thy presents or spoils)."
But in speeches and epic poems the exordia provide a sample of the subject, in order that the hearers may know beforehand what it is about, and that the mind may not be kept in suspense, for that which is undefined leads astray; so then he who puts the beginning, so to say, into the hearer's hand enables him, if he holds fast to it, to follow the story. Hence the following exordia:
"Sing the wrath, O Muse."
"Tell me of the man, O Muse."
"Inspire me with another theme, how from the land of Asia a great war crossed into Europe."
Similarly, tragic poets make clear the subject of their drama, if not at the outset, like Euripides, at least somewhere in the prologue, like Sophocles, "My father was Polybus."
It is the same in comedy. So then the most essential and special function of the exordium is to make clear what is the end or purpose of the speech; wherefore it should not be employed, if the subject is quite clear or unimportant. All the other forms of exordia in use are only remedies, and are common to all three branches of Rhetoric. These are derived from the speaker, the hearer, the subject, and the opponent. From the speaker and the opponent, all that helps to destroy or create prejudice. But this must not be done in the same way; for the defendant must deal with this at the beginning, the accuser in the epilogue. The reason is obvious. The defendant, when about to introduce himself, must remove all obstacles, so that he must first clear away all prejudice; the accuser must create prejudice in the epilogue, that his hearers may have a livelier recollection of it.
The object of an appeal to the hearer is to make him well disposed or to arouse his indignation, and sometimes to engage his attention or the opposite; for it is not always expedient to engage his attention, which is the reason why many speakers try to make their hearers laugh. As for rendering the hearers tractable, everything will lead up to it if a person wishes, including the appearance of respectability, because respectable

persons command more attention. Hearers pay most attention to things that are important, that concern their own interests, that are astonishing, that are agreeable; wherefore one should put the idea into their heads that the speech deals with such subjects. To make his hearers inattentive, the speaker must persuade them that the matter is unimportant, that it does not concern them, that it is painful.

But we must not lose sight of the fact that all such things are outside the question, for they are only addressed to a hearer whose judgement is poor and who is ready to listen to what is beside the case; for if he is not a man of this kind, there is no need of an exordium, except just to make a summary statement of the subject, so that, like a body, it may have a head. Further, engaging the hearers' attention is common to all parts of the speech, if necessary; for attention slackens everywhere else rather than at the beginning. Accordingly, it is ridiculous to put this at the beginning, at a time when all listen with the greatest attention. Wherefore, when the right moment comes, one must say, "And give me your attention, for it concerns you as much as myself"; and, "I will tell you such a thing as you have never yet" heard of, so strange and wonderful. This is what Prodicus used to do; whenever his hearers began to nod, he would throw in a dash of his fifty-drachma lecture. But it is clear that one does not speak thus to the hearer qua hearer; for all in their exordia endeavor either to arouse prejudice or to remove their own apprehensions:

"O prince, I will not say that with haste [I have come breathless]."
"Why this preamble?"

This is what those also do who have, or seem to have, a bad case; for it is better to lay stress upon anything rather than the case itself. That is why slaves never answer questions directly but go all round them, and indulge in preambles. We have stated how the hearer's goodwill is to be secured and all other similar states of mind. And since it is rightly said,

"Grant that on reaching the Phaeacians I may find friendship or compassion,"

the orator should aim at exciting these two feelings.

In epideictic exordia, one must make the hearer believe that he shares the praise, either himself, or his family, or his pursuits, or at any rate in some way or other. For Socrates says truly in his Funeral Oration that "it is easy to praise Athenians in the presence of Athenians, but not in the presence of Lacedaemonians."

Deliberative oratory borrows its exordia from forensic, but naturally they are very uncommon in it. For in fact the hearers are acquainted with the subject, so that the case needs no exordium, except for the orator's own sake, or on account of his adversaries, or if the hearers attach too much or too little importance to the question according to his idea. Wherefore he must either excite or remove prejudice, and magnify or minimize the importance of the subject. Such are the reasons for exordia; or else they merely serve the purpose of ornament, since their absence makes the speech appear offhand. For such is the encomium on the Eleans, in which Gorgias, without any preliminary sparring or movements, starts off at once, "Elis, happy city."

# Chapter 15

One way of removing prejudice is to make use of the arguments by which one may clear oneself from disagreeable suspicion; for it makes no difference whether this suspicion has been openly expressed or not; and so this may be taken as a general rule. Another way consists in contesting the disputed points, either by denying the fact or its harmfulness, at least to the plaintiff; or by asserting that its importance is exaggerated; or that it is not unjust at all, or only slightly so; or neither disgraceful nor important. These are the possible points of dispute: as Iphicrates, in answer to Nausicrates, admitted that he had done what the prosecutor alleged and inflicted damage, but denied that he had been guilty of wrongdoing. Again, one may strike the balance, when guilty of wrongdoing, by maintaining that although the action was injurious it was honorable, painful but useful, or anything else of the kind.

Another method consists in saying that it was a case of error, misfortune, or necessity; as, for example, Sophocles said that he trembled, not, as the accuser said, in order to appear old, but from necessity, for it was against his wish that he was eighty years of age. One may also substitute one motive for another, and say that one did not mean to injure but to do something else, not that of which one was accused, and that the wrongdoing was accidental: "I should deserve your hatred, had I acted so as to bring this about."

Another method may be employed if the accuser, either himself or one closely related to him, has been involved in a similar charge, either now or formerly; or, if others are involved who are admittedly not exposed to the charge; for instance, if it is argued that so-and-so is an adulterer, because he is a dandy, then so-and-so must be.

Again, if the accuser has already similarly accused others, or himself been accused by others; or if others, without being formally accused, have been suspected as you are now, and their innocence has been proved.

Another method consists in counter-attacking the accuser; for it would be absurd to believe the words of one who is himself unworthy of belief.

Another method is to appeal to a verdict already given, as Euripides did in the case about the exchange of property; when Hygiaenon accused him of impiety as having advised perjury in the verse,

"My tongue hath sworn, but my mind is unsworn,"
Euripides replied that his accuser did wrong in transferring the decisions of the court of Dionysus to the law courts; for he had already rendered an account of what he had said there, or was still ready to do so, if his adversary desired to accuse him.

Another method consists in attacking slander, showing how great an evil it is, and this because it alters the nature of judgements, and that it does not rely on the real facts of the case.

Common to both parties is the topic of tokens, as in the Teucer, Odysseus reproaches Teucer with being a relative of Priam, whose sister his mother Hesione was; to which Teucer replied that his father Telamon was the enemy of Priam, and that he himself did not denounce the spies.

Another method, suitable for the accuser, is to praise something unimportant at great length, and to condemn something important concisely; or, putting forward several things that are praiseworthy in the opponent, to condemn the one thing that has an important bearing upon the case. Such methods are most artful and unfair; for by their use men endeavor to make what is good in a man injurious to him, by mixing it up with what is bad.

Another method is common to both accuser and defender. Since the same thing may have been done from several motives, the accuser must disparage it by taking it in the worse sense, while the defender must take it in the better sense. For instance, when Diomedes chose Odysseus for his companion, it may be said on the one hand that he did so because he considered him to be the bravest of men, on the other, that it was because Odysseus was the only man who was no possible rival for him, since he was a poltroon. Let this suffice for the question of prejudice.

## Chapter 16

In the epideictic style the narrative should not be consecutive, but disjointed; for it is necessary to go through the actions which form the subject of the speech. For a speech is made up of one part that is inartificial (the speaker being in no way the author of the actions which he relates), and of another that does depend upon art. The latter consists in showing that the action did take place, if it be incredible, or that it is of a certain kind, or of a certain importance, or all three together. This is why it is sometimes right not to narrate all the facts consecutively, because a demonstration of this kind is difficult to remember. From some facts a man may be shown to be courageous, from others wise or just. Besides, a speech of this kind is simpler, whereas the other is intricate and not plain. It is only necessary to recall famous actions; wherefore most people have no need of narrative—for instance, if you wish to praise Achilles; for everybody knows what he did, and it is only necessary to make use of it. But if you wish to praise Critias, narrative is necessary, for not many people know what he did....

But at the present day it is absurdly laid down that the narrative should be rapid. And yet, as the man said to the baker when he asked whether he was to knead bread hard or soft, "What! is it impossible to knead it well?" so it is in this case; for the narrative must not be long, nor the exordium, nor the proofs either. For in this case also propriety does not consist either in rapidity or conciseness, but in a due mean; that is, one must say all that will make the facts clear, or create the belief that they have happened or have done injury or wrong, or that they are as important as you wish to make them. The opposite party must do the opposite. And you should incidentally narrate anything that tends to show your own virtue, for instance, "I always recommended him to act rightly, not to forsake his children"; or the wickedness of your opponent, for instance, "but he answered that, wherever he might be, he would always find other children," an answer attributed by Herodotus to the Egyptian rebels; or anything which is likely to please the dicasts.

In defence, the narrative need not be so long; for the points at issue are either that the fact has not happened or that it was neither injurious nor wrong nor so important as asserted, so that one should not waste time over what all are agreed upon, unless anything tends to prove that, admitting the act, it is not wrong. Again, one should only mention such past things as are likely to excite pity or indignation if described as actually happening; for instance, the story of Alcinous, because in the presence of Penelope it is reduced to sixty lines, and the way in which Phayllus dealt with the epic cycle, and the prologue to the Oeneus.

And the narrative should be of a moral character, and in fact it will be so, if we know what effects this. One thing is to make clear our moral purpose; for as is the moral purpose, so is the character, and as is the end, so is the moral purpose. For this reason mathematical treatises have no moral character, because neither have they moral purpose; for they have no moral end. But the Socratic dialogues have; for they discuss such questions. Other ethical indications are the accompanying peculiarities of each individual character; for instance, "He was talking and walking on at the same time," which indicates effrontery and boorishness. Nor should we speak as if from the intellect, after the manner of present-day orators; but from moral purpose: "But I wished it, and I preferred it; and even if I profited nothing, it is better." The first statement indicates prudence, the second virtue; for prudence consists in the pursuit of what is useful, virtue in that of what is honorable. If anything of the kind seems incredible, then the reason must be added; of this Sophocles gives an example, where his

Antigone says that she cared more for her brother than for her husband or children; for the latter can be replaced after they are gone,
"but when father and mother are in the grave, no brother can ever be born."
If you have no reason, you should at least say that you are aware that what you assert is incredible, but that it is your nature; for no one believes that a man ever does anything of his own free will except from motives of self-interest.
Further, the narrative should draw upon what is emotional by the introduction of such of its accompaniments as are well known, and of what is specially characteristic of either yourself or of the adversary: "And he went off looking grimly at me"; and as Aeschines says of Cratylus, that he hissed violently and violently shook his fists. Such details produce persuasion because, being known to the hearer, they become tokens of what he does not know. Numerous examples of this may be found in Homer:
"Thus she spoke, and the aged nurse covered her face with her hands;"
for those who are beginning to weep lay hold on their eyes. And you should at once introduce yourself and your adversary as being of a certain character, that the hearers may regard you or him as such; but do not let it be seen. That this is easy is perfectly clear from the example of messengers; we do not yet know what they are going to say, but nevertheless we have an inkling of it.
Again, the narrative should be introduced in several places, sometimes not at all at the beginning. In deliberative oratory narrative is very rare, because no one can narrate things to come; but if there is narrative, it will be of things past, in order that, being reminded of them, the hearers may take better counsel about the future. This may be done in a spirit either of blame or of praise; but in that case the speaker does not perform the function of the deliberative orator. If there is anything incredible, you should immediately promise both to give a reason for it at once and to submit it to the judgement of any whom the hearers approve; as, for instance, Jocasta in the Oedipus of Carcinus is always promising, when the man who is looking for her son makes inquiries of her; and similarly Haemon in Sophocles.

## Chapter 17

Proofs should be demonstrative, and as the disputed points are four, the demonstration should bear upon the particular point disputed; for instance, if the fact is disputed, proof of this must be brought at the trial before anything else; or if it is maintained that no injury has been done; or that the act was not so important as asserted; or was just, then this must be proved, the three last questions being matters of dispute just as the question of fact. But do not forget that it is only in the case of a dispute as to this question of fact that one of the two parties must necessarily be a rogue; for ignorance is not the cause, as it might be if a question of right or wrong were the issue; so that in this case one should spend time on this topic, but not in the others.

In epideictic speeches, amplification is employed, as a rule, to prove that things are honorable or useful; for the facts must be taken on trust, since proofs of these are rarely given, and only if they are incredible or the responsibility is attributed to another.

In deliberative oratory, it may be maintained either that certain consequences will not happen, or that what the adversary recommends will happen, but that it will be unjust, inexpedient, or not so important as supposed. But one must also look to see whether he makes any false statements as to things outside the issue; for these look like evidence that he makes misstatements about the issue itself as well.

Examples are best suited to deliberative oratory and enthymemes to forensic. The first is concerned with the future, so that its examples must be derived from the past; the second with the question of the existence or non-existence of facts, in which demonstrative and necessary proofs are more in place; for the past involves a kind of necessity. One should not introduce a series of enthymemes continuously but mix them up; otherwise they destroy one another. For there is a limit of quantity; thus, "Friend, since thou hast said as much as a wise man would say," where Homer does not say τοιαῦτα (such things as), but τόσα (as many things as). Nor should you try to find enthymemes about everything; otherwise you will be imitating certain philosophers, who draw conclusions that are better known and more plausible than the premises from which they are drawn. And whenever you wish to arouse emotion, do not use an enthymeme, for it will either drive out the emotion or it will be useless; for simultaneous movements drive each other out, the result being their mutual destruction or weakening. Nor should you look for an enthymeme at the time when you wish to give the speech an ethical character; for demonstration involves neither moral character nor moral purpose.

Moral maxims, on the other hand, should be used in both narrative and proof; for they express moral character; for instance, "I gave him the money and that although I knew that one ought not to trust." Or, to arouse emotion: "I do not regret it, although I have been wronged; his is the profit, mine the right."

Deliberative speaking is more difficult than forensic, and naturally so, because it has to do with the future; whereas forensic speaking has to do with the past, which is already known, even by diviners, as Epimenides the Cretan said; for he used to divine, not the future, but only things that were past but obscure. Further, the law is the subject in forensic speaking; and when one has a starting-point, it is easier to find a demonstrative proof. Deliberative speaking does not allow many opportunities for lingering—for instance, attacks on the adversary, remarks about oneself, or attempts to arouse emotion. In this branch of Rhetoric there is less room for these than in any other, unless the speaker wanders from the subject. Therefore, when at a loss for topics, one must do as the orators at Athens, amongst them Isocrates, for even when deliberating, he brings accusations against the Lacedaemonians, for instance, in the Panegyricus, and against Chares in the Symmachikos (On the Peace).

Epideictic speeches should be varied with laudatory episodes, after the manner of Isocrates, who is always bringing somebody in. This is what Gorgias meant when he said that he was never at a loss for something to say; for, if he is speaking of Peleus, he praises Achilles, then Aeacus, then the god; similarly courage, which does this and that, or is of such a kind. If you have proofs, then, your language must be both ethical and demonstrative; if you have no enthymemes, ethical only. In fact, it is more fitting that a virtuous man should show himself good than that his speech should be painfully exact.

Refutative enthymemes are more popular than demonstrative, because, in all cases of refutation, it is clearer that a logical conclusion has been reached; for opposites are more noticeable when placed in juxtaposition. The refutation of the opponent is not a particular kind of proof; his arguments should be refuted partly by objection, partly by counter-syllogism. In both deliberative and forensic rhetoric he who speaks first should state his own proofs and afterwards meet the arguments of the opponent, refuting or pulling them to pieces beforehand. But if the opposition is varied, these arguments should be dealt with first, as Callistratus did in the Messenian assembly; in fact, it was only after he had first refuted what his opponents were likely to say that he put forward his own proofs. He who replies should first state the arguments against the opponent's speech, refuting and answering it by syllogisms, especially if his arguments have met with approval. For as the mind is ill-disposed towards one against whom prejudices have been raised beforehand, it is equally so towards a speech, if the adversary is thought to have spoken well. One must therefore make room in the hearer's mind for the speech one intends to make; and for this purpose you must destroy the impression made by the adversary. Wherefore it is only after having combated all the arguments, or the most important, or those which are plausible, or most easy to refute, that you should substantiate your own case:
"I will first defend the goddesses, for I [do not think] that Hera"

in this passage the poet has first seized upon the weakest argument.
So much concerning proofs. In regard to moral character, since sometimes, in speaking of ourselves, we render ourselves liable to envy, to the charge of prolixity, or contradiction, or, when speaking of another, we may be accused of abuse or boorishness, we must make another speak in our place, as Isocrates does in the Philippus and in the Antidosis. Archilochus uses the same device in censure; for in his iambics he introduces the father speaking as follows of his daughter:
"There is nothing beyond expectation, nothing that can be sworn impossible,"
and the carpenter Charon in the iambic verse beginning
"I [care not for the wealth] of Gyges;"
Sophocles, also, introduces Haemon, when defending Antigone against his father, as if quoting the opinion of others. One should also sometimes change enthymemes into moral maxims; for instance, "Sensible men should become reconciled when they are prosperous; for in this manner they will obtain the greatest advantages," which is equivalent to the enthymeme "If men should become reconciled whenever it is most useful and advantageous, they should be reconciled in a time of prosperity."

# Chapter 18

In regard to interrogation, its employment is especially opportune, when the opponent has already stated the opposite, so that the addition of a question makes the result an absurdity; as, for instance, when Pericles interrogated Lampon about initiation into the sacred rites of the savior goddess. On Lampon replying that it was not possible for one who was not initiated to be told about them, Pericles asked him if he himself was acquainted with the rites, and when he said yes, Pericles further asked, "How can that be, seeing that you are uninitiated?" Again, interrogation should be employed when one of the two propositions is evident, and it is obvious that the opponent will admit the other if you ask him. But the interrogator, having obtained the second premise by putting a question, should not make an additional question of what is evident, but should state the conclusion. For instance, Socrates, when accused by Meletus of not believing in the gods, asked whether he did not say that there was a divine something; and when Meletus said yes, Socrates went on to ask if divine beings were not either children of the gods or something godlike. When Meletus again said yes, Socrates rejoined, "Is there a man, then, who can admit that the children of the gods exist without at the same time admitting that the gods exist?" Thirdly, when it is intended to show that the opponent either contradicts himself or puts forward a paradox.

Further, when the opponent can do nothing else but answer the question by a sophistical solution; for if he answers, "Partly yes, and partly no," "Some are, but some are not," "In one sense it is so, in another not," the hearers cry out against him as being in a difficulty. In other cases interrogation should not be attempted; for if the adversary raises an objection, the interrogator seems to be defeated; for it is impossible to ask a number of questions, owing to the hearer's weakness. Wherefore also we should compress our enthymemes as much as possible.

Ambiguous questions should be answered by defining them by a regular explanation, and not too concisely; those that appear likely to make us contradict ourselves should be solved at once in the answer, before the adversary has time to ask the next question or to draw a conclusion; for it is not difficult to see the drift of his argument. Both this, however, and the means of answering will be sufficiently clear from the Topics. If a conclusion is put in the form of a question, we should state the reason for our answer. For instance, Sophocles being asked by Pisander whether he, like the rest of the Committee of Ten, had approved the setting up of the Four Hundred, he admitted it. "What then?" asked Pisander, "did not this appear to you to be a wicked thing?" Sophocles admitted it. "So then you did what was wicked?" "Yes, for there was nothing better to be done." The Lacedaemonian, who was called to account for his ephoralty, being asked if he did not think that the rest of his colleagues had been justly put to death, answered yes. "But did not you pass the same measures as they did?" "Yes." "Would not you, then, also be justly put to death?" "No; for my colleagues did this for money; I did not, but acted according to my conscience." For this reason we should not ask any further questions after drawing the conclusion, nor put the conclusion itself as a question, unless the balance of truth is unmistakably in our favor.

As for jests, since they may sometimes be useful in debates, the advice of Gorgias was good—to confound the opponents' earnest with jest and their jest with earnest. We have stated in the Poetics how many kinds of jests there are, some of them becoming a gentleman, others not. You should therefore choose the kind that suits you. Irony is more gentlemanly than buffoonery; for the first is employed on one's own account, the second on that of another.

# Chapter 19

The epilogue is composed of four parts: to dispose the hearer favorably towards oneself and unfavorably towards the adversary; to amplify and depreciate; to excite the emotions of the hearer; to recapitulate. For after you have proved that you are truthful and that the adversary is false, the natural order of things is to praise ourselves, blame him, and put the finishing touches. One of two things should be aimed at, to show that you are either relatively or absolutely good and the adversary either relatively or absolutely bad. The topics which serve to represent men as good or bad have already been stated. After this, when the proof has once been established, the natural thing is to amplify or depreciate; for it is necessary that the facts should be admitted, if it is intended to deal with the question of degree; just as the growth of the body is due to things previously existing. The topics of amplification and depreciation have been previously set forth. Next, when the nature and importance of the facts are clear, one should rouse the hearer to certain emotions—pity, indignation, anger, hate, jealousy, emulation, and quarrelsomeness. The topics of these also have been previously stated, so that all that remains is to recapitulate what has been said. This may appropriately be done at this stage in the way certain rhetoricians wrongly recommend for the exordium, when they advise frequent repetition of the points, so that they may be easily learnt. In the exordium we should state the subject, in order that the question to be decided may not escape notice, but in the epilogue we should give a summary statement of the proofs.

We should begin by saying that we have kept our promise, and then state what we have said and why. Our case may also be closely compared with our opponent's; and we may either compare what both of us have said on the same point, or without direct comparison: "My opponent said so-and-so, and I said so-and-so on this point and for these reasons." Or ironically, as for instance, "He said this and I answered that; what would he have done, if he had proved this, and not simply that?" Or by interrogation: "What is there that has not been proved?" or, "What has my opponent proved?" We may, therefore, either sum up by comparison, or in the natural order of the statements, just as they were made, our own first, and then again, separately, if we so desire, what has been said by our opponent. To the conclusion of the speech the most appropriate style is that which has no connecting particles, in order that it may be a peroration, but not an oration: "I have spoken; you have heard; you know the facts; now give your decision."

# The Poetics of Aristotle

## Preface

In the tenth book of the Republic, when Plato has completed his final burning denunciation of Poetry, the false Siren, the imitator of things which themselves are shadows, the ally of all that is low and weak in the soul against that which is high and strong, who makes us feed the things we ought to starve and serve the things we ought to rule, he ends with a touch of compunction: 'We will give her champions, not poets themselves but poet-lovers, an opportunity to make her defence in plain prose and show that she is not only sweet—as we well know—but also helpful to society and the life of man, and we will listen in a kindly spirit. For we shall be gainers, I take it, if this can be proved.' Aristotle certainly knew the passage, and it looks as if his treatise on poetry was an answer to Plato's challenge.

Few of the great works of ancient Greek literature are easy reading. They nearly all need study and comment, and at times help from a good teacher, before they yield up their secret. And the Poetics cannot be accounted an exception. For one thing the treatise is fragmentary. It originally consisted of two books, one dealing with Tragedy and Epic, the other with Comedy and other subjects. We possess only the first. For another, even the book we have seems to be unrevised and unfinished. The style, though luminous, vivid, and in its broader division systematic, is not that of a book intended for publication. Like most of Aristotle's extant writing, it suggests the MS. of an experienced lecturer, full of jottings and adscripts, with occasional phrases written carefully out, but never revised as a whole for the general reader. Even to accomplished scholars the meaning is often obscure, as may be seen by a comparison of the three editions recently published in England, all the work of savants of the first eminence, (1) or, still more strikingly, by a study of the long series of misunderstandings and overstatements and corrections which form the history of the Poetics since the Renaissance.

(1) Prof. Butcher, 1895 and 1898; Prof. Bywater, 1909; and Prof. Margoliouth, 1911.

But it is of another cause of misunderstanding that I wish principally to speak in this preface. The great edition from which the present translation is taken was the fruit of prolonged study by one of the greatest Aristotelians of the nineteenth century, and is itself a classic among works of scholarship. In the hands of a student who knows even a little Greek, the translation, backed by the commentary, may lead deep into the mind of Aristotle. But when the translation is used, as it doubtless will be, by readers who are quite without the clue provided by a knowledge of the general habits of the Greek language, there must arise a number of new difficulties or misconceptions.

To understand a great foreign book by means of a translation is possible enough where the two languages concerned operate with a common stock of ideas, and belong to the same period of civilization. But between ancient Greece and modern England there yawn immense gulfs of human history; the establishment and the partial failure of a common European religion, the barbarian invasions, the feudal system, the regrouping of modern Europe, the age of mechanical invention, and the industrial revolution. In an average page of French or German philosophy nearly all the nouns can be translated directly into exact equivalents in English; but in Greek that is not so. Scarcely one in ten of the nouns on the first few pages of the Poetics has an exact English equivalent. Every proposition has to be reduced to its lowest terms of thought and then re-built. This is a difficulty which no translation can quite deal with; it must be left to a teacher who knows Greek. And there is a kindred difficulty which flows from it. Where words can be translated into equivalent words, the style of an original can be closely followed; but no translation which aims at being written in normal English can reproduce the style of Aristotle. I have sometimes played with the idea that a ruthlessly literal translation, helped out by bold punctuation, might be the best. For instance, premising that the words poesis, poetes mean originally 'making' and 'maker', one might translate the first paragraph of the Poetics thus:—

MAKING: kinds of making: function of each, and how the Myths ought to be put together if the Making is to go right.

Number of parts: nature of parts: rest of same inquiry.

Begin in order of nature from first principles.

Epos-making, tragedy-making (also comedy), dithyramb-making (and most fluting and harping), taken as a whole, are really not Makings but Imitations. They differ in three points; they imitate (a) different objects, (b) by different means, (c) differently (i.e. different manner).

Some artists imitate (i.e. depict) by shapes and colours. (Obs. sometimes by art, sometimes by habit.)Some by voice. Similarly the above arts all imitate by rhythm, language, and tune, and these either (1) separate or (2) mixed. Rhythm and tune alone, harping, fluting, and other arts with same effect—e.g. panpipes.

Rhythm without tune: dancing. (Dancers imitate characters, emotions, and experiences by means of rhythms expressed in form.)

Language alone (whether prose or verse, and one form of verse or many): this art has no name up to the present (i.e. there is no name to cover mimes and dialogues and any similar imitation made in iambics, elegiacs, &c. Commonly people attach the 'making' to the metre and say 'elegiac-makers', 'hexameter-makers,' giving them a common class-name by their metre, as if it was not their imitation that makes them 'makers').

Such an experiment would doubtless be a little absurd, but it would give an English reader some help in understanding both Aristotle's style and his meaning.

For example, their enlightenment in the literal phrase, 'how the myths ought to be put together.' The higher Greek poetry did not make up fictitious plots; its business was to express the heroic saga, the myths. Again, the literal translation of poetes, poet, as 'maker', helps to explain a term that otherwise seems a puzzle in the Poetics. If we wonder why Aristotle, and Plato before him, should lay such stress on the theory that art is imitation, it is a help to realize that common language called it 'making', and it was clearly not 'making' in the ordinary sense. The poet who was 'maker' of a Fall of Troy clearly did not make the real Fall of Troy. He made an imitation Fall of Troy. An artist who 'painted Pericles' really 'made an imitation Pericles by means of shapes and colours'. Hence we get started upon a theory of art which, whether finally satisfactory or not, is of immense importance, and are saved from the error of complaining that Aristotle did not understand the 'creative power' of art.

As a rule, no doubt, the difficulty, even though merely verbal, lies beyond the reach of so simple a tool as literal translation. To say that tragedy 'imitates good men' while comedy 'imitates bad men' strikes a modern reader as almost meaningless. The truth is that neither 'good' nor 'bad' is an exact equivalent of the Greek. It would be nearer perhaps to say that, relatively speaking, you look up to the characters of tragedy, and down upon those of comedy. High or low, serious or trivial, many other pairs of words would have to be called in, in order to cover the wide range of the common Greek words. And the point is important, because we have to consider whether in Chapter VI Aristotle really lays it down that tragedy, so far from being the story of un-happiness that we think it, is properly an imitation of eudaimonia—a word often translated 'happiness', but meaning something more like 'high life' or 'blessedness'. (1)

(1) See Margoliouth, p. 121. By water, with most editors, emends the text. Another difficult word which constantly recurs in the Poetics is prattein or praxis, generally translated 'to act' or 'action'. But prattein, like our 'do', also has an intransitive meaning 'to fare' either well or ill; and Professor Margoliouth has pointed out that it seems more true to say that tragedy shows how men 'fare' than how they 'act'. It shows their experiences or fortunes rather than merely their deeds. But one must not draw the line

too bluntly. I should doubt whether a classical Greek writer was ordinarily conscious of the distinction between the two meanings. Certainly it is easier to regard happiness as a way of faring than as a form of action. Yet Aristotle can use the passive of prattein for things 'done' or 'gone through' (e.g. 52a, 22, 29: 55a, 25).

The fact is that much misunderstanding is often caused by our modern attempts to limit too strictly the meaning of a Greek word. Greek was very much a live language, and a language still unconscious of grammar, not, like ours, dominated by definitions and trained upon dictionaries. An instance is provided by Aristotle's famous saying that the typical tragic hero is one who falls from high state or fame, not through vice or depravity, but by some great hamartia. Hamartia means originally a 'bad shot' or 'error', but is currently used for 'offence' or 'sin'. Aristotle clearly means that the typical hero is a great man with 'something wrong' in his life or character; but I think it is a mistake of method to argue whether he means 'an intellectual error' or 'a moral flaw'. The word is not so precise. Similarly, when Aristotle says that a deed of strife or disaster is more tragic when it occurs 'amid affections' or 'among people who love each other', no doubt the phrase, as Aristotle's own examples show, would primarily suggest to a Greek feuds between near relations. Yet some of the meaning is lost if one translates simply 'within the family'.

There is another series of obscurities or confusions in the Poetics which, unless I am mistaken, arises from the fact that Aristotle was writing at a time when the great age of Greek tragedy was long past, and was using language formed in previous generations. The words and phrases remained in the tradition, but the forms of art and activity which they denoted had sometimes changed in the interval. If we date the Poetics about the year 330 B.C., as seems probable, that is more than two hundred years after the first tragedy of Thespis was produced in Athens, and more than seventy after the death of the last great masters of the tragic stage. When we remember that a training in music and poetry formed a prominent part of the education of every wellborn Athenian, we cannot be surprised at finding in Aristotle, and to a less extent in Plato, considerable traces of a tradition of technical language and even of aesthetic theory. It is doubtless one of Aristotle's great services that he conceived so clearly the truth that literature is a thing that grows and has a history. But no writer, certainly no ancient writer, is always vigilant. Sometimes Aristotle analyses his terms, but very often he takes them for granted; and in the latter case, I think, he is sometimes deceived by them. Thus there seem to be cases where he has been affected in his conceptions of fifth-century tragedy by the practice of his own day, when the only living form of drama was the New Comedy.

For example, as we have noticed above, true Tragedy had always taken its material from the sacred myths, or heroic sagas, which to the classical Greek constituted history. But the New Comedy was in the habit of inventing its plots. Consequently Aristotle falls into using the word mythos practically in the sense of 'plot', and writing otherwise in a way that is unsuited to the tragedy of the fifth century. He says that tragedy adheres to 'the historical names' for an aesthetic reason, because what has happened is obviously possible and therefore convincing. The real reason was that the drama and the myth were simply two different expressions of the same religious kernel (p. 44). Again, he says of the Chorus (p. 65) that it should be an integral part of the play, which is true; but he also says that it' should be regarded as one of the actors', which shows to what an extent the Chorus in his day was dead and its technique forgotten. He had lost the sense of what the Chorus was in the hands of the great masters, say in the Bacchae or the Eumenides. He mistakes, again, the use of that epiphany of a God which is frequent at the end of the single plays of Euripides, and which seems to have been equally so at the end of the trilogies of Aeschylus. Having lost the living tradition, he sees neither the ritual origin nor the dramatic value of these divine epiphanies. He thinks of the convenient gods and abstractions who sometimes spoke the prologues of the New Comedy, and imagines that the God appears in order to unravel the plot. As a matter of fact, in one play which he often quotes, the Iphigenia Taurica, the plot is actually distorted at the very end in order to give an opportunity for the epiphany.(1)

(1) See my Euripides and his Age, pp. 221-45.

One can see the effect of the tradition also in his treatment of the terms Anagnorisis and Peripeteia, which Professor Bywater translates as 'Discovery and Peripety' and Professor Butcher as 'Recognition and Reversal of Fortune'. Aristotle assumes that these two elements are normally present in any tragedy, except those which he calls 'simple'; we may say, roughly, in any tragedy that really has a plot. This strikes a modern reader as a very arbitrary assumption. Reversals of Fortune of some sort are perhaps usual in any varied plot, but surely not Recognitions? The clue to the puzzle lies, it can scarcely be doubted, in the historical origin of tragedy. Tragedy, according to Greek tradition, is originally the ritual play of Dionysus, performed at his festival, and representing, as Herodotus tells us, the 'sufferings' or 'passion' of that God. We are never directly told what these 'sufferings' were which were so represented; but Herodotus remarks that he found in Egypt a ritual that was 'in almost all points the same'. (1) This was the well-known ritual of Osiris, in which the god was torn in pieces, lamented, searched for, discovered or recognized, and the mourning by a sudden Reversal turned into joy. In any tragedy which still retained the stamp of its Dionysiac

origin, this Discovery and Peripety might normally be expected to occur, and to occur together. I have tried to show elsewhere how many of our extant tragedies do, as a matter of fact, show the marks of this ritual.(2)
(1) Cf. Hdt. ii. 48; cf. 42,144. The name of Dionysus must not be openly mentioned in connexion with mourning (ib. 61, 132, 86). This may help to explain the transference of the tragic shows to other heroes.
(2) In Miss Harrison's Themis, pp. 341-63.
I hope it is not rash to surmise that the much-debated word _katharsis_, 'purification' or 'purgation', may have come into Aristotle's mouth from the same source. It has all the appearance of being an old word which is accepted and re-interpreted by Aristotle rather than a word freely chosen by him to denote the exact phenomenon he wishes to describe. At any rate the Dionysus ritual itself was a katharmos or katharsis—a purification of the community from the taints and poisons of the past year, the old contagion of sin and death. And the words of Aristotle's definition of tragedy in Chapter VI might have been used in the days of Thespis in a much cruder and less metaphorical sense. According to primitive ideas, the mimic representation on the stage of 'incidents arousing pity and fear' did act as a katharsis of such 'passions' or 'sufferings' in real life. (For the word pathemata means 'sufferings' as well as 'passions'.) It is worth remembering that in the year 361 B.C., during Aristotle's lifetime, Greek tragedies were introduced into Rome, not on artistic but on superstitious grounds, as a katharmos against a pestilence (Livy vii. 2). One cannot but suspect that in his account of the purpose of tragedy Aristotle may be using an old traditional formula, and consciously or unconsciously investing it with a new meaning, much as he has done with the word mythos.
Apart from these historical causes of misunderstanding, a good teacher who uses this book with a class will hardly fail to point out numerous points on which two equally good Greek scholars may well differ in the mere interpretation of the words. What, for instance, are the 'two natural causes' in Chapter IV which have given birth to Poetry? Are they, as our translator takes them, (1) that man is imitative, and (2) that people delight in imitations? Or are they (1) that man is imitative and people delight in imitations, and (2) the instinct for rhythm, as Professor Butcher prefers? Is it a 'creature' a thousand miles long, or a 'picture' a thousand miles long which raises some trouble in Chapter VII? The word zoon means equally 'picture' and 'animal'. Did the older poets make their characters speak like 'statesmen', politikoi, or merely like ordinary citizens, politai, while the moderns made theirs like 'professors of rhetoric'? (Chapter VI, p. 38; cf. Margoliouth's note and glossary).
It may seem as if the large uncertainties which we have indicated detract in a ruinous manner from the value of the Poetics to us as a work of criticism. Certainly if any young writer took this book as a manual of rules by which

to 'commence poet', he would find himself embarrassed. But, if the book is properly read, not as a dogmatic text-book but as a first attempt, made by a man of astounding genius, to build up in the region of creative art a rational order like that which he established in logic, rhetoric, ethics, politics, physics, psychology, and almost every department of knowledge that existed in his day, then the uncertainties become rather a help than a discouragement. They give us occasion to think and use our imagination. They make us, to the best of our powers, try really to follow and criticize closely the bold gropings of an extraordinary thinker; and it is in this process, and not in any mere collection of dogmatic results, that we shall find the true value and beauty of the Poetics.

The book is of permanent value as a mere intellectual achievement; as a store of information about Greek literature; and as an original or first-hand statement of what we may call the classical view of artistic criticism. It does not regard poetry as a matter of unanalysed inspiration; it makes no concession to personal whims or fashion or ennui. It tries by rational methods to find out what is good in art and what makes it good, accepting the belief that there is just as truly a good way, and many bad ways, in poetry as in morals or in playing billiards. This is no place to try to sum up its main conclusions. But it is characteristic of the classical view that Aristotle lays his greatest stress, first, on the need for Unity in the work of art, the need that each part should subserve the whole, while irrelevancies, however brilliant in themselves, should be cast away; and next, on the demand that great art must have for its subject the great way of living. These judgements have often been misunderstood, but the truth in them is profound and goes near to the heart of things.

Characteristic, too, is the observation that different kinds of art grow and develop, but not indefinitely; they develop until they 'attain their natural form'; also the rule that each form of art should produce 'not every sort of pleasure but its proper pleasure'; and the sober language in which Aristotle, instead of speaking about the sequence of events in a tragedy being 'inevitable', as we bombastic moderns do, merely recommends that they should be 'either necessary or probable' and 'appear to happen because of one another'.

Conceptions and attitudes of mind such as these constitute what we may call the classical faith in matters of art and poetry; a faith which is never perhaps fully accepted in any age, yet, unlike others, is never forgotten but lives by being constantly criticized, re-asserted, and rebelled against. For the fashions of the ages vary in this direction and that, but they vary for the most part from a central road which was struck out by the imagination of Greece.

*G. M*

# Aristotle on the Art of Poetry

## 1

Our subject being Poetry, I propose to speak not only of the art in general but also of its species and their respective capacities; of the structure of plot required for a good poem; of the number and nature of the constituent parts of a poem; and likewise of any other matters in the same line of inquiry. Let us follow the natural order and begin with the primary facts. Epic poetry and Tragedy, as also Comedy, Dithyrambic poetry, and most flute-playing and lyre-playing, are all, viewed as a whole, modes of imitation. But at the same time they differ from one another in three ways, either by a difference of kind in their means, or by differences in the objects, or in the manner of their imitations.
I. Just as form and colour are used as means by some, who (whether by art or constant practice) imitate and portray many things by their aid, and the voice is used by others; so also in the above-mentioned group of arts, the means with them as a whole are rhythm, language, and harmony—used, however, either singly or in certain combinations. A combination of rhythm and harmony alone is the means in flute-playing and lyre-playing, and any other arts there may be of the same description, e.g. imitative piping. Rhythm alone, without harmony, is the means in the dancer's imitations; for even he, by the rhythms of his attitudes, may represent men's characters, as well as what they do and suffer. There is further an art which imitates by language alone, without harmony, in prose or in verse, and if in verse, either in some one or in a plurality of metres. This form of imitation is to this day without a name. We have no common name for a mime of Sophron or Xenarchus and a Socratic Conversation; and we should still be without one even if the imitation in the two instances were in trimeters or elegiacs or some other kind of verse—though it is the way with people to tack on 'poet' to the name of a metre, and talk of elegiac-poets and epic-poets, thinking that they call them poets not by reason of the imitative nature of their work, but indiscriminately by reason of the metre they write in. Even if a theory of medicine or physical philosophy be put forth in a metrical form, it is usual to describe the writer in this way; Homer and Empedocles, however, have really nothing in common apart from their metre; so that, if the one is to be called a poet, the other should be termed a physicist rather than a poet. We should be in the same position also, if the imitation in these instances were in all the metres, like the Centaur (a rhapsody in a medley of all metres) of Chaeremon; and Chaeremon one has to recognize as a poet. So much, then, as to these arts. There are, lastly, certain other arts, which combine all the means

enumerated, rhythm, melody, and verse, e.g. Dithyrambic and Nomic poetry, Tragedy and Comedy; with this difference, however, that the three kinds of means are in some of them all employed together, and in others brought in separately, one after the other. These elements of difference in the above arts I term the means of their imitation.

## 2

II. The objects the imitator represents are actions, with agents who are necessarily either good men or bad—the diversities of human character being nearly always derivative from this primary distinction, since the line between virtue and vice is one dividing the whole of mankind. It follows, therefore, that the agents represented must be either above our own level of goodness, or beneath it, or just such as we are in the same way as, with the painters, the personages of Polygnotus are better than we are, those of Pauson worse, and those of Dionysius just like ourselves. It is clear that each of the above-mentioned arts will admit of these differences, and that it will become a separate art by representing objects with this point of difference. Even in dancing, flute-playing, and lyre-playing such diversities are possible; and they are also possible in the nameless art that uses language, prose or verse without harmony, as its means; Homer's personages, for instance, are better than we are; Cleophon's are on our own level; and those of Hegemon of Thasos, the first writer of parodies, and Nicochares, the author of the Diliad, are beneath it. The same is true of the Dithyramb and the Nome: the personages may be presented in them with the difference exemplified in the... of... and Argas, and in the Cyclopses of Timotheus and Philoxenus. This difference it is that distinguishes Tragedy and Comedy also; the one would make its personages worse, and the other better, than the men of the present day.

## 3

III. A third difference in these arts is in the manner in which each kind of object is represented. Given both the same means and the same kind of object for imitation, one may either (1) speak at one moment in narrative and at another in an assumed character, as Homer does; or (2) one may remain the same throughout, without any such change; or (3) the imitators may represent the whole story dramatically, as though they were actually doing the things described.
As we said at the beginning, therefore, the differences in the imitation of these arts come under three heads, their means, their objects, and their manner.

So that as an imitator Sophocles will be on one side akin to Homer, both portraying good men; and on another to Aristophanes, since both present their personages as acting and doing. This in fact, according to some, is the reason for plays being termed dramas, because in a play the personages act the story. Hence too both Tragedy and Comedy are claimed by the Dorians as their discoveries; Comedy by the Megarians—by those in Greece as having arisen when Megara became a democracy, and by the Sicilian Megarians on the ground that the poet Epicharmus was of their country, and a good deal earlier than Chionides and Magnes; even Tragedy also is claimed by certain of the Peloponnesian Dorians. In support of this claim they point to the words 'comedy' and 'drama'. Their word for the outlying hamlets, they say, is comae, whereas Athenians call them demes—thus assuming that comedians got the name not from their comoe or revels, but from their strolling from hamlet to hamlet, lack of appreciation keeping them out of the city. Their word also for 'to act', they say, is dran, whereas Athenians use prattein.

So much, then, as to the number and nature of the points of difference in the imitation of these arts.

# 4

It is clear that the general origin of poetry was due to two causes, each of them part of human nature. Imitation is natural to man from childhood, one of his advantages over the lower animals being this, that he is the most imitative creature in the world, and learns at first by imitation. And it is also natural for all to delight in works of imitation. The truth of this second point is shown by experience: though the objects themselves may be painful to see, we delight to view the most realistic representations of them in art, the forms for example of the lowest animals and of dead bodies. The explanation is to be found in a further fact: to be learning something is the greatest of pleasures not only to the philosopher but also to the rest of mankind, however small their capacity for it; the reason of the delight in seeing the picture is that one is at the same time learning—gathering the meaning of things, e.g. that the man there is so-and-so; for if one has not seen the thing before, one's pleasure will not be in the picture as an imitation of it, but will be due to the execution or colouring or some similar cause. Imitation, then, being natural to us—as also the sense of harmony and rhythm, the metres being obviously species of rhythms—it was through their original aptitude, and by a series of improvements for the most part gradual on their first efforts, that they created poetry out of their improvisations.

Poetry, however, soon broke up into two kinds according to the differences of character in the individual poets; for the graver among them would represent noble actions, and those of noble personages; and the meaner sort the actions of the ignoble. The latter class produced invectives at first, just as others did hymns and panegyrics. We know of no such poem by any of the pre-Homeric poets, though there were probably many such writers among them; instances, however, may be found from Homer downwards, e.g. his Margites, and the similar poems of others. In this poetry of invective its natural fitness brought an iambic metre into use; hence our present term 'iambic', because it was the metre of their 'iambs' or invectives against one another. The result was that the old poets became some of them writers of heroic and others of iambic verse. Homer's position, however, is peculiar: just as he was in the serious style the poet of poets, standing alone not only through the literary excellence, but also through the dramatic character of his imitations, so too he was the first to outline for us the general forms of Comedy by producing not a dramatic invective, but a dramatic picture of the Ridiculous; his Margites in fact stands in the same relation to our comedies as the Iliad and Odyssey to our tragedies. As soon, however, as Tragedy and Comedy appeared in the field, those naturally drawn to the one line of poetry became writers of comedies instead of iambs, and those naturally drawn to the other, writers of tragedies instead of epics, because these new modes of art were grander and of more esteem than the old.

If it be asked whether Tragedy is now all that it need be in its formative elements, to consider that, and decide it theoretically and in relation to the theatres, is a matter for another inquiry.

It certainly began in improvisations—as did also Comedy; the one originating with the authors of the Dithyramb, the other with those of the phallic songs, which still survive as institutions in many of our cities. And its advance after that was little by little, through their improving on whatever they had before them at each stage. It was in fact only after a long series of changes that the movement of Tragedy stopped on its attaining to its natural form. (1) The number of actors was first increased to two by Aeschylus, who curtailed the business of the Chorus, and made the dialogue, or spoken portion, take the leading part in the play. (2) A third actor and scenery were due to Sophocles. (3) Tragedy acquired also its magnitude. Discarding short stories and a ludicrous diction, through its passing out of its satyric stage, it assumed, though only at a late point in its progress, a tone of dignity; and its metre changed then from trochaic to iambic. The reason for their original use of the trochaic tetrameter was that their poetry was satyric and more connected with dancing than it now is. As soon, however, as a spoken part came in, nature herself found the appropriate metre. The iambic, we know, is the most speakable of metres, as is shown by the fact that we very often fall into it in conversation, whereas we rarely talk hexameters, and only when we depart from the speaking tone of voice. (4) Another change was a plurality of episodes or acts. As for the remaining matters, the superadded embellishments and the account of their introduction, these must be taken as said, as it would probably be a long piece of work to go through the details.

## 5

As for Comedy, it is (as has been observed) an imitation of men worse than the average; worse, however, not as regards any and every sort of fault, but only as regards one particular kind, the Ridiculous, which is a species of the Ugly. The Ridiculous may be defined as a mistake or deformity not productive of pain or harm to others; the mask, for instance, that excites laughter, is something ugly and distorted without causing pain.

Though the successive changes in Tragedy and their authors are not unknown, we cannot say the same of Comedy; its early stages passed unnoticed, because it was not as yet taken up in a serious way. It was only at a late point in its progress that a chorus of comedians was officially granted by the archon; they used to be mere volunteers. It had also already certain definite forms at the time when the record of those termed comic poets begins. Who it was who supplied it with masks, or prologues, or a plurality of actors and the like, has remained unknown. The invented Fable, or Plot, however, originated in Sicily, with Epicharmus and Phormis; of Athenian poets Crates was the first to drop the Comedy of invective and frame stories of a general and non-personal nature, in other words, Fables or Plots.

Epic poetry, then, has been seen to agree with Tragedy to this extent, that of being an imitation of serious subjects in a grand kind of verse. It differs from it, however, (1) in that it is in one kind of verse and in narrative form; and (2) in its length—which is due to its action having no fixed limit of time, whereas Tragedy endeavours to keep as far as possible within a single circuit of the sun, or something near that. This, I say, is another point of difference between them, though at first the practice in this respect was just the same in tragedies as in epic poems. They differ also (3) in their constituents, some being common to both and others peculiar to Tragedy—hence a judge of good and bad in Tragedy is a judge of that in epic poetry also. All the parts of an epic are included in Tragedy; but those of Tragedy are not all of them to be found in the Epic.

## 6

Reserving hexameter poetry and Comedy for consideration hereafter, let us proceed now to the discussion of Tragedy; before doing so, however, we must gather up the definition resulting from what has been said. A tragedy, then, is the imitation of an action that is serious and also, as having magnitude, complete in itself; in language with pleasurable accessories, each kind brought in separately in the parts of the work; in a dramatic, not in a narrative form; with incidents arousing pity and fear, wherewith to accomplish its catharsis of such emotions. Here by 'language with pleasurable accessories' I mean that with rhythm and harmony or song superadded; and by 'the kinds separately' I mean that some portions are worked out with verse only, and others in turn with song.

I. As they act the stories, it follows that in the first place the Spectacle (or stage-appearance of the actors) must be some part of the whole; and in the second Melody and Diction, these two being the means of their imitation. Here by 'Diction' I mean merely this, the composition of the verses; and by 'Melody', what is too completely understood to require explanation. But further: the subject represented also is an action; and the action involves agents, who must necessarily have their distinctive qualities both of character and thought, since it is from these that we ascribe certain qualities to their actions. There are in the natural order of things, therefore, two causes, Character and Thought, of their actions, and consequently of their success or failure in their lives. Now the action (that which was done) is represented in the play by the Fable or Plot. The Fable, in our present sense of the term, is simply this, the combination of the incidents, or things done in the story; whereas Character is what makes us ascribe certain moral qualities to the agents; and Thought is shown in all they say when proving a particular point or, it may be, enunciating a general truth. There are six parts consequently of every tragedy, as a whole, that is, of such or such quality, viz. a Fable or Plot, Characters, Diction, Thought, Spectacle and Melody; two of them arising from the means, one from the manner, and three from the objects of the dramatic imitation; and there is nothing else besides these six. Of these, its formative elements, then, not a few of the dramatists have made due use, as every play, one may say, admits of Spectacle, Character, Fable, Diction, Melody, and Thought.

II. The most important of the six is the combination of the incidents of the story.

Tragedy is essentially an imitation not of persons but of action and life, of happiness and misery. All human happiness or misery takes the form of action; the end for which we live is a certain kind of activity, not a quality. Character gives us qualities, but it is in our actions—what we do—that we are happy or the reverse. In a play accordingly they do not act in order to portray the Characters; they include the Characters for the sake of the action. So that it is the action in it, i.e. its Fable or Plot, that is the end and purpose of the tragedy; and the end is everywhere the chief thing. Besides this, a tragedy is impossible without action, but there may be one without

Character. The tragedies of most of the moderns are characterless—a defect common among poets of all kinds, and with its counterpart in painting in Zeuxis as compared with Polygnotus; for whereas the latter is strong in character, the work of Zeuxis is devoid of it. And again: one may string together a series of characteristic speeches of the utmost finish as regards Diction and Thought, and yet fail to produce the true tragic effect; but one will have much better success with a tragedy which, however inferior in these respects, has a Plot, a combination of incidents, in it. And again: the most powerful elements of attraction in Tragedy, the Peripeties and Discoveries, are parts of the Plot. A further proof is in the fact that beginners succeed earlier with the Diction and Characters than with the construction of a story; and the same may be said of nearly all the early dramatists. We maintain, therefore, that the first essential, the life and soul, so to speak, of Tragedy is the Plot; and that the Characters come second—compare the parallel in painting, where the most beautiful colours laid on without order will not give one the same pleasure as a simple black-and-white sketch of a portrait. We maintain that Tragedy is primarily an imitation of action, and that it is mainly for the sake of the action that it imitates the personal agents. Third comes the element of Thought, i.e. the power of saying whatever can be said, or what is appropriate to the occasion. This is what, in the speeches in Tragedy, falls under the arts of Politics and Rhetoric; for the older poets make their personages discourse like statesmen, and the moderns like rhetoricians. One must not confuse it with Character. Character in a play is that which reveals the moral purpose of the agents, i.e. the sort of thing they seek or avoid, where that is not obvious—hence there is no room for Character in a speech on a purely indifferent subject. Thought, on the other hand, is shown in all they say when proving or disproving some particular point, or enunciating some universal proposition. Fourth among the literary elements is the Diction of the personages, i.e. as before explained, the expression of their thoughts in words, which is practically the same thing with verse as with prose. As for the two remaining parts, the Melody is the greatest of the pleasurable accessories of Tragedy. The Spectacle, though an attraction, is the least artistic of all the parts, and has least to do with the art of poetry. The tragic effect is quite possible without a public performance and actors; and besides, the getting-up of the Spectacle is more a matter for the costumier than the poet.

# 7

Having thus distinguished the parts, let us now consider the proper construction of the Fable or Plot, as that is at once the first and the most important thing in Tragedy. We have laid it down that a tragedy is an imitation of an action that is complete in itself, as a whole of some magnitude; for a whole may be of no magnitude to speak of. Now a whole is that which has beginning, middle, and end. A beginning is that which is not itself necessarily after anything else, and which has naturally something else after it; an end is that which is naturally after something itself, either as its necessary or usual consequent, and with nothing else after it; and a middle, that which is by nature after one thing and has also another after it. A well-constructed Plot, therefore, cannot either begin or end at any point one likes; beginning and end in it must be of the forms just described. Again: to be beautiful, a living creature, and every whole made up of parts, must not only present a certain order in its arrangement of parts, but also be of a certain definite magnitude. Beauty is a matter of size and order, and therefore impossible either (1) in a very minute creature, since our perception becomes indistinct as it approaches instantaneity; or (2) in a creature of vast size—one, say, 1,000 miles long—as in that case, instead of the object being seen all at once, the unity and wholeness of it is lost to the beholder.

Just in the same way, then, as a beautiful whole made up of parts, or a beautiful living creature, must be of some size, a size to be taken in by the eye, so a story or Plot must be of some length, but of a length to be taken in by the memory. As for the limit of its length, so far as that is relative to public performances and spectators, it does not fall within the theory of poetry. If they had to perform a hundred tragedies, they would be timed by water-clocks, as they are said to have been at one period. The limit, however, set by the actual nature of the thing is this: the longer the story, consistently with its being comprehensible as a whole, the finer it is by reason of its magnitude. As a rough general formula, 'a length which allows of the hero passing by a series of probable or necessary stages from misfortune to happiness, or from happiness to misfortune', may suffice as a limit for the magnitude of the story.

## *8*

The Unity of a Plot does not consist, as some suppose, in its having one man as its subject. An infinity of things befall that one man, some of which it is impossible to reduce to unity; and in like manner there are many actions of one man which cannot be made to form one action. One sees, therefore, the mistake of all the poets who have written a Heracleid, a Theseid, or similar poems; they suppose that, because Heracles was one man, the story also of Heracles must be one story. Homer, however, evidently understood this point quite well, whether by art or instinct, just in the same way as he excels the rest in every other respect. In writing an Odyssey, he did not make the poem cover all that ever befell his hero—it befell him, for instance, to get wounded on Parnassus and also to feign madness at the time of the call to arms, but the two incidents had no probable or necessary connexion with one another—instead of doing that, he took an action with a Unity of the kind we are describing as the subject of the Odyssey, as also of the Iliad. The truth is that, just as in the other imitative arts one imitation is always of one thing, so in poetry the story, as an imitation of action, must represent one action, a complete whole, with its several incidents so closely connected that the transposal or withdrawal of any one of them will disjoin and dislocate the whole. For that which makes no perceptible difference by its presence or absence is no real part of the whole.

## 9

From what we have said it will be seen that the poet's function is to describe, not the thing that has happened, but a kind of thing that might happen, i.e. what is possible as being probable or necessary. The distinction between historian and poet is not in the one writing prose and the other verse—you might put the work of Herodotus into verse, and it would still be a species of history; it consists really in this, that the one describes the thing that has been, and the other a kind of thing that might be. Hence poetry is something more philosophic and of graver import than history, since its statements are of the nature rather of universals, whereas those of history are singulars. By a universal statement I mean one as to what such or such a kind of man will probably or necessarily say or do— which is the aim of poetry, though it affixes proper names to the characters; by a singular statement, one as to what, say, Alcibiades did or had done to him. In Comedy this has become clear by this time; it is only when their plot is already made up of probable incidents that they give it a basis of proper names, choosing for the purpose any names that may occur to them, instead of writing like the old iambic poets about particular persons. In Tragedy, however, they still adhere to the historic names; and for this reason: what convinces is the possible; now whereas we are not yet sure as to the possibility of that which has not happened, that which has happened is manifestly possible, else it would not have come to pass. Nevertheless even in Tragedy there are some plays with but one or two known names in them, the rest being inventions; and there are some without a single known name, e.g. Agathon'sAnthens, in which both incidents and names are of the poet's invention; and it is no less delightful on that account. So that one must not aim at a rigid adherence to the traditional stories on which tragedies are based. It would be absurd, in fact, to do so, as even the known stories are only known to a few, though they are a delight none the less to all.

It is evident from the above that, the poet must be more the poet of his stories or Plots than of his verses, inasmuch as he is a poet by virtue of the imitative element in his work, and it is actions that he imitates. And if he should come to take a subject from actual history, he is none the less a poet for that; since some historic occurrences may very well be in the probable and possible order of things; and it is in that aspect of them that he is their poet.

Of simple Plots and actions the episodic are the worst. I call a Plot episodic when there is neither probability nor necessity in the sequence of episodes. Actions of this sort bad poets construct through their own fault, and good ones on account of the players. His work being for public performance, a good poet often stretches out a Plot beyond its capabilities, and is thus obliged to twist the sequence of incident.

Tragedy, however, is an imitation not only of a complete action, but also of incidents arousing pity and fear. Such incidents have the very greatest effect on the mind when they occur unexpectedly and at the same time in consequence of one another; there is more of the marvellous in them then than if they happened of themselves or by mere chance. Even matters of chance seem most marvellous if there is an appearance of design as it were in them; as for instance the statue of Mitys at Argos killed the author of Mitys' death by falling down on him when a looker-on at a public spectacle; for incidents like that we think to be not without a meaning. A Plot, therefore, of this sort is necessarily finer than others.

## 10

Plots are either simple or complex, since the actions they represent are naturally of this twofold description. The action, proceeding in the way defined, as one continuous whole, I call simple, when the change in the hero's fortunes takes place without Peripety or Discovery; and complex, when it involves one or the other, or both. These should each of them arise out of the structure of the Plot itself, so as to be the consequence, necessary or probable, of the antecedents. There is a great difference between a thing happening propter hoc and post hoc.

## 11

A Peripety is the change from one state of things within the play to its opposite of the kind described, and that too in the way we are saying, in the probable or necessary sequence of events; as it is for instance in Oedipus: here the opposite state of things is produced by the Messenger, who, coming to gladden Oedipus and to remove his fears as to his mother, reveals the secret of his birth. And in Lynceus: just as he is being led off for execution, with Danaus at his side to put him to death, the incidents preceding this bring it about that he is saved and Danaus put to death. A Discovery is, as the very word implies, a change from ignorance to knowledge, and thus to either love or hate, in the personages marked for good or evil fortune. The finest form of Discovery is one attended by Peripeties, like that which goes with the Discovery in Oedipus. There are no doubt other forms of it; what we have said may happen in a way in reference to inanimate things, even things of a very casual kind; and it is also possible to discover whether some one has done or not done something. But the form most directly connected with the Plot and the action of the piece is the first-mentioned. This, with a Peripety, will arouse either pity or fear—actions of that nature being what Tragedy is assumed to represent; and it will also serve to bring about the happy or unhappy ending. The Discovery, then, being of persons, it may be that of one party only to the other, the latter being already known; or both the parties may have to discover themselves. Iphigenia, for instance, was discovered to Orestes by sending the letter; and another Discovery was required to reveal him to Iphigenia.

Two parts of the Plot, then, Peripety and Discovery, are on matters of this sort. A third part is Suffering; which we may define as an action of a destructive or painful nature, such as murders on the stage, tortures, woundings, and the like. The other two have been already explained.

## 12

The parts of Tragedy to be treated as formative elements in the whole were mentioned in a previous Chapter. From the point of view, however, of its quantity, i.e. the separate sections into which it is divided, a tragedy has the following parts: Prologue, Episode, Exode, and a choral portion, distinguished into Parode and Stasimon; these two are common to all tragedies, whereas songs from the stage and Commoe are only found in some. The Prologue is all that precedes the Parode of the chorus; an Episode all that comes in between two whole choral songs; the Exode all that follows after the last choral song. In the choral portion the Parode is the whole first statement of the chorus; a Stasimon, a song of the chorus without anapaests or trochees; a Commas, a lamentation sung by chorus and actor in concert. The parts of Tragedy to be used as formative elements in the whole we have already mentioned; the above are its parts from the point of view of its quantity, or the separate sections into which it is divided. '

# 13

The next points after what we have said above will be these: (1) What is the poet to aim at, and what is he to avoid, in constructing his Plots? and (2) What are the conditions on which the tragic effect depends?

We assume that, for the finest form of Tragedy, the Plot must be not simple but complex; and further, that it must imitate actions arousing pity and fear, since that is the distinctive function of this kind of imitation. It follows, therefore, that there are three forms of Plot to be avoided. (1) A good man must not be seen passing from happiness to misery, or (2) a bad man from misery to happiness.

The first situation is not fear-inspiring or piteous, but simply odious to us. The second is the most untragic that can be; it has no one of the requisites of Tragedy; it does not appeal either to the human feeling in us, or to our pity, or to our fears. Nor, on the other hand, should (3) an extremely bad man be seen falling from happiness into misery. Such a story may arouse the human feeling in us, but it will not move us to either pity or fear; pity is occasioned by undeserved misfortune, and fear by that of one like ourselves; so that there will be nothing either piteous or fear-inspiring in the situation. There remains, then, the intermediate kind of personage, a man not pre-eminently virtuous and just, whose misfortune, however, is brought upon him not by vice and depravity but by some error of judgement, of the number of those in the enjoyment of great reputation and prosperity; e.g. Oedipus, Thyestes, and the men of note of similar families. The perfect Plot, accordingly, must have a single, and not (as some tell us) a double issue; the change in the hero's fortunes must be not from misery to happiness, but on the contrary from happiness to misery; and the cause of it must lie not in any depravity, but in some great error on his part; the man himself being either such as we have described, or better, not worse, than that. Fact also confirms our theory. Though the poets began by accepting any tragic story that came to hand, in these days the finest tragedies are always on the story of some few houses, on that of Alemeon, Oedipus, Orestes, Meleager, Thyestes, Telephus, or any others that may have been involved, as either agents or sufferers, in some deed of horror. The theoretically best tragedy, then, has a Plot of this description. The critics, therefore, are wrong who blame Euripides for taking this line in his tragedies, and giving many of them an unhappy ending. It is, as we have said, the right line to take. The best proof is this: on the stage, and in the public performances, such plays, properly worked out, are seen to be the most truly tragic; and Euripides, even if his elecution be faulty in every other point, is seen to be nevertheless the most tragic certainly of the dramatists. After this comes the construction of Plot which some rank first, one with a double story (like the Odyssey) and an opposite issue for the good and the bad personages. It is ranked as first only through the weakness of the audiences; the poets merely follow their public, writing as its wishes dictate. But the pleasure here is not that of Tragedy. It belongs rather to Comedy, where the bitterest enemies in the piece (e.g. Orestes and Aegisthus) walk off good friends at the end, with no slaying of any one by any one.

## 14

The tragic fear and pity may be aroused by the Spectacle; but they may also be aroused by the very structure and incidents of the play—which is the better way and shows the better poet. The Plot in fact should be so framed that, even without seeing the things take place, he who simply hears the account of them shall be filled with horror and pity at the incidents; which is just the effect that the mere recital of the story in Oedipus would have on one. To produce this same effect by means of the Spectacle is less artistic, and requires extraneous aid. Those, however, who make use of the Spectacle to put before us that which is merely monstrous and not productive of fear, are wholly out of touch with Tragedy; not every kind of pleasure should be required of a tragedy, but only its own proper pleasure. The tragic pleasure is that of pity and fear, and the poet has to produce it by a work of imitation; it is clear, therefore, that the causes should be included in the incidents of his story. Let us see, then, what kinds of incident strike one as horrible, or rather as piteous. In a deed of this description the parties must necessarily be either friends, or enemies, or indifferent to one another. Now when enemy does it on enemy, there is nothing to move us to pity either in his doing or in his meditating the deed, except so far as the actual pain of the sufferer is concerned; and the same is true when the parties are indifferent to one another. Whenever the tragic deed, however, is done within the family—when murder or the like is done or meditated by brother on brother, by son on father, by mother on son, or son on mother—these are the situations the poet should seek after. The traditional stories, accordingly, must be kept as they are, e.g. the murder of Clytaemnestra by Orestes and of Eriphyle by Alcmeon. At the same time even with these there is something left to the poet himself; it is for him to devise the right way of treating them. Let us explain more clearly what we mean by 'the right way'. The deed of horror may be done by the doer knowingly and consciously, as in the old poets, and in Medea's murder of her children in Euripides. Or he may do it, but in ignorance of his relationship, and discover that afterwards, as does the Oedipus in Sophocles. Here the deed is outside the play; but it may be within it, like the act of the Alcmeon in Astydamas, or that of the Telegonus in Ulysses Wounded. A third possibility is for one meditating some deadly injury to

another, in ignorance of his relationship, to make the discovery in time to draw back. These exhaust the possibilities, since the deed must necessarily be either done or not done, and either knowingly or unknowingly.
The worst situation is when the personage is with full knowledge on the point of doing the deed, and leaves it undone. It is odious and also (through the absence of suffering) untragic; hence it is that no one is made to act thus except in some few instances, e.g. Haemon and Creon in Antigone. Next after this comes the actual perpetration of the deed meditated. A better situation than that, however, is for the deed to be done in ignorance, and the relationship discovered afterwards, since there is nothing odious in it, and the Discovery will serve to astound us. But the best of all is the last; what we have in Cresphontes, for example, where Merope, on the point of slaying her son, recognizes him in time; in Iphigenia, where sister and brother are in a like position; and in Helle, where the son recognizes his mother, when on the point of giving her up to her enemy.
This will explain why our tragedies are restricted (as we said just now) to such a small number of families. It was accident rather than art that led the poets in quest of subjects to embody this kind of incident in their Plots. They are still obliged, accordingly, to have recourse to the families in which such horrors have occurred.
On the construction of the Plot, and the kind of Plot required for Tragedy, enough has now been said.

# 15

In the Characters there are four points to aim at. First and foremost, that they shall be good. There will be an element of character in the play, if (as has been observed) what a personage says or does reveals a certain moral purpose; and a good element of character, if the purpose so revealed is good. Such goodness is possible in every type of personage, even in a woman or a slave, though the one is perhaps an inferior, and the other a wholly worthless being. The second point is to make them appropriate. The Character before us may be, say, manly; but it is not appropriate in a female Character to be manly, or clever. The third is to make them like the reality, which is not the same as their being good and appropriate, in our sense of the term. The fourth is to make them consistent and the same throughout; even if inconsistency be part of the man before one for imitation as presenting that form of character, he should still be consistently inconsistent. We have an instance of baseness of character, not required for the story, in the Menelaus in Orestes; of the incongruous and unbefitting in the lamentation of Ulysses in Scylla, and in the (clever) speech of Melanippe; and of inconsistency in Iphigenia at Aulis, where Iphigenia the suppliant is utterly unlike the later Iphigenia. The right thing, however, is in the Characters just as in the incidents of the play to endeavour always after the necessary or the probable; so that whenever such-and-such a personage says or does such-and-such a thing, it shall be the probable or necessary outcome of his character; and whenever this incident follows on that, it shall be either the necessary or the probable consequence of it. From this one sees (to digress for a moment) that the Denouement also should arise out of the plot itself, arid not depend on a stage-artifice, as in Medea, or in the story of the (arrested) departure of the Greeks in the Iliad. The artifice must be reserved for matters outside the play—for past events beyond human knowledge, or events yet to come, which require to be foretold or announced; since it is the privilege of the Gods to know everything. There should be nothing improbable among the actual incidents. If it be unavoidable, however, it should be outside the tragedy, like the improbability in the Oedipus of Sophocles. But to return to the Characters. As Tragedy is an imitation of personages better than the ordinary man, we in our way should follow the example of good portrait-painters, who reproduce the distinctive features of a man, and at the same time, without losing the likeness, make him handsomer than he is. The poet in like manner, in portraying men quick or slow to anger, or with similar infirmities of character, must know how to represent them as such, and at the same time as good men, as Agathon and Homer have represented Achilles.

All these rules one must keep in mind throughout, and further, those also for such points of stage-effect as directly depend on the art of the poet, since in these too one may often make mistakes. Enough, however, has been said on the subject in one of our published writings.

## 16

Discovery in general has been explained already. As for the species of Discovery, the first to be noted is (1) the least artistic form of it, of which the poets make most use through mere lack of invention, Discovery by signs or marks. Of these signs some are congenital, like the 'lance-head which the Earth-born have on them', or 'stars', such as Carcinus brings in in his Thyestes; others acquired after birth—these latter being either marks on the body, e.g. scars, or external tokens, like necklaces, or to take another sort of instance, the ark in the Discovery in Tyro. Even these, however, admit of two uses, a better and a worse; the scar of Ulysses is an instance; the Discovery of him through it is made in one way by the nurse and in another by the swineherds. A Discovery using signs as a means of assurance is less artistic, as indeed are all such as imply reflection; whereas one bringing them in all of a sudden, as in the Bath-story, is of a better order. Next after these are (2) Discoveries made directly by the poet; which are inartistic for that very reason; e.g. Orestes' Discovery of himself in Iphigenia: whereas his sister reveals who she is by the letter, Orestes is made to say himself what the poet rather than the story demands. This, therefore, is not far removed from the first-mentioned fault, since he might have presented certain tokens as well. Another instance is the 'shuttle's voice' in the Tereus of Sophocles. (3) A third species is Discovery through memory, from a man's consciousness being awakened by something seen or heard. Thus in The Cyprioe of Dicaeogenes, the sight of the picture makes the man burst into tears; and in the Tale of Alcinous, hearing the harper Ulysses is reminded of the past and weeps; the Discovery of them being the result. (4) A fourth kind is Discovery through reasoning; e.g. in The Choephoroe: 'One like me is here; there is no one like me but Orestes; he, therefore, must be here.' Or that which Polyidus the Sophist suggested for Iphigenia; since it was natural for Orestes to reflect: 'My sister was sacrificed, and I am to be sacrificed like her.' Or that in the Tydeus of Theodectes: 'I came to find a son, and am to die myself.' Or that in The Phinidae: on seeing the place the women inferred their fate, that they were to die there, since they had also been exposed there. (5) There is, too, a composite Discovery arising from bad reasoning on the side of the other party. An instance of it is in Ulysses the False Messenger: he said he should know the bow—which he had not seen; but to suppose from that that he would know it again (as though he had once seen it) was bad reasoning. (6) The best of all Discoveries, however, is that arising from the incidents themselves, when the great surprise comes about through a probable incident, like that in the Oedipus of Sophocles; and also in Iphigenia; for it was not improbable that she should wish to have a letter taken home. These last are the only Discoveries independent of the artifice of signs and necklaces. Next after them come Discoveries through reasoning.

## 17

At the time when he is constructing his Plots, and engaged on the Diction in which they are worked out, the poet should remember (1) to put the actual scenes as far as possible before his eyes. In this way, seeing everything with the vividness of an eye-witness as it were, he will devise what is appropriate, and be least likely to overlook incongruities. This is shown by what was censured in Carcinus, the return of Amphiaraus from the sanctuary; it would have passed unnoticed, if it had not been actually seen by the audience; but on the stage his play failed, the incongruity of the incident offending the spectators. (2) As far as may be, too, the poet should even act his story with the very gestures of his personages. Given the same natural qualifications, he who feels the emotions to be described will be the most convincing; distress and anger, for instance, are portrayed most truthfully by one who is feeling them at the moment. Hence it is that poetry demands a man with special gift for it, or else one with a touch of madness in him; the former can easily assume the required mood, and the latter may be actually beside himself with emotion. (3) His story, again, whether already made or of his own making, he should first simplify and reduce to a universal form, before proceeding to lengthen it out by the insertion of episodes. The following will show how the universal element in Iphigenia, for instance, may be viewed: A certain maiden having been offered in sacrifice, and spirited away from her sacrificers into another land, where the custom was to sacrifice all strangers to the Goddess, she was made there the priestess of this rite. Long after that the brother of the priestess happened to come; the fact, however, of the oracle having for a certain reason bidden him go thither, and his object in going, are outside the Plot of the play. On his coming he was arrested, and about to be sacrificed, when he revealed who he was—either as Euripides puts it, or (as suggested by Polyidus) by the not improbable exclamation, 'So I too am doomed to be sacrificed, as my sister was'; and the disclosure led to his salvation. This done, the next thing, after the proper names have been fixed as a basis for the story, is to work in episodes or accessory incidents. One must mind, however, that the episodes are appropriate, like the fit of madness in Orestes, which led to his arrest, and the purifying, which brought about his salvation. In plays, then, the episodes are short; in epic poetry they serve to lengthen out the poem. The argument of the Odyssey is not a long one.

A certain man has been abroad many years; Poseidon is ever on the watch for him, and he is all alone. Matters at home too have come to this, that his substance is being wasted and his son's death plotted by suitors to his wife. Then he arrives there himself after his grievous sufferings; reveals himself, and falls on his enemies; and the end is his salvation and their death. This being all that is proper to the Odyssey, everything else in it is episode.

## 18

(4) There is a further point to be borne in mind. Every tragedy is in part Complication and in part Denouement; the incidents before the opening scene, and often certain also of those within the play, forming the Complication; and the rest the Denouement. By Complication I mean all from the beginning of the story to the point just before the change in the hero's fortunes; by Denouement, all from the beginning of the change to the end. In the Lynceus of Theodectes, for instance, the Complication includes, together with the presupposed incidents, the seizure of the child and that in turn of the parents; and the Denouement all from the indictment for the murder to the end. Now it is right, when one speaks of a

tragedy as the same or not the same as another, to do so on the ground before all else of their Plot, i.e. as having the same or not the same Complication and Denouement. Yet there are many dramatists who, after a good Complication, fail in the Denouement. But it is necessary for both points of construction to be always duly mastered. (5) There are four distinct species of Tragedy—that being the number of the constituents also that have been mentioned: first, the complex Tragedy, which is all Peripety and Discovery; second, the Tragedy of suffering, e.g. the Ajaxes and Ixions; third, the Tragedy of character, e.g. The Phthiotides and Peleus. The fourth constituent is that of 'Spectacle', exemplified in The Phorcides, in Prometheus, and in all plays with the scene laid in the nether world. The poet's aim, then, should be to combine every element of interest, if possible, or else the more important and the major part of them. This is now especially necessary owing to the unfair criticism to which the poet is subjected in these days. Just because there have been poets before him strong in the several species of tragedy, the critics now expect the one man to surpass that which was the strong point of each one of his predecessors. (6) One should also remember what has been said more than once, and not write a tragedy on an epic body of incident (i.e. one with a plurality of stories in it), by attempting to dramatize, for instance, the entire story of the Iliad. In the epic owing to its scale every part is treated at proper length; with a drama, however, on the same story the result is very disappointing. This is shown by the fact that all who have dramatized the fall of Ilium in its entirety, and not part by part, like Euripides, or the whole of the Niobe story, instead of a portion, like Aeschylus, either fail utterly or have but ill success on the stage; for that and that alone was enough to ruin a play by Agathon. Yet in their Peripeties, as also in their simple plots, the poets I mean show wonderful skill in aiming at the kind of effect they desire—a tragic situation that arouses the human feeling in one, like the clever villain (e.g. Sisyphus) deceived, or the brave wrongdoer worsted. This is probable, however, only in Agathon's sense, when he speaks of the probability of even improbabilities coming to pass. (7) The Chorus too should be regarded as one of the actors; it should be an integral part of the whole, and take a share in the action—that which it has in Sophocles rather than in Euripides. With the later poets, however, the songs in a play of theirs have no more to do with the Plot of that than of any other tragedy. Hence it is that they are now singing intercalary pieces, a practice first introduced by Agathon. And yet what real difference is there between singing such intercalary pieces, and attempting to fit in a speech, or even a whole act, from one play into another?

# 19

The Plot and Characters having been discussed, it remains to consider the Diction and Thought. As for the Thought, we may assume what is said of it in our Art of Rhetoric, as it belongs more properly to that department of inquiry. The Thought of the personages is shown in everything to be effected by their language—in every effort to prove or disprove, to arouse emotion (pity, fear, anger, and the like), or to maximize or minimize things. It is clear, also, that their mental procedure must be on the same lines in their actions likewise, whenever they wish them to arouse pity or horror, or have a look of importance or probability. The only difference is that with the act the impression has to be made without explanation; whereas with the spoken word it has to be produced by the speaker, and result from his language. What, indeed, would be the good of the speaker, if things appeared in the required light even apart from anything he says?

As regards the Diction, one subject for inquiry under this head is the turns given to the language when spoken; e.g. the difference between command and prayer, simple statement and threat, question and answer, and so forth. The theory of such matters, however, belongs to Elocution and the professors of that art. Whether the poet knows these things or not, his art as a poet is never seriously criticized on that account. What fault can one see in Homer's 'Sing of the wrath, Goddess'?—which Protagoras has criticized as being a command where a prayer was meant, since to bid one do or not do, he tells us, is a command. Let us pass over this, then, as appertaining to another art, and not to that of poetry.

# 20

The Diction viewed as a whole is made up of the following parts: the Letter (or ultimate element), the Syllable, the Conjunction, the Article, the Noun, the Verb, the Case, and the Speech. (1) The Letter is an indivisible sound of a particular kind, one that may become a factor in an intelligible sound. Indivisible sounds are uttered by the brutes also, but no one of these is a Letter in our sense of the term. These elementary sounds are either vowels, semivowels, or mutes. A vowel is a Letter having an audible sound without the addition of another Letter. A semivowel, one having an audible sound by the addition of another Letter; e.g. S and R. A mute, one having no sound at all by itself, but becoming audible by an addition, that of one of the Letters which have a sound of some sort of their own; e.g. D and G. The Letters differ in various ways: as produced by different conformations or in different regions of the mouth; as aspirated, not aspirated, or sometimes one and sometimes the other; as long, short, or of variable quantity; and further as having an acute grave, or intermediate accent.

The details of these matters we must leave to the metricians. (2) A Syllable is a nonsignificant composite sound, made up of a mute and a Letter having a sound (a vowel or semivowel); for GR, without an A, is just as much a Syllable as GRA, with an A. The various forms of the Syllable also belong to the theory of metre. (3) A Conjunction is (a) a non-significant sound which, when one significant sound is formable out of several, neither hinders nor aids the union, and which, if the Speech thus formed stands by itself (apart from other Speeches) must not be inserted at the beginning of it; e.g. men, de, toi, de. Or (b) a non-significant sound capable of combining two or more significant sounds into one; e.g. amphi, peri, etc. (4) An Article is a non-significant sound marking the beginning, end, or dividing-point of a Speech, its natural place being either at the extremities or in the middle.
(5) A Noun or name is a composite significant sound not involving the idea of time, with parts which have no significance by themselves in it. It is to be remembered that in a compound we do not think of the parts as having a significance also by themselves; in the name 'Theodorus', for instance, the doron means nothing to us.
(6) A Verb is a composite significant sound involving the idea of time, with parts which (just as in the Noun) have no significance by themselves in it. Whereas the word 'man' or 'white' does not imply when, 'walks' and 'has walked' involve in addition to the idea of walking that of time present or time past.
(7) A Case of a Noun or Verb is when the word means 'of or 'to' a thing, and so forth, or for one or many (e.g. 'man' and 'men'); or it may consist merely in the mode of utterance, e.g. in question, command, etc. 'Walked?' and 'Walk!' are Cases of the verb 'to walk' of this last kind. (8) A Speech is a composite significant sound, some of the parts of which have a certain significance by themselves. It may be observed that a Speech is not always made up of Noun and Verb; it may be without a Verb, like the definition of man; but it will always have some part with a certain significance by itself. In the Speech 'Cleon walks', 'Cleon' is an instance of such a part. A Speech is said to be one in two ways, either as signifying one thing, or as a union of several Speeches made into one by conjunction. Thus the Iliad is one Speech by conjunction of several; and the definition of man is one through its signifying one thing.

## 21

Nouns are of two kinds, either (1) simple, i.e. made up of non-significant parts, like the word ge, or (2) double; in the latter case the word may be made up either of a significant and a non-significant part (a distinction which disappears in the compound), or of two significant parts. It is possible also to have triple, quadruple or higher compounds, like most of our amplified names; e.g.' Hermocaicoxanthus' and the like.

Whatever its structure, a Noun must always be either (1) the ordinary word for the thing, or (2) a strange word, or (3) a metaphor, or (4) an ornamental word, or (5) a coined word, or (6) a word lengthened out, or (7) curtailed, or (8) altered in form. By the ordinary word I mean that in general use in a country; and by a strange word, one in use elsewhere. So that the same word may obviously be at once strange and ordinary, though not in reference to the same people; sigunos, for instance, is an ordinary word in Cyprus, and a strange word with us. Metaphor consists in giving the thing a name that belongs to something else; the transference being either from genus to species, or from species to genus, or from species to species, or on grounds of analogy. That from genus to species is eXemplified in 'Here stands my ship'; for lying at anchor is the 'standing' of a particular kind of thing. That from species to genus in 'Truly ten thousand good deeds has Ulysses wrought', where 'ten thousand', which is a particular large number, is put in place of the generic 'a large number'. That from species to species in 'Drawing the life with the bronze', and in 'Severing with the enduring bronze'; where the poet uses 'draw' in the sense of 'sever' and 'sever' in that of 'draw', both words meaning to 'take away' something. That from analogy is possible whenever there are four terms so related that the second (B) is to the first (A), as the fourth (D) to the third (C); for one may then metaphorically put B in lieu of D, and D in lieu of B. Now and then, too, they qualify the metaphor by adding on to it that to which the word it supplants is relative. Thus a cup (B) is in relation to Dionysus (A) what a shield (D) is to Ares (C). The cup accordingly will be metaphorically described as the 'shield of Dionysus' (D + A), and the shield as the 'cup of Ares' (B + C). Or to take another instance: As old age (D) is to life (C), so is evening (B) to day (A). One will accordingly describe evening (B) as the 'old age of the day' (D + A)—or by the Empedoclean equivalent; and old age (D) as the 'evening' or 'sunset of life'' (B + C). It may be that some of the terms thus related have no special name of their own, but for all that they will be metaphorically described in just the same way. Thus to cast forth seed-corn is called 'sowing'; but to cast forth its flame, as said of the sun, has no special name. This nameless act (B), however, stands in just the same relation to its object, sunlight (A), as sowing (D) to the seed-corn (C). Hence the expression in the poet, 'sowing around a god-created flame' (D + A). There is also another form of qualified metaphor. Having given the thing the alien name, one may by a negative addition deny of it one of the attributes naturally associated with its new name. An instance of this would be to call the shield not the 'cup of Ares,' as in the former case, but a 'cup that holds no wine'. * * * A coined word is a name which, being quite unknown among a people, is given by the poet himself; e.g. (for there are some words that seem to be of this origin) hernyges for horns, and areter for priest. A word is said to be lengthened out, when it has a short vowel made long, or an extra syllable inserted; e. g. polleos for poleos, Peleiadeo for Peleidon. It is said to be curtailed, when it has lost a part; e.g. kri, do, and ops in miaginetaiamphoteron ops. It is an altered word, when part is left as it was and part is of the poet's making; e.g. dexiteron for dexion, in dexiteron kata maxon.

The Nouns themselves (to whatever class they may belong) are either masculines, feminines, or intermediates (neuter). All ending in N, P, S, or in the two compounds of this last, PS and X, are masculines. All ending in the invariably long vowels, H and O, and in A among the vowels that may be long, are feminines. So that there is an equal number of masculine and feminine terminations, as PS and X are the same as S, and need not be counted. There is no Noun, however, ending in a mute or in either of the two short vowels, E and O. Only three (meli, kommi, peperi) end in I, and five in T. The intermediates, or neuters, end in the variable vowels or in N, P, X.

## 22

The perfection of Diction is for it to be at once clear and not mean. The clearest indeed is that made up of the ordinary words for things, but it is mean, as is shown by the poetry of Cleophon and Sthenelus. On the other hand the Diction becomes distinguished and non-prosaic by the use of unfamiliar terms, i.e. strange words, metaphors, lengthened forms, and everything that deviates from the ordinary modes of speech.—But a whole statement in such terms will be either a riddle or a barbarism, a riddle, if made up of metaphors, a barbarism, if made up of strange words. The very nature indeed of a riddle is this, to describe a fact in an impossible combination of words (which cannot be done with the real names for things, but can be with their metaphorical substitutes); e.g. 'I saw a man glue brass on another with fire', and the like. The corresponding use of strange words results in a barbarism.—A certain admixture, accordingly, of unfamiliar terms is necessary. These, the strange word, the metaphor, the ornamental equivalent, etc..will save the language from seeming mean and prosaic, while the ordinary words in it will secure the requisite clearness. What helps most, however, to render the Diction at once clear and non-prosaic is the use of the lengthened, curtailed, and altered forms of words. Their deviation from the ordinary words will, by making the language unlike that in general use give it a non-prosaic appearance; and their having much in common with the words in general use will give it the quality of clearness. It is not right, then, to condemn these modes of speech, and ridicule the poet for using them, as some have done; e.g. the elder

Euclid, who said it was easy to make poetry if one were to be allowed to lengthen the words in the statement itself as much as one likes—a procedure he caricatured by reading 'EpixarhoneidonMarathonadeBadi—gonta, and oukhan g' eramenos ton ekeinouhelle boron as verses. A too apparent use of these licences has certainly a ludicrous effect, but they are not alone in that; the rule of moderation applies to all the constituents of the poetic vocabulary; even with metaphors, strange words, and the rest, the effect will be the same, if one uses them improperly and with a view to provoking laughter. The proper use of them is a very different thing. To realize the difference one should take an epic verse and see how it reads when the normal words are introduced. The same should be done too with the strange word, the metaphor, and the rest; for one has only to put the ordinary words in their place to see the truth of what we are saying. The same iambic, for instance, is found in Aeschylus and Euripides, and as it stands in the former it is a poor line; whereas Euripides, by the change of a single word, the substitution of a strange for what is by usage the ordinary word, has made it seem a fine one. Aeschylus having said in his Philoctetes:
phagedaina he monsarkashesthieipodos
Euripides has merely altered the hesthiei here into thoinatai. Or suppose
nun de m' heonholigostekaioutidanoskaihaeikos
to be altered by the substitution of the ordinary words into
nun de m' heonmikrostekaihasthenikoskaiheidos
Or the line
diphronhaeikelionkatatheisolingentetrapexan
into
diphronmoxtheronkatatheismikrantetrapexan
Or heionesboosin into heioneskraxousin. Add to this that Ariphrades used to ridicule the tragedians for introducing expressions unknown in the language of common life, doeatonhapo (for apodomaton), sethen, hego de nin, Achilleosperi (for periAchilleos), and the like. The mere fact of their not being in ordinary speech gives the Diction a non-prosaic character; but Ariphrades was unaware of that. It is a great thing, indeed, to make a proper use of these poetical forms, as also of compounds and strange words. But the greatest thing by far is to be a master of metaphor. It is the one thing that cannot be learnt from others; and it is also a sign of genius, since a good metaphor implies an intuitive perception of the similarity in dissimilars.

Of the kinds of words we have enumerated it may be observed that compounds are most in place in the dithyramb, strange words in heroic, and metaphors in iambic poetry. Heroic poetry, indeed, may avail itself of them all. But in iambic verse, which models itself as far as possible on the spoken language, only those kinds of words are in place which are allowable also in an oration, i.e. the ordinary word, the metaphor, and the ornamental equivalent.

Let this, then, suffice as an account of Tragedy, the art imitating by means of action on the stage.

# 23

As for the poetry which merely narrates, or imitates by means of versified language (without action), it is evident that it has several points in common with Tragedy.

I. The construction of its stories should clearly be like that in a drama; they should be based on a single action, one that is a complete whole in itself, with a beginning, middle, and end, so as to enable the work to produce its own proper pleasure with all the organic unity of a living creature. Nor should one suppose that there is anything like them in our usual histories. A history has to deal not with one action, but with one period and all that happened in that to one or more persons, however disconnected the several events may have been. Just as two events may take place at the same time, e.g. the sea-fight off Salamis and the battle with the Carthaginians in Sicily, without converging to the same end, so too of two consecutive events one may sometimes come after the other with no one end as their common issue. Nevertheless most of our epic poets, one may say, ignore the distinction.

Herein, then, to repeat what we have said before, we have a further proof of Homer's marvellous superiority to the rest. He did not attempt to deal even with the Trojan war in its entirety, though it was a whole with a definite beginning and end—through a feeling apparently that it was too long a story to be taken in in one view, or if not that, too complicated from the variety of incident in it. As it is, he has singled out one section of the whole; many of the other incidents, however, he brings in as episodes, using the Catalogue of the Ships, for instance, and other episodes to relieve the uniformity of his narrative. As for the other epic poets, they treat of one man, or one period; or else of an action which, although one, has a multiplicity of parts in it. This last is what the authors of the Cypria and Little Iliad have done. And the result is that, whereas the Iliad or Odyssey supplies materials for only one, or at most two tragedies, the Cypria does that for several, and the Little Iliad for more than eight: for an Adjudgment of Arms, a Philoctetes, a Neoptolemus, a Eurypylus, a Ulysses as Beggar, a Laconian Women, a Fall of Ilium, and a Departure of the Fleet; as also a Sinon, and Women of Troy.

II. Besides this, Epic poetry must divide into the same species as Tragedy; it must be either simple or complex, a story of character or one of suffering. Its parts, too, with the exception of Song and Spectacle, must be the same, as it requires Peripeties, Discoveries, and scenes of suffering just like Tragedy. Lastly, the Thought and Diction in it must be good in their way. All these elements appear in Homer first; and he has made due use of them. His two poems are each examples of construction, the Iliad simple and a story of suffering, the Odyssey complex (there is Discovery throughout it) and a story of character. And they are more than this, since in Diction and Thought too they surpass all other poems.

There is, however, a difference in the Epic as compared with Tragedy, (1) in its length, and (2) in its metre. (1) As to its length, the limit already suggested will suffice: it must be possible for the beginning and end of the work to be taken in in one view—a condition which will be fulfilled if the poem be shorter than the old epics, and about as long as the series of tragedies offered for one hearing. For the extension of its length epic poetry has a special advantage, of which it makes large use. In a play one cannot represent an action with a number of parts going on simultaneously; one is limited to the part on the stage and connected with the actors. Whereas in epic poetry the narrative form makes it possible for one to describe a number of simultaneous incidents; and these, if germane to the subject, increase the body of the poem. This then is a gain to the Epic, tending to give it grandeur, and also variety of interest and room for episodes of diverse kinds. Uniformity of incident by the satiety it soon creates is apt to ruin tragedies on the stage. (2) As for its metre, the heroic has been assigned it from experience; were any one to attempt a narrative poem in some one, or in several, of the other metres, the incongruity of the thing would be apparent. The heroic; in fact is the gravest and weightiest of metres—which is what makes it more tolerant than the rest of strange words and metaphors, that also being a point in which the narrative form of poetry goes beyond all others. The iambic and trochaic, on the other hand, are metres of movement, the one representing that of life and action, the other that of the dance. Still more unnatural would it appear, it one were to write an epic in a medley of metres, as Chaeremon did. Hence it is that no one has ever written a long story in any but heroic verse; nature herself, as we have said, teaches us to select the metre appropriate to such a story.

Homer, admirable as he is in every other respect, is especially so in this, that he alone among epic poets is not unaware of the part to be played by the poet himself in the poem. The poet should say very little in propria persona, as he is no imitator when doing that. Whereas the other poets are perpetually coming forward in person, and say but little, and that only here and there, as imitators, Homer after a brief preface brings in forthwith a man, a woman, or some other Character—no one of them characterless, but each with distinctive characteristics.

The marvellous is certainly required in Tragedy. The Epic, however, affords more opening for the improbable, the chief factor in the marvellous, because in it the agents are not visibly before one. The scene of the pursuit of Hector would be ridiculous on the stage—the Greeks halting instead of pursuing him, and Achilles shaking his head to stop them; but in the poem the absurdity is overlooked. The marvellous, however, is a cause of pleasure, as is shown by the fact that we all tell a story with additions, in the belief that we are doing our hearers a pleasure.

Homer more than any other has taught the rest of us the art of framing lies in the right way. I mean the use of paralogism. Whenever, if A is or happens, a consequent, B, is or happens, men's notion is that, if the B is, the A also is—but that is a false conclusion. Accordingly, if A is untrue, but there is something else, B, that on the assumption of its truth follows as its consequent, the right thing then is to add on the B. Just because we know the truth of the consequent, we are in our own minds led on to the erroneous inference of the truth of the antecedent. Here is an instance, from the Bath-story in the Odyssey.

A likely impossibility is always preferable to an unconvincing possibility. The story should never be made up of improbable incidents; there should be nothing of the sort in it. If, however, such incidents are unavoidable, they should be outside the piece, like the hero's ignorance in Oedipus of the circumstances of Lams' death; not within it, like the report of the Pythian games in Electra, or the man's having come to Mysia from Tegea without uttering a word on the way, in The Mysians. So that it is ridiculous to say that one's Plot would have been spoilt without them, since it is fundamentally wrong to make up such Plots. If the poet has taken such a Plot, however, and one sees that he might have put it in a more probable form, he is guilty of absurdity as well as a fault of art. Even in the Odyssey the improbabilities in the setting-ashore of Ulysses would be clearly intolerable in the hands of an inferior poet. As it is, the poet conceals them, his other excellences veiling their absurdity. Elaborate Diction, however, is required only in places where there is no action, and no Character or Thought to be revealed. Where there is Character or Thought, on the other hand, an over-ornate Diction tends to obscure them.

## 25

As regards Problems and their Solutions, one may see the number and nature of the assumptions on which they proceed by viewing the matter in the following way. (1) The poet being an imitator just like the painter or other maker of likenesses, he must necessarily in all instances represent things in one or other of three aspects, either as they were or are, or as they are said or thought to be or to have been, or as they ought to be. (2) All this he does in language, with an admixture, it may be, of strange words and metaphors, as also of the various modified forms of words, since the use of these is conceded in poetry. (3) It is to be remembered, too, that there is not the same kind of correctness in poetry as in politics, or indeed any other art. There is, however, within the limits of poetry itself a possibility of two kinds of error, the one directly, the other only accidentally connected with the art. If the poet meant to describe the thing correctly, and failed through lack of power of expression, his art itself is at fault. But if it was through his having meant to describe it in some incorrect way (e.g. to make the horse in movement have both right legs thrown forward) that the technical error (one in a matter of, say, medicine or some other special science), or impossibilities of whatever kind they may be, have got into his description, his error in that case is not in the essentials of the poetic art. These, therefore, must be the premisses of the Solutions in answer to the criticisms involved in the Problems.

I. As to the criticisms relating to the poet's art itself. Any impossibilities there may be in his descriptions of things are faults. But from another point of view they are justifiable, if they serve the end of poetry itself—if (to assume what we have said of that end) they make the effect of some portion of the work more astounding. The Pursuit of Hector is an instance in point. If, however, the poetic end might have been as well or better attained without sacrifice of technical correctness in such matters, the impossibility is not to be justified, since the description should be, if it can, entirely free from error. One may ask, too, whether the error is in a matter directly or only accidentally connected with the poetic art; since it is a lesser error in an artist not to know, for instance, that the hind has no horns, than to produce an unrecognizable picture of one.

II. If the poet's description be criticized as not true to fact, one may urge perhaps that the object ought to be as described—an answer like that of Sophocles, who said that he drew men as they ought to be, and Euripides as they were. If the description, however, be neither true nor of the thing as it ought to be, the answer must be then, that it is in accordance with opinion. The tales about Gods, for instance, may be as wrong as Xenophanes thinks, neither true nor the better thing to say; but they are certainly in accordance with opinion. Of other statements in poetry one may perhaps say, not that they are better than the truth, but that the fact was so at the time; e.g. the description of the arms: 'their spears stood upright, butt-end upon the ground'; for that was the usual way of fixing them then, as it is still with the Illyrians. As for the question whether something said or done in a poem is morally right or not, in dealing with that one should consider not only the intrinsic quality of the actual word or deed, but also the person who says or does it, the person to whom he says or does it, the time, the means, and the motive of the agent—whether he does it to attain a greater good, or to avoid a greater evil.

III. Other criticisms one must meet by considering the language of the poet: (1) by the assumption of a strange word in a passage like oureas men proton, where by oureas Homer may perhaps mean not mules but sentinels. And in saying of Dolon, hosp etoieidos men heenkakos, his meaning may perhaps be, not that Dolon's body was deformed, but that his face was ugly, as eneidos is the Cretan word for handsome-faced. So, too, goroteron de keraie may mean not 'mix the wine stronger', as though for topers, but 'mix it quicker'. (2) Other expressions in Homer may be explained as metaphorical; e.g. in halloi men ratheoitekaianereseudon (hapantes) pannux as compared with what he tells us at the same time, e toi hot hespedion to Troikonhathreseien, aulonsuriggon *tehomadon* the word hapantes 'all', is metaphorically put for 'many', since 'all' is a species of 'many '. So also his oie d' ammoros is metaphorical, the best known standing 'alone'. (3) A change, as Hippias suggested, in the mode of reading a word will solve the difficulty in didomen de oi, and to men oukataputhetaihombro. (4) Other difficulties may be solved by another punctuation; e.g. in Empedocles, aipsa de thnetephyonto, ta prinmathonathanataxorateprinkekreto. Or (5) by the assumption of an equivocal term, as in parocheken de pleonux, where pleo in equivocal.Or (6) by an appeal to the custom of language. Wine-and-water we call 'wine'; and it is on the same principle that Homer speaks of a knemisneoteuktoukassiteroio, a 'greave of new-wrought tin.' A worker in iron we call a 'brazier'; and it is on the same principle that Ganymede is described as the 'wine-server' of Zeus, though the Gods do not drink wine. This latter, however, may be an instance of metaphor. But whenever also a word seems to imply some contradiction, it is necessary to reflect how many ways there may be of understanding it in the passage in question; e.g. in Homer's te r' hesxetoxalkeonhegxos one should consider the possible senses of 'was stopped there'—whether by taking it in this sense or in that one will best avoid the fault of which Glaucon speaks: 'They start with some improbable presumption; and having so decreed it themselves, proceed to draw inferences, and censure the poet as though he had actually said whatever they happen to believe, if his statement conflicts with their own notion of things.' This is how Homer's silence about Icarius has been treated. Starting with, the notion of his having been a Lacedaemonian, the critics think it strange for Telemachus not to have met him when he went to Lacedaemon. Whereas the fact may have been as the Cephallenians say, that the wife of Ulysses was of a Cephallenian family, and that her father's name was Icadius, not Icarius. So that it is probably a mistake of the critics that has given rise to the Problem.

Speaking generally, one has to justify (1) the Impossible by reference to the requirements of poetry, or to the better, or to opinion. For the purposes of poetry a convincing impossibility is preferable to an unconvincing possibility; and if men such as Zeuxis depicted be impossible, the answer is that it is better they should be like that, as the artist ought to improve on his model. (2) The Improbable one has to justify either by showing it to be in accordance with opinion, or by urging that at times it is not improbable; for there is a probability of things happening also against probability. (3) The contradictions found in the poet's language one should first test as one does an opponent's confutation in a dialectical argument, so as to see whether he means the same thing, in the same relation, and in the same sense, before admitting that he has contradicted either something he has said himself or what a man of sound sense assumes as true. But there is no possible apology for improbability of Plot or depravity of character, when they are not necessary and no use is made of them, like the improbability in the appearance of Aegeus in Medea and the baseness of Menelaus in Orestes.

The objections, then, of critics start with faults of five kinds: the allegation is always that something in either (1) impossible, (2) improbable, (3) corrupting, (4) contradictory, or (5) against technical correctness. The answers to these objections must be sought under one or other of the above-mentioned heads, which are twelve in number.

## 26

The question may be raised whether the epic or the tragic is the higher form of imitation. It may be argued that, if the less vulgar is the higher, and the less vulgar is always that which addresses the better public, an art addressing any and every one is of a very vulgar order. It is a belief that their public cannot see the meaning, unless they add something themselves, that causes the perpetual movements of the performers—bad flute-players, for instance, rolling about, if quoit-throwing is to be represented, and pulling at the conductor, if Scylla is the subject of the piece. Tragedy, then, is said to be an art of this order—to be in fact just what the later actors were in the eyes of their predecessors; for Myrmiscus used to call Callippides 'the ape', because he thought he so overacted his parts; and a similar view was taken of Pindarus also. All Tragedy, however, is said to stand to the Epic as the newer to the older school of actors. The one, accordingly, is said to address a cultivated 'audience, which does not need the accompaniment of gesture; the other, an uncultivated one. If, therefore, Tragedy is a vulgar art, it must clearly be lower than the Epic.

The answer to this is twofold. In the first place, one may urge (1) that the censure does not touch the art of the dramatic poet, but only that of his interpreter; for it is quite possible to overdo the gesturing even in an epic recital, as did Sosistratus, and in a singing contest, as did Mnasitheus of Opus. (2) That one should not condemn all movement, unless one means to condemn even the dance, but only that of ignoble people—which is the point of the criticism passed on Callippides and in the present day on others, that their women are not like gentlewomen. (3) That Tragedy may produce its effect even without movement or action in just the same way as Epic poetry; for from the mere reading of a play its quality may be seen. So that, if it be superior in all other respects, this element of inferiority is not a necessary part of it.

In the second place, one must remember (1) that Tragedy has everything that the Epic has (even the epic metre being admissible), together with a not inconsiderable addition in the shape of the Music (a very real factor in the pleasure of the drama) and the Spectacle. (2) That its reality of presentation is felt in the play as read, as well as in the play as acted. (3) That the tragic imitation requires less space for the attainment of its end; which is a great advantage, since the more concentrated effect is more pleasurable than one with a large admixture of time to dilute it—consider the Oedipus of Sophocles, for instance, and the effect of expanding it into the number of lines of the Iliad. (4) That there is less unity in the imitation of the epic poets, as is proved by the fact that any one work of theirs supplies matter for several tragedies; the result being that, if they take what is really a single story, it seems curt when briefly told, and thin and waterish when on the scale of length usual with their verse. In saying that there is less unity in an epic, I mean an epic made up of a plurality of actions, in the same way as the Iliad and Odyssey have many such parts, each one of them in itself of some magnitude; yet the structure of the two Homeric poems is as perfect as can be, and the action in them is as nearly as possible one action. If, then, Tragedy is superior in these respects, and also besides these, in its poetic effect (since the two forms of poetry should give us, not any or every pleasure, but the very special kind we have mentioned), it is clear that, as attaining the poetic effect better than the Epic, it will be the higher form of art.

So much for Tragedy and Epic poetry—for these two arts in general and their species; the number and nature of their constituent parts; the causes of success and failure in them; the Objections of the critics, and the Solutions in answer to them.

Made in the USA
San Bernardino, CA
08 January 2018